CIRCLES OF RECOVERY
Self-Help Organizations for Addictions

Self-help organizations across the world, such as Alcoholics Anonymous, Croix d'Or, The Links, Moderation Management, Narcotics Anonymous, and SMART Recovery, have attracted tens of millions of individuals seeking to address addiction problems with drugs or alcohol. For the first time, this book provides an integrative, international review of research on these organizations, focusing in particular on the critical questions as to how they affect individual members and whether self-help groups and formal healthcare systems can work together to combat substance abuse. Keith Humphreys reviews over 500 studies into the efficacy of self-help groups as an alternative and voluntary form of treatment. In addition to offering a critical, state-of-the-art review of the international body of research in this area, he provides practical strategies for individual clinicians and treatment systems to interact with self-help organizations in a way that improves outcomes for patients and for communities as a whole.

KEITH HUMPHREYS is Associate Professor of Psychiatry at the Stanford University School of Medicine, and Director of the Program Evaluation and Resource Center. He has received national and international awards for his work, and has served on expert consultant panels for the Center for Mental Health Services, the National Institute of Alcohol Abuse and Alcoholism, the Office of Behavioral and Social Science Research, the Department of Veterans Affairs, and the Office of Juvenile Justice and Delinquency Prevention.

INTERNATIONAL RESEARCH MONOGRAPHS IN THE ADDICTIONS (IRMA)

Series Editor
Professor Griffith Edwards
National Addiction Centre
Institute of Psychiatry, London

This is a series of volumes presenting important research from major centers around the world on the basic sciences, both biological and behavioral, that have a bearing on the addictions. It also addresses the clinical and public health applications of such research. The series will cover alcohol, illicit drugs, psychotropics, and tobacco. It is an important resource for clinicians, researchers, and policy makers.

Also in this series

Cannabis and Cognitive Functioning
Nadia Solowij
ISBN 0 521 159114 7

Alcohol and the Community: A Systems Approach to Prevention
Harold D. Holder
ISBN 0 521 59187 2

A Community Reinforcement Approach to Addiction Treatment
Robert J. Meyers and William R. Miller
ISBN 0 521 77107 2

Treatment Matching in Alcoholism
Thomas F. Babor and Frances K. Del Boca
ISBN 0 521 65112 3

CIRCLES OF RECOVERY

Self-Help Organizations for Addictions

KEITH HUMPHREYS

Department of Psychiatry
Stanford University School of Medicine

CAMBRIDGE
UNIVERSITY PRESS

CAMBRIDGE UNIVERSITY PRESS
Cambridge, New York, Melbourne, Madrid, Cape Town,
Singapore, São Paulo, Delhi, Tokyo, Mexico City

Cambridge University Press
The Edinburgh Building, Cambridge CB2 8RU, UK

Published in the United States of America by Cambridge University Press, New York

www.cambridge.org
Information on this title: www.cambridge.org/9780521176378

© Cambridge University Press 2004

First published 2004
First paperback edition 2011

A catalogue record for this publication is available from the British Library

Library of Congress Cataloguing in Publication data
Humphreys, Keith.
Circles of recovery: self-help organizations for addictions / Keith Humphreys.
    p. ; cm. – (International research monographs in the addictions)
Includes bibliographical references and index.
ISBN 0 521 79277 0 (hardback)
1. Substance abuse – Treatment.   2. Substance abuse – Patients – Rehabilitation.   3. Self-help
groups.   4. Addicts – Services for.   5. Alcoholics – Services for.   I. Title.   II. Series.
[DNLM: 1. Self-Help Groups.   2. Substance-Related Disorders – therapy.   3. Program
Evaluation. WM 270 H927c 2004]
RC564.H85   2004
362.29'18 – dc21   2003043935

ISBN 978-0-521-79277-6 Hardback
ISBN 978-0-521-17637-8 Paperback

Contents

Acknowledgements   x

1 Definitions, scope, and origin of the health-related self-help group
   movement   1
   Points of departure   1
   Goals of this book   2
       Goal 1: to describe addiction-related self-help organizations   2
       Goal 2: to evaluate how self-help group involvement affects members 3
       Goal 3: to provide guidelines for clinical and policy interaction with
           self-help groups   4
       Goal 4: to bring science to bear on controversial issues in the field 5
   The scope of this book   7
       Range of societies examined   8
       Benefits and challenges of an international scope   9
       Range of addiction-related and non-addiction-related self-help
           organizations addressed   11
       Range of disciplines covered   12
   What self-help organizations are and what they are not   12
       Nomenclature   12
       Essential characteristics of self-help organizations   13
       Optional features of self-help organizations   17
       Differentiating self-help organizations from other interventions   21
   Generic factors behind the development of the self-help group movement
       in the modern world   24
   Five inter-related forces that have fostered the modern self-help group
       movement   26
       Improved public health and wealth   26
       Weakening of familial ties   27

Limits of professional assistance 28
The rise of consumerism in health care 30
Benefits of participation 31

2 An international tour of addiction-related mutual-help organizations 33
Background and context 33
Origins, philosophy, and membership of addiction-related self-help
  organizations 35
  Alcoholics Anonymous 35
  Abstainers Clubs 43
  Al-Anon Family Groups 46
  All Nippon Sobriety Association/the Sobriety Friends Society
    (Danshukai) 51
  Blue Cross (Croix Bleue) 54
  Clubs of Treated Alcoholics 57
  Double Trouble in Recovery 60
  Free Life (Vie Libre) 63
  Jewish Alcoholics, Chemically Dependent Persons, and Significant
    Others 65
  The Links 67
  Moderation Management 70
  Narcotics Anonymous 74
  Nicotine Anonymous 77
  Oxford Houses 78
  Pui Hong Self-Help Association 80
  Rational Recovery 82
  SMART Recovery 84
  SOS/LifeRing Secular Recovery 86
  Women for Sobriety 88
Comparisons and contrasts 90

3 Does self-help group participation lead to positive addiction-related,
  psychiatric, and medical outcomes? 94
Conceptual background 94
  The case for evaluating whether addiction self-help groups
    "really work" 94
  Evaluating self-help groups as analogous to professional healthcare
    interventions 95

Randomized clinical trials as a regulating ideal in treatment research 96
  Randomized trials are not necessarily the best guide to useful
    knowledge 96
  Randomized trials have additional shortcomings specific to self-help
    group evaluation 97
  Correlational studies and quasi-experiments are no panacea either 98
Outcome studies of specific addiction-related mutual-help
organizations 99
  Al-Anon Family Groups 100
  All Nippon Sobriety Association and the Sobriety Friends
    Society (Danshukai) 102
  Clubs of Treated Alcoholics 103
  Double Trouble in Recovery 103
  Moderation Management 104
  Narcotics Anonymous 104
  Nicotine Anonymous 106
  Oxford Houses 107
  Pui Hong Self-Help Association 108
  Rational Recovery 108
  Secular Organization for Sobriety 109
  Women for Sobriety 109
Outcome studies of AA 109
  Experimental and quasi-experimental studies of AA as a sole
    intervention 111
  Longitudinal studies of AA's effectiveness in combination with
    treatment 115
  Summary of AA effectiveness studies 119
Three intriguing questions about AA's effectiveness 119
  Mediators of AA's influence on drinking outcomes 119
  AA's potential for population-level benefits 123
  Weaknesses and possible harms of AA 125
Summary 126

4 A different perspective on change in self-help organizations:
   spirituality, identity, life stories, friendship networks, and
   politicization 128
   Moving beyond the treatment-outcome perspective 128
   Scope and background 130

Domain 1: spiritual change   131
  Understanding spiritual change in substance-abuse-related self-help
    organizations   137
Domain 2: identity and life-story transformation   141
Domain 3: friendship-network composition   144
Domain 4: politicization and empowerment   146
Summary   148

5 How should government agencies, healthcare organizations, and
   clinicians interact with self-help organizations?   149
   External support of self-help organizations: benefits and risks   149
     Direct health benefits   149
     Healthcare cost reductions   150
     Challenges to collaboration   152
     Summary: moving carefully forward   154
   Strategies for governmental support of addiction-related self-help
     organizations   154
     Legitimating rhetoric   155
     Direct financial support of self-help organizations   156
     In-kind resource provision   156
     Investments in self-help support organizations   157
     Media and information campaigns   159
     Training and education for professional helpers   160
     Research support   161
     Self-help groups as participants in relevant policy arenas   163
   Strategies for individual clinicians and treatment agencies   163
     The need for a collaborative mindset   164
   Avenues for collaboration   166
     Making effective referrals   167
     Empirically supported referral strategies   167
     Consultation and an experimental attitude over a priori matching   168
     Common worries about referral   169
     Helping to start self-help groups   174
     Technical assistance, lectures, research help, and media referral
       person   174
     Attending self-help groups as a professional   175

Epilogue: summing up, moving forward   177
   Some answers for the Martian   177

Contents

What are addiction-related self-help organizations and where do
they come from?   177
What effects do self-help organizations have?   179
How might professionals interact with self-help organizations?   180
Toward a better tomorrow   180

References   182
Index   219

Acknowledgements

Anyone who writes a book has many people to thank for its virtues, and only himself to blame for its shortcomings. My greatest debt for this book is to Peter Mendel, who must have inhaled ten decades' worth of library dust while scouring the interdisciplinary literature on self-help organizations. Peter's trenchant analysis of prior self-help group research was essential groundwork for this book. Doyanne Horst also did heroic service by proof reading the entire manuscript and reference list, and by obtaining Spanish grey literature. Colleen Loomis caught many typographical errors that had escaped my eyes and also helped me to obtain and understand some French articles. Tomofumi Oka offered the same assistance with some Japanese literature, and also patiently answered my series of niggling questions on the distinctions between Danshukai, Danshu-Tomo-no-Kai, and Zenzoku Danshu Renmei. A number of scholars graciously took the time to critique draft sections of the text and to provide important insights into self-help organizations. My warmest thanks for such assistance goes to James Awbrey, Ehab El-Kharrat, A. Thomas Horvath, Lee Ann Kaskutas, Ernest Kurtz, Noriko Kurube, Linda Kurtz, Alexandre Laudet, Klaus Mäkelä, and Josef Ruzek. Series editor Griffith Edwards richly deserves the title of "honorary midwife" for inspiring me with intellectual and personal support throughout the entire process of conceptualizing and revising the book. Last, but certainly not least, I am also indebted to Alcoholics Anonymous, Blue Cross, and Jewish Alcoholics, Chemically Dependent Persons and Significant Others for clarifying specific aspects of their organizations, as I am to the hundreds of members of various self-help organizations who have shared their stories with me over the years.

1

Definitions, scope, and origin of the health-related self-help group movement

Points of departure

The use and abuse of alcohol, opiates, cocaine, nicotine, and other substances is arguably the greatest threat to public health in the developed world. Substance use causes half a million deaths annually in the USA alone, and is a contributing factor to countless morbidities, not to mention tremendous human suffering (Horgan, Skwara, & Strickler, 2001). Accordingly, developed societies have created complex networks of professionally operated health and social welfare programs to help the millions of individuals whose substance use harms themselves and others. Individuals with substance-abuse problems can thus seek help from addiction-treatment professionals in acute inpatient treatment programs, detoxification units, day hospitals, evening intensive outpatient programs, residential therapeutic communities, halfway houses, psychiatric clinics, psychologists' offices, social work agencies, and primary medical care practices, among many other settings. Help-seekers also can avail themselves of the advice of religious leaders, trusted friends, family members, and co-workers. Yet no matter how sparsely or generously all of the above potential sources of help are provided in a given society, a significant number of addicted individuals turn to each other for support, guidance, understanding, practical advice, and a sense of belonging by joining self-help organizations.

The mutual-help organizations with which addicted individuals affiliate vary enormously in their histories, structures, philosophies, procedures, and membership. Abstainers Clubs broadcast members' life stories on Polish television, whereas Alcoholics Anonymous shuns all efforts at media promotion. The All Nippon Sobriety Association receives grants from the Japanese government, whereas Cocaine Anonymous refuses outside financial support. Moderation Management allows members to attempt controlled drinking; Women for Sobriety insists on abstinence. Croix Bleue self-help groups conceptualize substance abuse as a spiritual and moral problem, whereas Rational Recovery and SMART Recovery view it as simply an unhealthy behavioral habit. Yet within this diversity, all mutual-help organizations make the same, much-debated, claim of improving the lives of their members.

Given this claim, and the fact that mutual-help organizations engage millions of addicted individuals throughout the world, one might suspect that they have been a major focus of healthcare and public health policy planning, but this is not the case. For the same reasons, one might assume that scientists have studied self-help groups as intensely as they have professional treatments for addiction, but they have not. Indeed, if a Martian came to earth and looked upon addiction-related research and policy from his completely naive vantage point, he would probably be puzzled by the relatively minimal amount of attention experts in the field have paid to mutual-help initiatives (Humphreys, 1997a). He might ask, "What are these mutual help organizations? Where do they come from? Do they really help anyone? And how should professionals in the field work with them, if they should even do so at all?". This book is one Earthling's answer to the puzzled Martian, as well as an invitation for conversation to any fellow Earthlings who have pondered the same questions.

Goals of this book

This book has four interrelated goals: (1) to describe a variety of addiction-related mutual-help organizations, (2) to evaluate how addicted individuals are affected by their involvement in self-help groups, (3) to provide guidelines for clinicians and policy makers concerning how to interact with such organizations, and (4) to bring scientific knowledge to bear on hotly debated issues in the field. The importance of pursuing these goals stems from the tremendous harm done by substance abuse and the tremendous potential of self-help organizations to help address it.

Goal 1: to describe addiction-related self-help organizations

This book surveys the international literature on self-help organizations for individuals who have problems due to their own or a loved one's use of alcohol, nicotine, and illicit drugs. Such organizations will be shorthanded here as "addiction-related" purely for convenience of communication, recognizing that this term is sometimes used more narrowly (e.g., only for individuals meeting formal diagnostic criteria for substance dependence) or more broadly (e.g., to apply to individuals who gamble, overeat, or engage in compulsive sexual behavior).

Three realities suggest that an effort to integrate the international literature on addiction-related self-help organizations is worthwhile. First, "self-help" is used to describe so many different activities in the addiction field as to make the term almost meaningless at worst, confusing at best. Such confusion blocks integration of diverse knowledge bases. Second, many professionals lack knowledge about self-help organizations, including about what they might contribute to the amelioration of substance-abuse problems. Third, many people's understanding of addiction-related self-help is based on information about only one self-help organization (most commonly, Alcoholics Anonymous) in one country (most commonly, the USA), which is falsely assumed to be representative of all organizations in all nations.

This book will address these issues by defining precisely what constitutes a self-help organization, by integrating literatures that were previously considered separate, and by covering the wide range of organizations that exist in all their diversity. It is hoped this will grant readers a more thorough understanding of a complex, multi-faceted, international phenomenon in the addiction field.

Goal 2: to evaluate how self-help group involvement affects members

As mentioned, although self-help groups differ enormously, all claim to benefit participants. One of the central tasks of this book is to summarize the scientific evidence on whether this claim is warranted. This will involve answering this question from the same perspective from which researchers often evaluate professional treatments for addiction (e.g., does participation reduce substance use?), as well as from the perspective from which one might evaluate voluntary community associations (e.g., does participation build friendships and make life more meaningful?), because, as will be explored, self-help organizations share characteristics with both of these analogues. Given this substantive focus, in selecting literature for discussion, highest priority will be given to reports of empirical efforts to assess how individuals involved in self-help groups change over time.

This book's focus on the group–participant interaction differentiates it from other volumes that analyze self-help organizations as social movements (Bloomfield, 1994). Such a perspective directs greater attention than will be the case here to topics such as how self-help organizations influence other cultural institutions, diffuse across societies, manage finances, structure internal bureaucracy, and promote organizational growth (Borkman, 1999). The magnificent work of the International Collaborative Study of Alcoholics Anonymous in eight societies (Eisenbach-Stangl & Rosenqvist, 1998; Mäkelä *et al.*, 1996) demonstrated beyond doubt the value of a social movement perspective on self-help organizations. Hence, the decision to focus primarily on a different level of analysis here is not an implied criticism of the social movement perspective; rather it is an effort to complement it with new information and a different substantive focus. This book addresses some organizational issues related to professional/healthcare system interaction with self-help groups, but in general adopts a more clinical, psychological, and healthcare-oriented point of view by focusing on the interaction of the addicted individuals with their self-help groups and the consequences of that interaction for members' health and well-being.

Goal 3: to provide guidelines for clinical and policy interaction with self-help groups

The widespread lack of understanding of self-help organizations has made it difficult for their potential allies to know how to relate to them. Many clinicians are unsure of whether they should refer their substance-dependent patients to self-help groups, and if so, who should be referred and how. Even health professionals who have developed some expertise in this area are faced with difficult problems, such as how to respond when patients report that a self-help group is not helping them. Although a few empirical projects have addressed such issues, and individual suggestions for clinical strategies have appeared from time to time, they have not been assembled into a coherent set of "clinical practice guidelines" for interactions with self-help groups. This volume will attempt to remedy that lacuna.

Policy makers, public health department heads, and healthcare administrators usually have even less understanding of mutual-help organizations than do front-line clinicians. Whether they view self-help organizations as potential collaborators, competitors, or ignorable trivia, their attitudes are rarely grounded in empirical data or extensive experience. Even when attitudes are positive, implementation of self-help supportive policies that do more good than harm is no easy matter.

Primarily in Chapter 5, this book will provide empirically supported guidelines for how individual healthcare practitioners and health-related organizations can interact with self-help organizations in ways that reduce addiction-related problems while supporting the integrity of all parties. Even when formal studies have not been conducted, learning about policy efforts made in other countries – most of which have not been specific to addiction self-help organizations per se (e.g., Hatch & Kickbush, 1983; Surgeon General's Workshop on

Self-Help and Public Health, 1990) and are therefore unknown to many workers in that field – may stimulate readers to evaluate whether similar initiatives would be beneficial in their own setting.

This volume's guidelines for professional interaction with self-help organizations differ by design from available advice on how to minimize distinctions between self-help principles and professional treatment programs. A large literature advises treatment professionals on how to adopt the language and methods of self-help organizations into professional treatment. For example, many books and articles have addressed how clinicians can conduct "12-step psychotherapy" (e.g., Morgan, 1995; Zweben, 1986). This book takes a different perspective by assuming some separation between self-help organizations and professional treatment (Humphreys, 1993a). Hence, the effects of self-help groups per se will be evaluated not only as "adjuncts to treatment," and the guidelines for clinicians and policy makers will focus on interactions between self-help organizations and the professionally controlled helping system, rather than attempting to dissolve distinctions between the two.

Goal 4: to bring science to bear on controversial issues in the field

The final goal for this book is as much about process as outcome. That is, how shall the questions implicit in the first three goals be addressed, and under what rules shall differences of opinion be resolved? In short, data will be granted authority over opinion. Because this may seem a strangely prosaic, even unnecessary comment, some review of the unique intellectual issues related to addiction self-help groups is warranted.

The passion of individuals who have been helped to overcome substance abuse

The destructive effects of substance dependence can be all-consuming. The relief and gratitude that attend being helped out of addiction can be equally so. People who have been rescued from a disastrous situation sometimes become extremely passionate about the source of help; sometimes the source of assistance works to foster such feelings. Although certainly understandable, such emotions can lead individuals to believe that the approach that benefitted them will benefit everyone who has a problem which they perceive as similar to their own. Indeed, experimental studies have shown that when individuals are emotionally aroused, they are more prone to making automatic, oversimplified, and categorical judgements that do not take account of exceptions (Weick, 1984). Perhaps this accounts in part for the history of addiction treatment including many charismatic proselytizers of different interventions, including in some cases self-help organizations (White, 1998). In that vein, a vocal minority of people who have benefitted from addiction-related self-help groups come to see them as the right and only way to recovery (Tournier, 1979).

In this volume, popular enthusiasm for self-help groups in some quarters will be taken to reflect that at least some individuals' lives have been saved by such organizations, but that is all. That is, while not questioning any individual's opinion about what they have found helpful in dealing with addiction, this book will rely for its conclusions on research studies that reveal what benefits (or fails to benefit) a broad range of individuals.

In-group professional bias

Most professionals are aware of the potential bias of those who feel they owe their lives to self-help organizations. What many professionals appreciate less, and therefore deserves more description here, is the bias of professionals in favor of professionally controlled interventions (see Sarason, 1981, on "professional preciousness"), of which self-help organizations are obviously not one. Professionals attempt to cultivate an image of being dispassionate reasoners motivated solely by truth and the public good, but all professionals (the author, of course, included) are human beings with biases, flaws, and self-interests like anyone else.

In an overview of the history of research on Alcoholics Anonymous (AA), Ernest Kurtz sharply criticized individuals who have researched AA, noting for example widespread mis-citation, misquotation, and misunderstanding. E. Kurtz (1993) suggested that such errors stemmed from a fundamental lack of respect for AA among some researchers, including an unwillingness to accept that this non-professional organization might be beneficial.

Although an embarrassing "defense," those Kurtz criticizes could point out that mis-citation, misunderstanding, and mis-quotation are widespread across a range of scientific research areas. Further, many influential professionals have a very high opinion of AA (e.g., Du Pont, 1999). Every negative comment or error about AA and other self-help groups therefore cannot be attributed to bias or some other *ad hominem* problem.

At the same time, ample social psychological research has demonstrated "in group bias" with regard to judgements of performance (see Petty & Cacioppo, 1981, for a review). For example, given the same level of job performance, supervisors rate employees more highly when the employee is of their own gender

(Eagly, Makhijani, & Klonsky, 1992). Clinicians, researchers, and academics are all professionals, and thus may be inclined to judge the work of non-professional self-help groups by a higher standard than they judge their own (Levy, 1984).

Two examples illustrate how in-group bias operates within the mental health and addiction fields. Throughout the history of psychotherapy research, mental health professionals have attacked the methodologies of studies supporting the effectiveness of paraprofessional counselors – while praising other studies which use precisely the same methods but which find evidence of professional effectiveness (Christensen & Jacobson, 1994)! Turning to the addiction field, a distinguished group of scholars argued that because investigator bias may affect the results of research on self-help groups, researchers should ensure that diverse opinions about the effectiveness of self-help groups exist within their research teams (Emrick *et al.*, 1993). Yet no scholar has issued a parallel call for research teams studying professional interventions to include some researchers who do not believe in the effectiveness of professional treatment. In summary, it would behoove professionals to beware of pro-professional bias when judging self-help groups, particularly in situations where external pressures may predispose them to see non-professionals as rivals rather than collaborators.

This volume is written from the point of view that controversies around addiction-related self-help organizations should be evaluated with respect to their empirical underpinnings. The only alternative is to allow the aforementioned ideological extremes to carry the debate. Although the decision to rely on data is likely to disappoint polemicists on both sides, it provides a more trustworthy basis on which to develop policies and viewpoints that may have significant consequences for the lives of people who are substance-dependent.

The scope of this book

As will be described below, the scope of this book is very broad, providing a general introduction to addiction-related self-help organizations around the developed world. This involves some sacrifices in terms of depth, particularly relative to works that examine a single self-help organization in great detail (e.g., McCrady & Miller, 1993) or examine a variety of self-help organizations within a single society (e.g., Matzat, 2002; Robinson & Henry, 1977). However, the broad scope is intended to increase the value of this book in at least four respects: (1) the range of societies examined, (2) the benefits and challenges of an international scope, (3) the range of addiction-related and non-addiction-related self-help organizations addressed, and (4) the range of disciplines covered.

Range of societies examined

Only a few scholars have examined self-help groups in multiple societies, and even fewer have done so specifically for addiction (Room, 1998). To allow workers in different societies to learn from each other, and to create recognition of the worldwide nature of the self-help phenomena, this book will examine addiction-related self-help organizations in multiple countries. By necessity, societies were chosen for detailed attention based on substantive and practical reasons. Specifically, societies were included if they: (a) had significant self-help activity related to addiction, and (b) these organizations were well described in accessible literature. In some cases, it was not easy to determine which of these criteria ruled a society out of consideration. Most scientific literature emerges from the wealthier nations of the world, such that developing countries are not covered even though many of them are likely to have a rich mutual-help tradition. Even for some developed nations, exclusion from the present discussion could not always be traced distinctly to either of the above criteria. For example, the author was unable to locate any scientific literature describing addiction-related self-help organizations in Singapore or Slovakia, which may mean that: (a) such organizations are rare in those societies, (b) such organizations have not been the subject of significant attention, or (c) that the literature was not located during the author's library research. If the omission of any nation here leads a reader to highlight a literature on self-help groups that has been missed by the author and mainstream addiction research, then so much the better for the field's knowledge.

The definition of "accessible literature" deserves clarification. The author's language "skills" limited him to focusing primarily on English-language litera-ture, excepting a few minor ventures into key articles written in French, German, Spanish, or Japanese. Literature was identified through English-language com-puter databases (e.g., MEDLINE, ETOH), which were searched for material on addiction-related self-help groups, providing hundreds of citations from many nations. Most of this material, including a significant amount of grey literature, was obtained, often by contacting authors directly. Supplemental in-formation on the cultural context in which the work was done was sought where available from the author(s) of the work.

Through this process, it eventually became clear that the book could provide at least *some* detailed information on addiction-related self-help organizations in 20 countries: Australia, Austria, Belgium, Canada, Croatia, Denmark, France, Germany, Holland, Hong Kong, Israel, Italy, Japan, Mexico, Norway, Poland, Sweden, Switzerland, the UK, and the USA. Data from a number of other countries – among them Brazil, Finland, Iceland, India, Ireland, Russia, and Spain – are mentioned more briefly due to lack of availability. The amount of literature accessible to the author on each of the above nations of course varied widely on account of differences in production of English-language literature, level of research activity, and prevalence of addiction-related self-help organizations.

Benefits and challenges of an international scope

Just as a fish doesn't realize that it has been swimming until the first time it leaps from the water, one's culturally limited knowledge is only exposed as such when information on different cultures is acquired. Benjamin Gidron and Mark Chesler's (1994) framework for cross-cultural comparison notes the existence both of culturally universal aspects of self-help organizations as well as culturally specific aspects shaped by the societies in which organizations exist (see also Lavoie, Borkman, & Gidron, 1994). Similarly, though virtually all countries use severity of impairment and degree-of-deviance-from-norms as standards by which to judge substance use as a problem, beyond that generality countries vary dramatically on how they recognize, handle, and interpret addiction (Jaffe, 1980).

The cross-cultural diversity of addictive behavior and of self-help organizations has not always been well appreciated by researchers. The literature on addiction-related self-help groups is replete with generalizations that are clearly culturally limited (see, e.g., Norman Denzin's 1987, otherwise masterful, analysis of AA in a single community in Illinois, USA). As was demonstrated by the International Collaborative Study of Alcoholics Anonymous (Mäkelä, *et al.*, 1996), many statements about AA based on one culture are refuted by observing it in another. By covering an international array of literature, this volume hopes to increase awareness of the cultural contexts in which all observers view self-help organizations.

An international scope also offers an opportunity for societies to learn from one another's successes and failures. For example, the World Health Organization (WHO) and a network of western European scholars have analyzed quite carefully how different policy initiatives can strengthen the self-help sector (Hatch & Kickbush, 1983; Humble & Unell, 1989). Yet the substantial literature these workers have produced is rarely cited in the writings of Japanese,

American, or Australian scholars who have struggled with the same issues. Every nation thus wastes valuable resources "reinventing the wheel" – a price of not being familiar with what occurs beyond one's own borders.

An international scope also raises a formidable challenge. There is a level at which all comparative statements about "country X and country Y" seem shallow and absurd. All of the countries examined here comprise millions of residents, diverse cultural traditions, distinct regions, and multiple languages. How can entities that differ so much internally be discussed as meaningful wholes? The same might be asked of many addiction-related self-help organizations, which differ dramatically in process, structure, and membership not only across countries but within them. To complicate matters further, even within a single country and a single self-help organization, the nature of the organization may change so much over time that conclusions reached in one generation may be less applicable to the next (Mäkelä, 1993). Faced with this diversity, the cross-cultural self-help group analyst may be tempted to give up on all generalizations, or qualify each one with a long apologia on intra-cultural diversity and the limits of cross-national understanding.

The above coping strategies will be eschewed here in favor of putting some faith in readers' powers of discernment. All social and behavioral science studies occur in a context and reflect that context's nature in some way. In that sense, *all* empirical results have limits on their generalizability. In this book, conclusions about self-help organizations and the societies that surround them will be made based on research studies conducted in particular contexts. These conclusions will naturally be limited in generalizability as well. Rather than harangue readers repeatedly with sermons on this point, it will be assumed throughout that readers understand the inherent limits of efforts to make general statements about complex organizations and societies. If any reader has personal knowledge of how a conclusion drawn here does not apply in a particular group of the self-help organization concerned, the region of the country at issue, or a nation as whole, the best possible outcome would be for that person to document the exception, publish it, and let the scientific conversation continue.

The other primary challenge of an international scope is the disproportionate amount of literature produced by and about the USA, which exceeds that of all other nations combined. This does not make the US experience any more informative or representative than that of any other nation, however, so a conscious effort will be made to prefer examples from other nations when they are available.

Range of addiction-related and non-addiction-related self-help organizations addressed

Even though most substance-dependent persons use more than one substance, academic research is often organized into putatively distinct fields such as "alcohol research" published in "alcohol journals," "drug research" appearing in "drug journals," and "smoking research" gracing the pages of "smoking journals." As a result, individuals studying one substance are not necessarily aware of valuable lessons learned by those studying a different substance. This book will attempt to surmount this problem by reviewing research on addiction-related self-help organizations for all forms of substance-related problems.

The primary challenge of discussing a broad range of organizations is the fact that most research examines only one: Alcoholics Anonymous. If the USA is the "800 pound gorilla" of addiction research, Alcoholics Anonymous is its mate within self-help group research. As with the first gorilla, the author will not let the absolute size of the literature about AA per se preclude attention to other organizations. Multiple books solely devoted to AA are available, however (e.g., Denzin, 1987; Mäkelä et al., 1996; Maxwell, 1984; McCrady & Miller, 1993; Robinson, 1979; Rudy, 1986). Focusing relatively less on AA than have other works in the field will allow this book to attend more to those organizations which are similar to AA in many respects but which receive little attention (e.g., Al-Anon, Narcotics Anonymous), as well as to organizations with completely independent origins and approaches (e.g., Croix Bleue/Blue Cross). This approach should help counter-balance the mistaken belief that "discussion of AA exhausts the whole topic of mutual help for alcohol problems" (Rehm & Room, 1992, p. 556).

In addition to branching out to organizations for different substances of abuse, this volume will also make connections to the literature on self-help organizations addressing concerns other than addiction. Virtually every leading cause of morbidity and mortality in the developed world has at least one self-help organization addressed to it (Humphreys & Ribisl, 1999). With notable exceptions like the path-breaking books of David Robinson (1979; Robinson & Henry, 1977), literature on non-addiction self-help organizations is rarely cited or discussed in addiction-related works. This is unfortunate because substance dependence bears similarities to other problems (e.g., gambling, overeating, chronic psychiatric and medical disorders) for which self-help organizations are also available. Although such organizations are not the primary focus of the volume, where relevant, research upon them will be brought in to inform the discussion. This should also help to distinguish forces operative within and upon addiction-related self-help organizations that are related to addiction per se versus those that are generic.

Range of disciplines covered

The longer format of a book has the great virtue of allowing review of material from a range of disciplines. This volume collects insights from psychiatry, psychology, anthropology, public health, and sociology. The challenges to doing this are considerable, given the differences in method and foci across fields. However, as the heart of the book will attempt to demonstrate, the advantages are equally remarkable, because each discipline illuminates a different facet of the self-help phenomenon.

What self-help organizations are and what they are not

Defining the field of this book is made difficult by two problems. First, as mentioned, terms such as "self-help group" and "mutual-aid association" are used in inconsistent ways in the scientific literature as well as in popular discourse. Second, self-help organizations are complex and varied – in some ways looking like paraprofessional treatments, in other ways like community-based organizations, and in still other ways like social movements. Hence, a careful definition of terms and defining features is necessary.

Nomenclature

Taken literally, "Self-help" is a misnomer for what occurs in mutual-help groups. As a term, "self-help" has individualistic connotations, as reflected, for example, in "self-help" books that are focused on improving personal effectiveness or well-being, or in the Victorian English ideal of "self-made" men who pulled themselves up by their own bootstraps without society's help, as expressed in works like Samuel Smiles's *(undated) "Self-Help, with Illustrations of Character, Conduct and Perseverance."* Mutual-help organizations are, by definition, social rather than individualistic. Further, they are typically characterized by emotional supportiveness, cohesion, and the sensibility that help should be reciprocal (i.e., members should both give and receive help; Maton, 1988). Indeed, some mutual-help organizations, such as AA, specifically state that helping other members is essential to helping oneself (Alcoholics Anonymous, 1952/1953). None of these realities are captured by the term "self-help."

Because of the limitations of the term "self-help," some self-help group researchers have instead advocated the terms "mutual-help group" and "mutual-aid organization." Although these terms are more accurate, they have a disadvantage of their own in being different from the term used by many of the millions of people who participate in groups. Further, some leaders of self-help organizations feel that, for practical means of communication with the public, the term "self-help" is familiar and useful (Rappaport, 1993). This book employs the compromise solution of using the terms "mutual help" and "self-help" interchangeably, in the hopes that over time this will become a more common linguistic convention (Humphreys & Rappaport, 1994).

Distinguishing mutual help "groups" from "organizations" is another helpful convention. Here, "group" will be used to refer to the small number of individuals (i.e., perhaps a few dozen) who come together in a particular setting to address their substance-abuse problems, as in the Cocaine Anonymous "group" that meets every Thursday evening at the community center on Elm Street. Most groups meet face-to-face, but a small number occur over the Internet. Self-help groups are often nested within a larger structure, which will be called the self-help "organization." Organizations can be regional, national, or international in scope and engage in activities such as operating central offices, publishing literature, supporting efforts to start new groups, and the like. Some fledgling local self-help groups have no connection to a larger organizational structure (see, e.g., Schubert & Borkman, 1991; Sproule, O'Halloran, & Borkman, 2000), but such groups are usually too small and idiosyncratic to be the subject of evaluation research projects, and thus are not a focus of major attention in this volume.

Essential characteristics of self-help organizations

Mutual-help organizations are quite diverse, but this does not prevent characterization of certain essential features. Table 1 distinguishes universal characteristics of all self-help organizations from those present in only some of them.

Members share a problem or status

At the heart of all mutual-help efforts is faith in the power of individuals working together to address a shared problem, be it alcoholism, cancer, compulsive shopping, or bereavement (Richardson, 1983a; Rootes & Aanes, 1992). The need for the shared effort stems from the problem causing distress of some

Table 1. *Features of mutual-help organizations*

Universal features
Members share a problem or status
Self-directed leadership
Valuation of experiential knowledge
Norm of reciprocal helping
Lack of fees
Voluntary association
Inclusion of some personal-change goals
Optional features
Developed philosophy and program of change
Spiritual or religious emphasis
Groups nested within a larger organizational structure
Political advocacy
Internet presence
Membership by relations of the substance-abusing participant
Defined role for professionals
Acceptance of external funds
Residential structure

form, else there would be little cause for collective action. Importantly, this distress does not necessarily stem from the shared concern per se, but may be due to how individuals with the concern are treated in society. For example, virtually all mutual-help organizations for gay and lesbian people do not define being homosexual as a problem, but rather view it as a status that is distressing due to discrimination.

Self-directed leadership

Many helping models – ranging from surgery to witch doctors' healing rituals – rest on the presumption that an outside expert who does not have the problem should be in control of the helping interaction. In contrast, the self-help ethos places the individuals who have the problem or status in charge of the organization (Katz, 1981). Hence, drug-dependent people facilitate Narcotics Anonymous (NA) meetings and operate its service boards, parents whose child has died operate Compassionate Friends, and so on. Self-directed leadership in mutual-help organizations thus goes well beyond the level of control available in psychotherapies which are intended to foster self-control in patients but which still clearly distinguish the role of patient and care provider.

Self-help organizations facilitate the emergence of peer leadership in part by designing themselves as what the well-known ecological psychologist Roger Barker (1964) termed "undermanned settings" (literally, a behavior setting in which there were "not enough hands"). By having no designated class of expert helpers, self-help organizations create roles and pressures for individuals to take on responsibility for group tasks, which by itself may be beneficial to them (Montaño Fraire, 2000).

Valuation of experiential knowledge

Sociologists and anthropologists have long differentiated lay and professional knowledge. Lay knowledge represents commonsense ideas, folk knowledge, pop culture beliefs, and "recipe knowledge" (Berger & Luckmann, 1967), for example what the average person in a society believes to be the causes and solutions of alcohol problems. Professional knowledge, in contrast, is academically derived, analytic, and grounded in theory or scientific principles. Traditionally, these two types of knowledge have been viewed as exhaustive, sometimes to the subtle diminishment of what any non-professionals might think or know. In this intellectual context, the sociologist Thomasina Borkman (1976, 1990, 1999) developed a useful concept for understanding self-help groups: a third type of knowledge called "experiential."

According to Borkman, experiential knowledge is "grounded in lived experience, concrete and pragmatic," which differentiates it from the lay knowledge to which everyone has access, even without direct experience of the problem. Yet it also differs from professional knowledge because of its basis in specific experiences, and practicality. A particular individual or organization may possess all three types of knowledge, but Borkman argues persuasively that an emphasis on experiential knowledge is a defining characteristic of self-help organizations. Whereas treatment professionals point to licenses, graduate degrees, and "book learning" to demonstrate their expertise with those they would help, self-help group participants emphasize that their expertise comes from "having been there too."

Norm of reciprocal helping

Many helping interactions are "one-way," meaning that the roles of helper and helpee are fixed, as in the cases of a father reassuring his anxious 6-year-old about the first day of school, a priest listening to the confession of a parishioner, or a psychiatrist conducting psychoanalysis with a neurotic patient. In contrast, mutual-help organizations establish a norm of reciprocal helping under which each participant will both give and receive help. This reflects their optimistic view that even troubled people have assets and knowledge that can help others (Riessman, 1990). Yet this perspective is also realistic and practical, as the social support research literature almost uniformly indicates that people benefit from providing support as much as, or more than, they do from only receiving it (Maton, 1988; Schwartz & Sendor, 1999).

Within a culture of reciprocal helping, self-help group participants assume the role of peer organizational member rather than that of a service recipient. This aspect of the self-help ethos dramatically increases the number of potential helpers (Riessman & Carroll, 1995).

Lack of fees

Because self-help organizations do not have professional helpers, neither do they charge a fee. Money collected within self-help group meetings is typically of the "pass the hat" variety, meaning that small sums are contributed voluntarily in order to pay for routine expenses, such as room rental, beverages, and organizational literature. Lack of significant economic cost, combined with the absence of waiting lists and admission forms, make the barriers to entry to self-help groups intentionally low (Humphreys & Tucker, 2002; Riordan & Beggs, 1988). Traditions of financial giving vary within and across mutual-help organizations (Mäkelä *et al.*, 1996), and there is of course informal social pressure to support one's organization, but any organization which demands a set fee as a condition of attendance will be defined in this book as a professional service rather than a self-help organization.

Voluntary association

Self-help organizations are part of the "voluntary sector" of societies, also sometimes termed the "third sector" or "civil society" (Edwards & Foley, 1997, 1998). The voluntary sector is usually defined by what it is not, namely neither part of the private sector nor the state (cf. Bender, Bargal, & Gidron, 1986; Borkman, 1999). Functionally, this means that if independent citizens do not choose to create and maintain mutual-help groups, they will not exist. "Voluntary association" as a concept that describes an organization need not imply that all members attend free of outside pressure. Substance-dependent people are often subjected to substantial pressure to seek help by friends, family, and employers (Schmidt & Weisner, 1999), and in one country (the USA) they are sometimes legally required to attend self-help groups. Yet as long as the existence of the self-help organization and fundamental control of its operations are in the hands of private citizens, it remains accurate to term it a "third-sector voluntary association," despite the efforts of outside parties to use it for their own ends.

Inclusion of some personal-change goals

The essential features of self-help organizations outlined thus far apply to many other voluntary organizations that form for the sole purpose of changing the outside world in some way (e.g., political parties, labor unions, racial supremacist organizations). Self-help organizations should thus be further defined as always including at least some goals for change within members themselves. This does not imply that a self-help organization has to view members as the primary source of suffering. For example, organizations for stigmatized diseases (e.g., AIDS) may view many of their members' problems as stemming primarily from discrimination, but still expect members to change in some way, for example by reducing internalized self-hatred, learning new skills for coping with ill treatment, and so forth. This definition does not rule out externally focused advocacy by self-help organizations, in which many engage, as long as the organization also seeks to implement change within members.

Optional features of self-help organizations

The lower half of Table 1 lists characteristics that are found in some, but not all, self-help organizations. All of them thus represent dimensions of diversity within the whole.

Developed philosophy and program of change

Some self-help organizations focus primarily on providing fellowship, information, support, fun, and self-acceptance. Many organizations related to chronic illness (e.g., cancer, heart disease) fall into this category. Such organizations typically have not developed an overarching philosophy or "world view" (Antze, 1979, 1987; Humphreys, 1993b) beyond a general commitment to support each other in dealing with a challenging problem.

Other mutual-help organizations have sophisticated philosophies that address questions such as the origin of the problem, its nature, how it may be addressed, what constitutes "the good life," and so forth. This world view is typically accompanied by a well-developed program of individual change which is believed to better members' lives. For example, Recovery Inc. – a mutual-help organization for chronic psychiatric patients – has a program known as "Will Training," which provides detailed guidance on how to control symptoms of depression and anxiety (McFadden, Seidman, & Rappaport, 1992). AA has the "12 steps," which are intended to help members cease alcohol use, improve relationships with others, and grow spiritually. Thus, to use the language of AA, even though all self-help organizations offer "fellowship," only a subset also put forward a "program."

Spiritual or religious emphasis

Within those organizations that have a developed philosophy and program of change, a distinction can be made between those that have a secular versus a spiritual or religious philosophy (Room, 1998). Some self-help organizations occur within the context of a religious organization, restrict participation to members of one religious affiliation, and adopt their philosophy and rituals directly from the religion. For example, in the USA, some African-American churches have chronic-disease-focused self-help groups for parishioners who have an explicitly "Christ-centered" approach to recovery. Other self-help organizations, including many of those addressing life-threatening diseases, are not religiously affiliated but do make specific references to spiritual concerns and spiritual growth within their program of change. The above two types of self-help organizations can be contrasted with those that do not explicitly address spiritual or religious concerns in their philosophy, literature, or group meetings.

Groups nested within a larger organizational structure

As mentioned, some self-help groups are entirely local efforts created by ener-getic people working at the grassroots level. Long before AIDS-focused national organizations existed, for example, small groups of HIV-positive individuals gathered together regularly for mutual support in many European and US cities. Other self-help groups are nested within a larger organization that connects in-dividual chapters and geographic areas. These larger bodies develop and publish organizational literature, maintain group directories, and, among other activi-ties, may also convene conferences, set policy, and deal with external organiza-tions. The National Federation of the Societies of Links and the World Service Board of Al-Anon Family Groups are examples. Although they will not be analyzed extensively in this book, it is worth comment that, in general, the larger structure of self-help organizations usually reflects the non-hierarchical ethos present in individual chapters, with centralized control being intentionally weak.

Political advocacy

The best known addiction-related self-help organizations (e.g., AA, NA) have a tradition of not engaging in political advocacy, in part because they believe substance dependence arises entirely from sources inside of their members and not in the surrounding society. However, not all self-help organizations embrace this viewpoint. Most mutual-help organizations with a strong tradition of advocacy focus on problems other than substance abuse (e.g., serious mental illness, breast cancer). However, examples exist within the addiction field, e.g., Free Life (Vie Libre), which, in addition to promoting abstinence among members, embraces a mission of social advocacy (Bénichou, 1980) and officially endorses increases in public spending for addiction-related health care (Cerclé, 1984).

Internet presence

Making any comment about self-help organizations' presence on the Internet is hazardous because that rapidly changing medium may render it out of date in no time. At this writing at least, mutual-help organizations vary significantly in their use of the Internet. The Moderation Management self-help organization launched itself primarily by this route, with online meetings and a website that complemented a comparatively small network of face-to-face groups (Humphreys & Klaw, 2001; Klaw, Huebsch & Humphreys, 2000). Other organizations have less of a presence, either due to a long tradition of face-to-face meetings, or to a lack of Internet infrastructure in the countries in which they exist, or both.

Membership by relations of the substance-abusing participant

Mutual-help organizations vary on how broadly they define the shared status and the membership that flows from it (Room, 1998). For example, mutual-help organizations for incest survivors usually do not admit current sexual partners of victims, even though such individuals are often affected by members' status. In contrast, other self-help organizations (e.g., for low vision) extend membership to concerned relatives.

Defined role for professionals

Although self-help organizations are operated by members themselves, many establish supportive roles for professionals. Some organizations (e.g., Recovery Inc.) were largely created by professionals and later became self-sustaining mutual-help organizations, with professionals shifting to an advisory role. Others have always been entirely member-controlled, but invite in occasional professional speakers, work with hospital staff to secure meeting space, and ask professionals to refer patients or to serve on advisory boards. Finally, some self-help organizations are openly hostile to treatment professionals, though this is more prevalent among organizations for serious mental illness than for substance abuse (cf. Chamberlin, 1978).

More than any other characteristic, the role of professionals makes it difficult to define which organizations are truly self-help groups. Many helping professionals organize groups for which they themselves share the problem of interest (Medvene, Wituk, & Luke, 1999), which may or may not have a self-help ethos, depending on the professionals' behavior. A professional who has an anxiety disorder, who openly describes this fact, who does not control group interaction, and who both gives and receives help is no contradiction to the self-help ethos. However, a professional who does not reveal his disorder, does not operate as a peer, does not share control, etc., could better be described as volunteering time to run a free support group – a worthy activity to be sure but not the same as participating in a peer-operated self-help group.

These issues are made particularly complex in organizations that have blended professional–peer leadership, such as "Parents Anonymous" (Wordes *et al.*, 2002) in the USA and "Clubs for Treated Alcoholics" in the Adriatic countries (Hudolin, 1984). Within such organizations, individual groups may have the character of professional-controlled group psychotherapy in some regions and with some co-leaders, while operating as true peer-controlled self-help groups in other regions and with other co-leaders.

Political activist Sally Zinman (1987) raised the additional concern that, because "self-help," "consumer control," "empowerment," and similar terms have become trendy in some countries (e.g., Canada, France, England, USA), treatment professionals sometimes describe activities in which they are involved as "peer-operated," when in fact peer control is trivial. Buzzwords are far less important in differentiating self-help organizations from professional interventions than is the bread-and-butter reality of who has power within the organization.

Acceptance of external funds

One of the hottest debates within the self-help group movement concerns whether organizations can accept external funds and still maintain their grassroots, non-bureaucratic character. The founders of AA famously came to the conclusion that it was better for the organization to be entirely self-supporting, but this is by no means universal. Whether direct funding is a good strategy for self-help organizations and for potential supporters will be addressed in detail in Chapter 5; here it is sufficient to note the variance on this dimension.

Residential structure

Most self-help organizations offer support on an ambulatory basis, i.e., members come to attend group events and then leave. Other organizations offer a residential alternative that attempts to create a total mutual-help culture. Mental health consumer-run crisis residential units are a prominent example in the psychiatric field (Greenfield, Stoneking, & Sundby, 1996; Stroul, 1987). Residential self-help organizations for addicted individuals include the German Synanon (Fredersdorf, 2000), which allows long-term residence and a system of potential economic support (e.g., jobs), the Mexican AA "24-Hour-a-Day Movement" for homeless alcoholics (Rosovsky, 1998), and the US-based Oxford House organization (Jason *et al.*, 2001).

Differentiating self-help organizations from other interventions

The characteristics listed in Table 1 clarify how self-help organizations differ from many other organizations. Because of similarities in function and/or terminology, additional distinctions should be drawn with other interventions.

Self-help books

Self-help books are widely used, and can be helpful to individuals who have health and social problems, including substance abuse (Baldwin & McMillan, 1993; Marrs, 1995). Despite their name, they are not typically considered to be part of the self-help group literature. Self-help books are written by experts, rely on professional knowledge, and place the reader in the role of a service recipient who is not expected to help anyone other than him- or herself. These characteristics make self-help books more similar to professional intervention than to peer-controlled self-help organizations. The only genuine commonality between self-help books and self-help groups is faith that an individual can address a health problem without direct contact with a trained professional helper.

Voluntary care

Drawing on the work of the WHO regional office for Europe, Ilona Kickbush and Stephen Hatch (1983) distinguish self-help organizations from voluntary care. The latter involves various forms of non-professional help provided by community members to needy individuals (e.g., home visiting, child care, grocery shopping), is often organized under the egis of a charitable or religious organization, and in some countries is well-coordinated with state-provided services. Such programs value non-professional help and voluntary action, and are usually without fees, but are not mutual-help organizations because the individuals who have the problem of concern neither provide help nor have control over how the program operates. Hence, although productive links have been developed between many voluntary-care agencies and mutual-help initiatives, they are distinguishable forms of assistance (Kickbush & Hatch, 1983).

Professionally operated treatments, support groups, and patient-education programs

Many professional treatments, particularly in the addiction field, employ some concepts that are drawn from self-help organizations. Yet professionally operated treatments differ from self-help organizations even when they have surface similarities (Humphreys, 1993a, E. Kurtz, 1992; L. F. Kurtz, 1997a). Common terminology need not imply the same approach. A sample of professionals who described themselves as providing treatment from a "12-step, disease model perspective such as is found in AA" rated "reducing denial" as the most important aspect of treatment, and spiritual change as the least important aspect (Morgenstern & McCrady, 1993). Such professionals are apparently unaware that the term "denial" barely appears in AA literature and is actually derived from psychoanalytic writings, whereas spirituality is a central topic throughout AA's program and writings (Miller & Kurtz, 1994). Shared terms such as "12-step philosophy" and "the disease model" may make treatment and self-help groups sound more similar than they are, making some efforts at differentiation valuable in the name of accurate description (cf. Glaser, 1993).

The most fundamental difference between professional treatments and mutual-help organizations is that, in the former, expertise, power, and control emanate from professionals. This is true even in cases where a helping profes-sional has an addiction, because the professional is still in the dominant role of helper, is considered an expert, establishes the guidelines and location of the helping interaction, and receives a payment for services rendered.

Further, treatment professionals have legal and ethical constraints on their behavior that self-help groups do not. Professionals have to be licensed, as do the agencies in which they work. The ethics of many professional disciplines forbid professionals from forming lifelong friendships with patients, engaging in recreational activities with them, and all the other social interactions that are common within self-help organizations. Professionals have particular legal obligations to patients that groups do not have, for example to intervene aggres-sively when a patient is suicidal, to keep each patient's identity confidential, and to inform authorities when the patient reports certain types of information (e.g., the commission of certain crimes).

All of the above factors make the professional–patient interaction very differ-ent from peer–peer self-help group interaction. The idea that different helping interactions differ in structure, function, and effects seems neither novel nor shocking on its face. Nevertheless, some professionals bristle at the idea that self-help groups can do some things that professionals cannot. Why might this be so?

An unfortunate feature of the socialization of all professionals is implicit and explicit inculcation of the concept that professionals inherently improve those activities with which they become involved, particularly if such activities are operated by individuals "outside the guild." Hence, an empirical demonstra-tion to the contrary may be informative. Toro *et al.* (1988) compared the social environment and group norms in two types of groups operated by GROW – a mutual-help organization of individuals with serious psychiatric disorders. One set of groups was led by GROW members (i.e., individuals who had psy-chiatric problems), consistent with usual organizational practice, and the other set was led by professionals trained in social work, psychology, and related fields. The professionals were selected specifically because they were highly supportive of GROW, trained in its approach, and familiar with its philosophy. Nevertheless, results showed that GROW participants in peer-led groups rated the groups as higher in cohesion, expressiveness, and self-discovery than did participants in the professionally led groups. Outside observers rated partici-pants in peer-led groups as talking more, providing more information, and agreeing more often than did participants in professionally led groups. Even the professional leaders rated their groups as higher in leader control than did peer leaders.

The professional leaders in this study apparently unintentionally communicated expectations and role definitions that led GROW participants to act in ways consistent with the more passive role of "psychiatric patient." Given that GROW is intended to provide assistance that differs from that which is already available to psychiatric patients, these effects cannot be viewed as positive, even though they may have been quite appropriate for professionally controlled psychotherapy. The results serve not as a critique of professionally facilitated groups, which can be quite effective. Rather, in combination with similar findings from other studies (e.g., Wordes *et al.*, 2002), they are a cautionary tale for treatment professionals who assume that self-help groups provide nothing that professionals could not provide better themselves.

There is a large class of professional interventions in which professionals take the role of facilitator rather than leader/director, and such programs are usually neither viewed nor marketed as "treatment" per se. Such interventions include support groups and patient-education programs offered to individuals who have chronic health problems (see, e.g., Lorig *et al.*, 2001). Because such programs require active participation by patients and are intended to be less "scary" to participants than would an intervention labeled as a "psychological treatment," they are often called "self-help groups" by their organizers and in some empirical articles (e.g., Jensen, 1983). These programs are more akin to mutual-help organizations than are other professional interventions, but nevertheless are not mutual-help organizations because they differ significantly on critical dimensions (e.g., professional control, fees, etc.).

Generic factors behind the development of the self-help group movement in the modern world

The historical events and forces behind specific addiction-related self-help organizations will be reviewed in Chapter 2. As intriguing as such details are, they must be understood within a broader context. Self-help organizations addressing a plethora of health and life concerns blossomed in developed nations over the twentieth century. A small subset of the concerns self-help organizations address includes addictions, arthritis, bereavement, cancer, diabetes, grand-parenting, divorce, violence, and gay/lesbian identity. The following section explores those factors that have led to the creation of the multi-faceted self-help movement in developed nations.

In approaching this task, one must first wade through some non-substantive and unnecessary explanations for the emergence of self-help organizations. Like many complex social phenomena, the rise of self-help organizations in the developed world has been attributed to diverse factors. Some of these explanations are, in the author's opinion, overreaching and hard to verify empirically, for example Alfred Katz's (Katz, 1986; Katz & Bender, 1976) suggestions that the mutual-help group movement is in part a response to "rising depersonalization," "the loss of choices," alienation, malaise, and a widening generation gap, or the assertions (see Barath, 1991) that the European self-help group movement was a response to "greater appreciation of the small and fragile" and to "growing misery experienced by many people of all classes" (see also de Cocq, 1976, for equally vague remarks). One wonders whether, as a complex phenomenon whose boundaries are hard to establish, the self-help group movement is akin to a Rorschach inkblot upon which observers may project causal explanations reflecting their present-day gripes and biases. Zeitgeists are real and they shape social movements, but one must be cautious not to romanticize the past by implying that loneliness, alienation, powerlessness, family misery, etc., are modern inventions, particularly when the comparison is based on something hard to verify empirically like "increasing malaise in the air." Otherwise, one is engaging in a level of explanation that is no more elevated or precise than that of every generation's complaints about how "kids these days" are allegedly a step down from kids of previous days.

In addition to avoiding non-substantive explanations, self-help analysts should also beware non-necessary ones. Not all aspects of the self-help group movement *require* any particularly complex explanation, particularly the fact that groups involve human beings working together to solve common problems. The tendency to affiliate, to form organizations, and to solve basic problems of survival collectively has always been a fact of human existence. As the biologist Edmund Wilson (1988) has pointed out, these are evolutionary advantageous traits genetically encoded in certain species, including *Homo sapiens* (as well as, of course, ants, termites, and other creatures that most humans would prefer not to regard as genetic cousins). Coming from a very different viewpoint, the anarchist sociologist Peter Kropotkin (1955) made the historical argument that mutual aid is the central building block of civilization, whether it involves gathering food, raising a barn, or founding a village. Other scholars (e.g., Bender, 1986) made the similar point that, while the objects of mutual help vary across societies, its nature is always inherent in the process of social development. Hence, there is no real reason to explain the tendency of human beings to gather together, accumulate resources, and solve shared threats to survival per se. In contrast, what *does* require explanation is why, in recent decades, more individuals are engaging in mutual aid specifically in self-help groups, and why these groups focus upon certain specific problems.

Five inter-related forces that have fostered the modern self-help group movement

Of the many classes of explanations for the rise of the self-help group movement, five seem both the most specific and the most empirically verifiable. Particular factors are more important in some societies than in others, and the five interact in different ways at different times for different health problems. Yet a certain degree of generality can be attributed to all of them within those nations addressed in this book because they are essentially tied to societies that are becoming wealthier and more stable in the twentieth century than they were in previous eras.

What drives the self-help group movement must be distinguished at the outset from what makes policy makers and professionals show interest in the movement. This chapter focuses on the former question, whereas the issue of why self-help is periodically "re-discovered" (cf. Pancoast, Parker, & Froland,1983) by interested outsiders from time to time will be addressed in Chapter 5.

Improved public health and wealth

In 1900, life expectancy in western countries averaged around 50 years, and death or grievous injury from infectious diseases was a virtually constant threat (Breslow, 1990). Public health measures, improvements in clinical medicine, and rising wealth changed this situation dramatically over the twentieth century, allowing a much higher proportion of infants to live to adulthood, and, to a lesser but still significant extent, increasing the likelihood that adults would live to old age.

As marvelous as improved public health is, it has increased the prevalence of chronic health problems in at least three ways. First, as acute illness becomes less of a threat, human beings have wide new vistas available to kill themselves through long-term behavior patterns, for example smoking and overeating. Behavior patterns that, in a previous era, were considered unimportant because they usually took longer to end one's life than one expected to live became defined as "chronic behavioral health problems" as life expectancy increased. Second, chronic health problems (behavioral or not) have become more prevalent owing to medicine's increased ability to prevent or delay death for illnesses such as AIDS, cardiovascular disease, and cancer, among others (Surgeon General's Workshop on Self-Help and Public Health, 1990). Third, as a higher proportion of individuals live into old age, developing a chronic health problem and having to cope with it for an extended period become more normative human experiences (Riessman & Carroll, 1995).

Developed societies' public wealth has grown in tandem with public health over the past century, allowing more individuals to devote time and attention to problems other than immediate threats to survival. Modern citizens have more resources than did their forebears to attend to chronic illnesses, to gather health information, and to contemplate how illness affects personal identity (Mäkelä, 1991; Mäkelä *et al.*, 1996). For example, sickle cell anemia is a very serious illness, yet it was not until after World War II that African-Americans formed self-help groups to address it (Nash & Kramer, 1993). Prior African-American mutual-aid organizations focused primarily on creating basic economic resources for an oppressed population, such as life and disability insurance policies, monies for the legal defense of African-Americans falsely charged with crimes, and loan programs to support the education of African-American children and the development of African-American businesses (Humphreys & Hamilton, 1995; Neighbors, Elliott, & Gant, 1990). A sizable health- and identity-focused mutual-help movement may not have been possible until after class-based social movements (e.g., trade unions) had forced broader distribution of economic resources (Mäkelä *et al.*, 1996).

The prevalence of chronic illnesses and the increased resources of modern people to focus upon them have supported the growth of the self-help group movement in two ways. First, because most chronic illnesses cause physical and emotional distress, many individuals have the motivation to seek support, understanding, and knowledge from others who are coping with the same illnesses. Second, because chronic illnesses by definition last for extended periods, this provides a stable basis for self-help organizations to accrue members and develop an experienced leadership core.

Better public health has also increased the absolute size of the population, which of course has expanded the number of individuals from which self-help organizations can be formed. This is particularly important for self-help groups focused on very rare conditions like neurofibromatosis and retinitis pigmentosa (White & Madara, 1998), which otherwise would not have a sufficiently large number of affected individuals to form a stable membership base.

Weakening of familial ties

When upper-class Americans visited France in the late 1700s, they were unfavorably impressed with the "anti-family attitudes" of the French elite, whose marriages often produced no more than six children. The scandalized early Americans aside, the French were clearly ahead of the historical curve: the number of children per married couple has dropped precipitously in developed nations since. Other marked changes across developed nations include a much higher divorce rate, later age at first marriage, higher prevalence of never-married individuals living alone, and an increased tendency for multi-generation families to live in different geographical locations (Arnett, 2000).

Taken together, these data indicate that familial ties are weaker and less defining for modern individuals than they were in previous eras. This diminishment of familial ties (and relatedly, ties to the unrelated persons in the community in which one was born) is often cited as supporting the self-help group movement in the developed world (Borman, 1979). Whereas in developing nations, the problem of caring for sick and distressed individuals still falls almost entirely on family members, in developed societies such needs are more often met through seeking help from unrelated individuals, including self-help group members.

Limits of professional assistance

In a perceptive study conducted in the UK, Robinson and Henry (1977) analyzed the reasons why self-help organizations are founded. Dissatisfaction with professional services was a widely cited motivation across organizational founders. This general point requires analysis, as the "limits of professional assistance" are of different types.

Professional shortcomings

Many self-help organizations were founded by individuals who felt abused by healthcare professionals. For example, a major spur to the creation of organizations for parents of the mentally ill was justifiable anger at mental health professionals who asserted that autism, schizophrenia, and other serious illnesses were entirely the result of poor parenting. Similarly, individuals with many stigmatized conditions (e.g., sexually transmitted diseases, serious mental illness) have formed self-help organizations because they believe professional healthcare services are laden with the larger prejudices of society, reflected for example through neglect or outright abuse of patients with the condition (Zinman, Harp, & Budd, 1987).

Other self-help organizations are created in response to professional ignorance rather than ill intent. The conditions addressed by these organizations are usually rare, hard to diagnose, or both (e.g., achromatopsia, Gaucher's disease, lymphangiomyomatosis). Individuals founding mutual-help organizations of this sort usually attribute the shortcomings of the health care they receive to the special challenges of their illness rather than to professional biases or stigmatization. Such organizations therefore seek to educate professionals using their superior ability to pool information as a resource: 300 individuals with a very rare disease who regularly discuss it at self-help group meetings and integrate relevant medical research in their newsletter and website will know far more about the illness than will any primary care physician, who may see only one such patient in his or her career.

Independent of the behavior of any particular professional, the structure of health care also sometimes leads to dissatisfaction that spurs individuals to form alternative helping resources. Edward Madara, director of the American Self-help Clearinghouse, recently commented that, "some self-help groups came about because a group of patients were sitting together so long in a doctor's waiting room that they started to talk to each other about their disease instead." Lengthy admission forms, funding shortages, bureaucratic requirements, difficulty in obtaining appointments, etc., are near-universal within large healthcare systems, and can inspire frustrated patients to develop more accessible, less cumbersome, sources of support.

In summary, stigma, lack of knowledge, and red tape within professional health care have all contributed to the development of self-help organizations. Because all of these problems are in theory correctable, they may be legitimately viewed as professional shortcomings. Yet self-help organizations can also emerge in response to a different, intractable type of dissatisfaction with professional health care.

Realistic limitations on professional help

No-one would dispute the rights of healthcare consumers to ask that professional healthcare providers be respectful, knowledgeable, and accessible, or to form self-help groups as an independent resource when professional health care does not meet these standards. Nevertheless, it would be quite unfair to assume that professionals have failed in some way every time a self-help group is formed for a condition for which ample professional services exist.

Individuals often affiliate with self-help organizations to find a new community and long-term way of living (Humphreys & Rappaport, 1994; Miller & Kurtz, 1994; Robinson & Henry, 1977). For example, members may seek new friendships, new social activities, long-term value reorientation, and spiritual sustenance. Healthcare professionals cannot provide all these things (Dumont, 1974), nor should they be expected to. The resources societies provide for professional services could never be sufficient for every person with a health concern to develop a new community and system of living around professional help. And even if such resources were available, a network of paid supporters would not be comparable in an individual's experience to a supportive web of loved ones. Peer mutual help has existed in all societies before, during, and after any professional services were available because it meets essential needs and has essential functions orthogonal to those that can be professionalized. In the author's opinion, the idea that all human needs can be serviced by hired experts, or that they should be, is a technocratic fantasy that places absurd expectations on professionals (see Bender and colleagues, 1986, on this failed assumption of the classical welfare state).

If it is a mistake to assume that professional services could ever solve all human problems, then it is also a mistake to assume that self-help organizations are developed solely to be another, better, form of service. Self-help organizations are much more than an alternative form of treatment services – a point that will be developed further in Chapter 4. This realization makes sense of the apparently contradictory fact that some American commentators have stated that self-help organizations arise because of the USA's weak and inadequate public welfare safety net (Katz, 1981), whereas commentators from nations with stronger social welfare traditions (e.g., Israel) have argued that self-help groups are a response to the overreaching, intrusive, and paternalistic welfare state (Gidron & Bargal, 1986)!

The rise of consumerism in health care

The traditional framework of medical care could be parodied – with a not inconsiderable grain of truth – as "all-knowing professionals bestowing the miracle of their treatments from on high to their passive, deferent, and grateful patients." This model has come under significant criticism by health consumer movements in western European and North American nations over the past three decades, and the relationship between health professionals and individuals with health problems is being revised accordingly. Although health consumerism is much broader in scope than the rise of self-help group involvement, evidence from several societies indicates a synergy between the two.

For example, one of the main goals of the health consumer movement in Germany has been to "de-doctorize" control of health (Huber, 1983). Raising questions about the centrality of professional providers in caring for individuals' health problems implicitly endorses the mutual-help concept of keeping organizational control in the hands of peer members. The German health movement's theme of "increased personal control of health" also supports mutual help groups by implying that "the sick" still maintain some power to address their condition. Indeed, German self-help group advocates have explicitly tapped into such consumer movement themes in promoting their organizations (Huber, 1983; see also Trojan, Halves, & Wetendorf, 1986). Similar dynamics have affected healthcare policy in Quebec, where self-help group leaders have been a strong voice for greater consumer participation in all levels of the formal caregiving system and the taking of personal responsibility for health (Lavoie, 1983).

Similar health consumer movements are evident in most of the western societies covered in this volume. Self-help organizations can certainly come into existence without the presence of such movements, as they did in Japan, but when present, such movements help create a socio-political ethos that is favorable to self-help groups.

Benefits of participation

Prosaic explanations for social phenomena are often more compelling than the rococo attributions favored by many academic theorists. Self-help analysts should therefore not omit an obvious, powerful mechanism behind the expansion of self-help groups: they benefit their members. These benefits comprise those related to the explicit purpose of the group as well as those that are less explicit but equally important. The former set of rewards includes weight-reduction groups leading to weight loss (Peterson *et al.*, 1985; Stunkard *et al.*, 1970), caregiver groups improving coping with the stress of caring for seriously ill relatives (Fung & Chien, 2002; Toseland, Rossiter, & Labrecque, 1989), and psychiatric self-help organizations reducing hospitalizations (Gordon *et al.*, 1979). Among the latter set of rewards, research has identified subjective satisfaction with self-help groups among manic–depressive individuals (L. F. Kurtz, 1988) and among family members of mentally ill people (Biegel & Yamatani, 1987), in relation to friendship-making in groups for the elderly (Lieberman & Videka-Sherman, 1986), and with increased connection to cultural heritage among self-help groups for diabetic south Asian immigrants living in the UK (Simmons, 1992). It is a small intellectual leap that these benefits reinforce attendance and thereby strengthen self-help organizations. Whether similar reinforcements occur within addiction-related self-help groups is of course a major subject of chapters to follow.

Hans Toch (1965) offered an important expansion of the hypothesis that self-help group involvement is driven by obtained benefits in his classic book *"Social psychology of social movements."* Some self-change organizations attract members with the "provable and frequently proved" (p. 83) claim of effectiveness but also with the usually false claim of a *unique* benefit. Examining self-help organizations for obesity, psychiatric illness, and alcoholism, Toch notes many parallels in how different organizations operate, such that each group "may not be the only road to Rome" but "does know the way" (p. 83). To say that effectiveness may drive participation is only to support the first claim. The second is unlikely ever to be tested empirically because it would require forcing successful affiliates of one self-help group to leave and join another one.

2

An international tour of addiction-related mutual-help organizations

Background and context

The modern self-help group movement comprises many addiction-related organizations for all the reasons detailed in Chapter 1. Substance abuse is a chronic behavioral health problem and sufficiently prevalent to provide a large pool of potential self-help organization members. It cannot be addressed solely by professional resources because, as a stigmatized condition, it rarely commands a significant share of healthcare budgets, and, even when it does, many professionals do not know how, or simply do not want to, treat it. And in any case, many addicted individuals wish to change in ways that are hard to achieve with professional services alone, for example by building a new community that supports recovery.

These realities make it conceivable that addiction-related groups are the most common type of self-help organization. Support for this conjecture includes data showing that more than half of health-related self-help groups in the city of Hamburg, Germany, focused on substance abuse (Deneke, 1983). The only detailed national information on this question comes from the USA, where mutual-help group attendance is far more common than in other nations for which national data are available (e.g., Canada, see Gottlieb & Peters, 1991), and perhaps particularly so for addiction-related groups (Mäkelä et al., 1996). With that caution, the following nationally representative survey data, gathered by Ronald Kessler et al. (1997), is worthy of consideration. Of US adults aged 25–74 years, 18.7% had attended a self-help group in their lifetime, and 7.1% had done so in the past 12 months. Substance-abuse-related groups were the most prevalent type, with 6.4% lifetime participation and 2.6% participation in the past 12 months. Both the lifetime and past-12-months figures reveal that over a third of all Americans who have attended a self-help group have attended one focused on substance abuse. If one examines the number of self-help group *meetings* attended, the relative importance of addiction groups is even larger. Substance-related self-help group members attend an average of 76 meetings per year, which aggregates to 70% of all group meeting visits across the US self-help group movement. Whether these results generalize to other cultures is not known, but they clearly suggest that addiction-related groups have a major role in the modern self-help group movement.

Analysis of the self-help group movement in general, and of omnibus survey data such as the above, are informative, but knowing the history, philosophy, and membership of specific organizations is also necessary for understanding substance-abuse-related self-help organizations. To that end, the remainder of this chapter describes 19 such organizations operating in different parts of the developed world. These are obviously only a subset of all those that exist. Readers who are familiar with other organizations may wonder why they are not described. In a number of instances, a substance-abuse-related organization described in the literature as a self-help group proved instead, upon closer inspection, to be controlled by professionals who did not personally have the problem addressed by the group. Examples include Double Trouble (Caldwell & White, 1991), the UK-based version of Drinkwatchers (Barrison *et al.*, 1987; Ruzek, 1987; Ruzek & Vetter, 1983), and The Winner's Group (Bennett & Scholler-Jaquish, 1995). Other genuine self-help organizations were excluded because they appear to be defunct, including TRANX (Tattersall & Hallstrom, 1992) and the US-based version of Drinkwatchers (Winters, 1978). Still other self-help organizations were excluded due to there being little (or at least a failure to find) substantial scientific literature on them: Non-Al-Anon-Affiliated Adult Children of Alcoholics, Alcoholics Victorious, The Caritas Lok Heep Club (Porter *et al.*, 1999), Circle of Friends (Appel, 1996), Dual Disorders Anonymous, Free N' One Recovery, Kreuzbund, Marijuana Anonymous, Methadone Anonymous (Gilman, Galanter, & Dermatis, 2001), and PRIDE (Galanter *et al.*, 1984), to name a few. Even with these exclusions, there were many more substance-abuse-related self-help organizations to describe than could be included in a single volume. The 19 organizations below were chosen for detailed description from the subset of substance-abuse-related, peer-operated self-help organizations on which literature was available primarily on the basis of diversity, i.e., to show organizations operating in different parts of the world, engaging in a range of activities, with varied philosophies, for different populations and substances.

Two limitations of the following information should be borne in mind. First, a few organizations (e.g., Free Life, Pui Hong Self-Help Association) have been described in the English-language literature by only a few scholars, so their descriptions rely on a smaller number of observers than do those of organizations that have been the subject of more available research. Second, membership numbers should be viewed as estimates. When professional researchers conduct surveys of help-seeking, they typically ask many detailed questions about professional services and few or none about self-help group participation. This approach, which implicitly reflects the view that professional services are more important, results in poor data on self-help group participation. Further problems with membership numbers arise from mutual-help organizations themselves, who may use assessment approaches that understate or overstate their membership (perhaps at times intentionally), for example when they are making the case for public funds (Helmersson Bergmark, 1998). Finally, as more self-help organizations have established a presence on the Internet, membership has become harder to assess (i.e., should a person who logs onto an organization's website a few times a year be considered a member?). The numbers below reflect face-to-face group membership; to the author's knowledge, no self-help organization has yet included Internet-based participants in internal membership surveys.

The list below uses Anglicized names of groups for alphabetization. They are presented in alphabetical order except for AA, which is described first and at greater length because a detailed understanding of AA will facilitate discussion of the many other organizations it has influenced.

Origins, philosophy, and membership of addiction-related self-help organizations

Alcoholics Anonymous

Origins and history

The founding and development of AA have been recounted by the organization (Alcoholics Anonymous, 1952/1953, 1976) and by numerous scholars (e.g., Dumont, 1974; E. Kurtz, 1979/1991; Leach, 1973; Robertson, 1988; Robinson, 1979, 1980; Shaw, 1982; White, 1998). The following abbreviated history is amalgamated from the above works. Readers desiring a comprehensive treatment are referred to Ernest Kurtz's (1979/1991) classic study.

History records that AA was founded in 1935. However, as with most social phenomena, a full understanding of AA's origin requires one to go "before the beginning" (Sarason, 1972). The 1920s and 1930s witnessed the rise of a quasi-religious evangelical movement known as The Oxford Group, lead by a Lutheran minister named Frank Buchman. This movement began in north-eastern USA, and soon spread to other parts of the world where Lutheranism was influential (e.g., Sweden, see "The Links," p. 67). The Oxford Group attempted to recapture the spirit of early pietist Christianity, and valued confession of, and restitution for, sins among peers. Among its members were several alcoholics attempting to maintain sobriety, including Rowland Hazard and Edwin Thatcher. Hazard had been a patient of the Swiss psychoanalyst Carl Jung, who told him that his alcoholism could only be resolved through a spiritual transformation. Hazard communicated Jung's opinion to Thatcher, who was favorably impressed by it.

As part of his evangelical work as an Oxford Group member, Thatcher reached out in November, 1934, to an alcoholic friend named William Griffith Wilson (also known as AA co-founder "Bill W."). Wilson was unimpressed with Thatcher's account of the Oxford Group's and Jung's insights at the time, but came to appreciate them a few weeks later when he had a spiritual peak experience during yet another emergency detoxification. Hence, although Thatcher himself ultimately relapsed, he, along with Jung, Hazard, and Wilson's supportive physician William Silkworth, all had a role in leading Wilson to view recovery from alcoholism as a spiritual rather than merely a medical process.

Wilson participated in The Oxford Group after being released from the hospital and maintained abstinence for several months. However, in May, 1935, on a failed business trip to Akron, Ohio, his confidence left him and he found himself desperately wishing to soothe his pain with alcohol. He got in touch with Dr. Robert Holbrook Smith (now known as AA co-founder "Dr. Bob") – an Oxford Group member who had also struggled with alcoholism for many years. The two men met for several hours at the house of a sympathetic local woman named Henrietta Seiberling. Their conversation – now recognized as the first AA meeting – had a profound effect on them both. They discovered that they could identify with each other's stories, and provide each other strength and hope. A key lesson they drew from this experience was that the way for alcoholics to recover was for them to help other alcoholics.

Alcoholics held mutual-support meetings over the next few years under the auspices of the Oxford Group in New York City and Akron. However, the religiosity and rigidity of the Oxford Group began to rankle some members, particularly those in New York City. Wilson saw his own struggles, and those of other members, as stemming in part from their arrogant tendency to attempt superhuman tasks and then go into black depression when the inevitable failure occurred. The Oxford Group's demand for "absolute" honesty, "absolute" purity, "absolute" unselfishness and "absolute" love therefore seemed to exacerbate what, in Wilson's eyes, were the fundamental character problems of alcoholics. Desiring a program that was more flexible, and better suited to the needs of alcoholics as they saw it, AA's founders split off into their own mutual-help organization, which entered the public mind in 1939 with the publication of their book, *"Alcoholics Anonymous"* (known universally in AA simply as "The Big Book" because of the thick paper on which the first edition was printed). The appearance of AA's book was followed by positive media coverage of AA (e.g., in the *Saturday Evening Post*) and increased public awareness of alcoholism (e.g., *"Lost Weekend"* won the US Motion Picture Academy Awards for Best Picture, Director, and Actor in 1945), all of which helped to make the 1940s a decade of spectacular growth for AA. When the first edition of "The Big Book" was distributed, AA had at most several hundred members, whereas by the time Dr. Bob died in 1950, it had 50 000.

In addition to establishing new groups in new locations, AA's members continued to develop their philosophy and approach throughout the 1940s and 1950s. This evolutionary process was informed by ideas from the Oxford Group, William James, Carl Jung, and other outside sources, but its most important basis was members' experience of living with and recovering from alcoholism. Some aspects of AA, such as the practice of experienced members sponsoring newcomers, were developed specifically to help individual members recover. Others, such as AA's refusal to take any official stand on outside issues, were intended to help the organization as a whole survive and function effectively. (AA's founders knew that the earlier Washingtonian movement of "reformed drunkards" had engaged in internecine squabbles over outside political issues.) The development of AA's traditions and procedures was not without internal arguments, particularly when the entrepreneurial, outsized Wilson had to be reined in by Smith and other more prudent heads. Yet the tension was a productive one, resulting in a clear statement of AA's philosophy in the organization's second most important book, *"Twelve Steps and Twelve Traditions"* (Alcoholics Anonymous, 1952/1953).

AA has continued to grow steadily from the 1950s to the present day. Throughout this period, some of AA's ideas were adapted by other self-help organizations and professional treatment agencies (L. F. Kurtz, 1997a). In the former category are substance-abuse-related groups such as Narcotics Anonymous as well as organizations such as Emotions Anonymous (L. F. Kurtz & Chambon, 1987), Gamblers Anonymous (Browne, 1991; Petry & Armentano, 1999), and Overeaters Anonymous (Malenbaum, *et al.*, 1988; Suler & Barthelomew, 1986). Most notable among the latter are the "Minnesota Model" treatment programs, which, though distinct from AA, have facilitated its growth in societies such as Denmark (Steffen, 1994), Iceland (Ólafsdóttir, 1986, 2000), Israel, and Sweden. More commonly, AA spread to other societies through the efforts of individual AA members traveling abroad (see, e.g., Appel, 1996, on Germany; *Science*, on Russia, 1989), sometimes with support of members of the temperance movement (see, e.g., Oka, 1994b, on Japan; Voipio, 1987, on Finland).

AA has now spread from the USA to more than 50 other societies. A full description of AA's diffusion to, and particular character in, all of these societies would be beyond the scope of this book (indeed any one book). Some excellent sources for the interested reader, by country, are as follows. A two-volume work produced by the International Collaborative Study of Alcoholics Anonymous (Eisenbach-Stangl & Rosenqvist, 1998; Mäkelä *et al.*, 1996) provides invaluable data on AA in Austria, Canada, Iceland, Finland, Mexico, Poland, Sweden, and Switzerland. Informative accounts are also available about AA in Brazil (Jarrad, 1997), Denmark (Steffen, 1994), Germany (Appel, 1996; Rienhoff, 1979), India (Sharma & Mohan, 1994), Israel (Weiss, 1990, 1995), and the UK (Collins *et al.*, 1990; Robinson, 1979, 1980).

Philosophy and approach

AA views alcoholism as a disease with moral, physical, and spiritual components. More specifically, AA (1976) links alcoholism to "self-will run riot" and to related character flaws such as grandiosity, infantile narcissism, and selfishness. This focus on the essential being of the alcoholic implies that, in AA, one does not "have the disease of alcoholism" in the same manner that one would "have a cold." Rather, one *is* an alcoholic and there is no such thing as a cured, ex-alcoholic. Rather, there are only active alcoholics and those whose disease is in remission because they are abstinent and practicing AA's principles. This ineffable identity is emphasized by members when they speak in meetings using the introductory phrase, "My name is ___ and I am an alcoholic."

AA offers its members "fellowship," meaning a supportive network of recovering alcoholics, and a "program," meaning a method of ceasing alcohol consumption, improving moral character, and fostering spiritual growth. The 12 steps are the essence of AA's program of change (see Table 2). Only the first step mentions alcohol, which surprises observers who believe incorrectly that AA's sole purpose is to stop alcoholics from drinking. AA views cessation of alcohol use as necessary but not sufficient for recovery. Abstinence is "being dry," a mere stepping stone to "being sober." Attaining sobriety involves reducing

Table 2. *The 12 steps as used in Alcoholics Anonymous (1939)*

1. We admitted we were powerless over alcohol – that our lives had become unmanageable.
2. Came to believe that a power greater than ourselves could restore us to sanity.
3. Made a decision to turn our will and our lives over to the care of God *as we understood Him.*
4. Made a searching and fearless moral inventory of ourselves.
5. Admitted to God, to ourselves, and to another human being the exact nature of our wrongs.
6. Were entirely ready to have God remove all these defects of character.
7. Humbly asked Him to remove our shortcomings.
8. Made a list of all persons we had harmed, and became willing to make amends to them all.
9. Made direct amends to such people wherever possible, except when to do so would injure them or others.
10. Continued to take personal inventory and when we were wrong promptly admitted it.
11. Sought through prayer and meditation to improve our conscious contact with God *as we understood Him,* praying only for knowledge of His will for us and the power to carry that out.
12. Having had a spiritual awakening as a result of these steps, we tried to carry this message to alcoholics, and to practice these principles in all our affairs.

Source: From Alcoholics Anonymous (1939)

one's selfishness, treating others more fairly, and developing a relationship with a spiritual Higher Power.

AA's concept of "surrendering" to a Higher Power (Step 3) is often misunderstood. Surrender in AA is an acknowledgment of realistic limits on human control rather than an endorsement of irresponsibility. AA members are expected to take responsibility only for those things they can control, for example to give up trying to stop being an alcoholic but to start doing what one can (e.g., going to AA meetings). This "division of responsibility" is expressed in AA in a variety of ways, including in the slogan, "You do the legwork, your Higher Power takes care of the results," or the Serenity Prayer, "God grant me the serenity to accept the things I cannot change, the courage to change the things I can, and the wisdom to know the difference."

"Higher Power" in AA and in other 12-step organizations need not imply a deity. The Higher Power is simply help from outside the self. Accepting a Higher Power thus implies admitting that one is not personally all-powerful.

The Higher Power may be interpreted as the AA fellowship itself, as a spiritual force, as the Christian God, as Native American spirits, as the Catholic Saints etc., the key point being that it is not the member him- or herself (i.e., the member is "not-God," E. Kurtz, 1979/1991). This flexibility is emphasized in the steps, with God "as we understood him" being the only words set in italics.

Characterizing what "AA meetings are like" is difficult because of their diversity. Lee Ann Kaskutas (1998) conducted an ethnographic study of AA meetings in a single county in the USA and discovered many varieties of AA, ranging from the stereotypic smoke-filled, working-class gatherings in church basements, to elegant, upscale meetings at a yacht club attended by well-paid professionals. Some Native American AA meetings integrate native spirituality and are attended by whole families rather than by the alcoholic alone (Duran, 1994; Jilek-Aall, 1981). In Mexico City and in Latino-immigrant communities in Los Angeles, California, some AA meetings have a macho, confrontational atmosphere which members call the "terapia dura" ("rough therapy," see Hoffman, 1994; Rosovsky, 1998). AA meetings also vary by design within any cultural context. AA offers "open meetings" at which non-members learn about the organization, "closed meetings" for members only, "first-step meetings" oriented toward newcomers, "speaker's meetings" in which a single member tells his or her story at length, and "specialty meetings," for example those intended for gays, lesbians, women, men, etc.

These diversities notwithstanding, every meeting the author has observed or heard about has two features in common. All AA meetings conduct some ritual at the beginning and end of the meeting (e.g., a particular benediction, prayer, reading, group intonement, etc.). These rituals convey a sense of familiarity, make members more comfortable, and demarcate meetings as "sacred space" with values, norms, and purposes that are different from those of the outside world. Story-telling is the other universal feature of AA meetings (see Brandes, 2002; Cain, 1991; Humphreys, 2000a for extended discussions). AA stories may be about members' alcoholism, recovery, or struggles in living, or about AA itself. Indeed, most of AA's primary text is composed simply of members' stories. AA's founders valued story-telling and institutionalized it for several reasons. First, they believed that story-telling allowed potential members to identify with current members, and therefore to want to join AA (Alcoholics Anonymous, 1976; Humphreys, 2000a). Second, the founders' practical experience convinced them that direct advice to, and criticism of, alcoholics was rarely effective. Telling one's own story about one's own problems usually elides defensiveness in alcoholic listeners. Third, telling one's own story of alcoholism instills humility, whereas presuming to know other people's stories does not.

Membership

What qualifies an individual as a "member" of AA or of any other self-help organization is not always easy to define (McIntire, 2000). The AA World Service Organization counts as members those meeting attendees who complete AA's triennial survey. Using that methodology, AA estimated that in January of 2002 it had 100 100 groups, with 2.2 million members worldwide, 1.16 million of them in the USA. Membership could also be defined by the AA maxim that "a member is anyone who attends with a desire to stop drinking." This definition yields much higher membership estimates. Robin Room and Thomas Greenfield's (1993) analysis of a representative survey of US households showed that the number of Americans who attend AA for a personal drinking problem each year is three times AA's triennial survey-based membership estimate. This would place AA's total worldwide membership in the range of four to six million people, depending on what assumptions one makes about whether the discrepancy identified by Room and Greenfield (1993) is USA-specific or also occurs in other countries. Regardless of such conjectures' truth value, AA is the largest addiction-related self-help organization in the world.

AA is the most widely sought source of help for alcohol problems in the USA (Miller & McCrady, 1993) and probably in Mexico as well (López, 1988). The bulk of its members live in North America, but AA has spread throughout Europe, Central and South America, Oceania, and into parts of Asia and Africa (Mäkelä, 1991). Self-help organizations usually grow most rapidly when they are new within a society, because their pool of potential members equals the population prevalence of the problem the organization addresses (i.e., every living person who developed the problem at any time in the past could join). As the organization becomes well established over a period of years, its growth slows unless there is a surge in the incidence of new cases (i.e., the pool of new potential members). For this reason, AA's membership size may today be fairly stable within its "old world" (e.g., USA, Canada) whereas its growth may be concentrated in its "new world" (e.g., South America, Russia).

Using 1986 data, Klaus Mäkelä (1991) calculated each society's number of AA groups per million inhabitants. Within Europe, Ireland and Finland had the most AA groups per capita, whereas Austria and Poland had the fewest. In Central and South America, El Salvador and Costa Rica had the most AA groups, Chile and Bolivia none at all. Of the rest of the world's societies, AA was strongest in Australia, New Zealand, South Africa, and South Korea and was non-existent in the major Islamic societies (e.g., Indonesia, Saudi Arabia). Mäkelä's conclusions require two modifications in the light of developments subsequent to 1986. The break-up of the Soviet Union and the collapse of socialist governments in eastern Europe have allowed AA activities to increase in those regions (e.g., in East Germany; Von Appen, 1994). AA has also gained a foothold in Turkey, even though in general it remains a negligible presence within the Islamic world. Turkey is the only Islamic society that has an AA service office, which reports 22 AA groups with 500 regular members (personal communication, August 18, 2002). NA is currently expanding in Bahrain, Egypt, Kuwait, Lebanon, Morocco, Saudi Arabia, Qatar, and the United Arab Emirates, so 12-step groups can certainly take hold in Islamic societies (Ehab El-Kharrat, personal communication, September 21, 2002). However, the very low prevalence of alcohol dependence in most Islamic societies will likely always limit their number of AA groups.

In the USA and Canada, respondents to AA's 2001 membership survey were 88% Caucasian, 5% African-American, 4% Hispanic, 2% Native American, and 1% other backgrounds (Alcoholics Anonymous, 2002). Although reliable data on the race of AA members outside of the USA and Canada are not available, diversity is suggested simply by the number and variety of regions that have AA meetings. AA's appeal does not seem tied to socioeconomic level. Mäkelä (1991) points out that, in 1965, AA's strength was positively correlated with national wealth, whereas by 1986 this was no longer the case.

The proportion of women among AA members in different countries varies widely. At one extreme, data gathered around 1990 indicated that women constituted only 10% of Mexican AA members overall, and an even lower proportion in rural areas (Pérez-López *et al.*, 1992; Sutro, 1989). Women comprise more than a third of members in other societies (Austria, Canada, German-speaking Switzerland, and the USA; Alcoholics Anonymous, 2002; Mäkelä *et al.*, 1996; probably also Germany, based on pre-unification data provided by Rienhoff, 1979). The author's conjecture, based on attendance data provided by a number of scholars (e.g., Eisenbach-Stangl, 1996, 1997; Mäkelä *et al.*, 1996; Oka, 1994b; Rehm, 1996; Rienhoff, 1979), is that women alcoholics are particularly likely to attend AA in those countries where the alternative is a traditional male-oriented recovery movement in which most members are alcoholic men accompanied by their wives (e.g., All Nippon Sobriety Association in Japan; Blue Cross in Austria, German-speaking Switzerland and Germany; and Blue Cross and Free Life in France).

AA members typically have severe drinking problems before coming to the organization, with a high prevalence of physical dependence symptoms and histories of inpatient treatment. This was a main finding of a meta-analysis of studies performed primarily in the USA and Canada (Emrick *et al.*, 1993; see also Hasin & Grant, 1995). Studies from societies such as Mexico (del Carmen Mariño *et al.*, 1997; Rosovsky, Casanova, & Pérez, 1991) and the UK (Edwards *et al.*, 1966; Robinson, 1979) report parallel results.

Abstainers Clubs

Origins and history

Poland has had professional alcohol treatment programs since it regained sovereignty after World War I, but it has not always had self-help organizations (Morawski, 1992). Alcoholism was widely viewed as a moral defect and not an illness prior to the World War II, which stigmatized alcoholics and created an environment that was unsupportive of them operating mutual-help associations (Świątkiewicz & Zieliński, 1998). The universe of possibilities expanded after World War II as disease conceptions of substance abuse became more common and Polish healthcare workers learned about AA. Polish medical professionals started support organizations for alcoholic patients in the late 1940s and in the 1950s. Such organizations were called "self-help groups" or "AA clubs" (Mäkelä *et al.*, 1996), but departed significantly from the spirit of those terms. They were entirely under the control of non-alcoholic medical professionals and operated as an extension of professional treatment services. This was partly an outgrowth of Polish law making little allowance for voluntary, independent action by alcoholics, emphasizing instead the need for compulsory treatment under close professional supervision (Kurube, 1992b; Świątkiewicz, 1992). Further, although these early patient clubs often attempted to follow AA's approach, this was nearly impossible during the socialist period because references to spirituality and God were forbidden within alcohol treatment services (Świątkiewicz & Zieliński, 1998), as were organizations of anonymous persons not under state control (Woronowicz, 1992).

The precise founding date of modern-style Abstainers Clubs is unclear, but was probably between 1958 and 1960 (Kurube, 1992b; Woronowicz, 1992). These clubs were founded by alcoholics who were familiar with AA and who had a close relationship with treatment professionals within the humanistic and community psychiatry movements. This professional support of Abstainers Clubs was both helpful and paternalistic, in that many treatment providers offered clubs valuable assistance but ultimately were unwilling to let them become independent of their influence (Mäkelä *et al.*, 1996).

Truly autonomous alcohol self-help organizations received a major boost in Poland with the arrival of the Solidarity Period (Woronowicz, 1992). This era witnessed a cultural backlash against authoritarian controls and, indeed, toward many things simply because they were associated with past practice (Świątkiewicz & Zieliński, 1998). Such sentiments were obviously unsupportive of professional control within patient clubs. In addition, alcohol-treatment system reform legislation that was enacted in 1982 specifically endorsed the value of peer-controlled self-help initiatives (Morawski, 1992; Świątkiewicz & Zieliński, 1998). The formation of an independent Federation of Abstainers Clubs in 1984 formalized the liberation of truly peer-operated Abstainers Clubs from professional control. This sparked a sharp increase in the number of Abstainers Clubs in Poland in the 1980s (Morawski, 1992), and also facilitated the growth of AA groups, with which Abstainers Clubs often maintained a symbiotic relationship.

Philosophy and approach

It would be desirable for present purposes to describe only those Abstainers Clubs that are genuine self-help groups autonomous of professionals. To the self-help analyst, a peer-controlled Abstainers Club operated by "members" clearly differs from a professionally controlled club composed of alcoholic "patients." However, this point of view is not necessarily shared either by members of these clubs or by scholars who write about them. Some members do not even perceive a distinction between Abstainer Clubs and AA either (Woronowicz, 1992). Rather than attempting to force the phenomenon to fit his perspective, the author will describe Abstainer Clubs as a whole, recognizing that, like Clubs of Treated Alcoholics in the Adriatic countries (see p. 57), "Abstainers Clubs" comprise true self-help organizations, professionally controlled organizations, and the shades of grey between the two.

The change program within Abstainers Clubs is called the "Way of Sobriety." Noriko Kurube (1992b) describes it as more psychosocial in nature than AA's approach, even though many Abstainers Clubs consider it equivalent to the "12 steps." Abstainers Clubs also differ from AA in preferring to call members "abstainers" rather than "alcoholics," in order to focus on present successes rather than past problems (Woronowicz, 1992). These distinctions notwithstanding, most Abstainers Club members are exposed to AA's philosophy because at least 40% report co-membership (Świątkiewicz, 1992), and some

Abstainers Clubs view holding AA meetings as one of their activities, and select a common leader for their club and AA meetings (Kurube, 1992b; Woronowicz, 1992). Whether connected to AA or not, as implied by their name Abstainers Clubs view abstinence as the only appropriate drinking goal.

Most clubs hold social, recreational, educational, and supportive activities 2–5 days per week (Morawski, 1992), in which both problem drinkers and their families participate (Kurube, 1992b). In addition to mutual-help meetings, activities include publishing literature and engaging in public education efforts. Personal appearances on television are the most interesting aspect of the organization's outreach efforts. Club members' faces are clearly visible during such television programs, as in Abstainers Clubs there is no AA-style tradition of anonymity to the public (Mäkelä *et al.*, 1996).

Abstainers Clubs maintain a close relationship with professional and governmental agencies. In addition to donations, Abstainers' Clubs receive governmental funding to support their activities (Świątkiewicz & Zieliński, 1998), which at times provokes criticism from Polish AA members (Woronowicz, 1992). During periods of fiscal or political crisis in the government, this funding has not always been assured, which at times puts significant strain on the organization (Świątkiewicz, 1992).

Membership

Although they bear some similarity to the Clubs for Treated Alcoholics of the Adriatic countries, Abstainers Clubs as such appear to operate entirely in Poland. The number of clubs oscillates between 250 and 300 (Woronowicz, 1992). Jacek Morawski (1992) estimated membership in Abstainer's Clubs at 3000 in 1986, 2350 of which were former problem drinkers. A subsequent estimate by placed membership at 7000–8000 persons (Świątkiewicz, 1992). In contrast, Kurube (1992b) reported a much higher 1990 estimate of 40 000 members. None of these estimates are recent or based on epidemiologic study; as mentioned, all probably combine membership in professionally controlled clubs with members in autonomous mutual-help organizations.

Limited information on members' characteristics is available, although it was gathered over a decade ago. Grażyna Świątkiewicz (1992) reported selected results from a study of a representative sample of 400 members conducted by Morawski. Most (86%) members were male, aged 31–40 years (54%), working class (63%), and had no university-level education (84%). Interestingly, none of the members were old-age pensioners. About half (52%) of the sample participated in the club with a family member, typically a wife. The clubs seem to have a significant group of experienced members, with 36% belonging for 2–5 years and 18% for more than 5 years.

Al-Anon Family Groups

Origins and history

In most societies today, AA meetings are attended by the alcoholic without his or her family members, but this was not originally the case. AA held meetings in the homes of members in its early years, with wives and children present (AA's initial group of members were all men; Wilson, 1979). The potential for a separate organization for family members was created in 1940 when AA began restricting attendance at meetings to alcoholics (Robertson, 1988; Wilson, 1979). According to Lois Wilson (1979), whose husband, Bill, was one of AA's co-founders, that same year in New York City the first Al-Anon meeting occurred during what was originally intended to be a card game between eight wives of alcoholics, held while their husbands were having an AA meeting. The wives recognized that they could benefit from their shared experience just as could their alcoholic husbands. Lois Wilson, Annie Smith (Dr. Robert Smith's wife), and Anne B. (Surname unknown) became the most important individuals in Al-Anon's early history (Robertson, 1988).

Such meetings became more common over the 1940s, and Al-Anon had almost 100 groups by the time Annie Smith died in 1948 (Martin, 1992). Lois Wilson and Anne B. created a separate meeting listing for family meetings, produced literature, and in 1951 created a new name for the organization: Al-Anon Family Groups. Membership grew steadily over the 1950s, aided in part by some positive media attention – particular multiple newspaper articles by the popular syndicated advice columnist Ann Landers (Robertson, 1988). Al-Anon achieved its first foothold abroad in 1953 when a group was founded in Finland (where it was originally called "Alva;" Rosenqvist, 1992). In 1957, a sufficient number of teenage children were interested in attending groups for the organization to form specialty groups for them under the name "Alateen."

Relative to AA, Al-Anon was slow to formalize its philosophy. The first edition of Al-Anon's collection of members' stories did not appear until 25 years after meetings began (Rehm & Room, 1992), and even this was an inchoate work which included many stories that made little reference to the 12 steps, a Higher Power, or other Al-Anon concepts (Martin, 1992). Some organizational uncertainty might also be inferred from one Al-Anon text switching its title repeatedly across editions between "*Living with an alcoholic*" and "*Al-Anon Family Groups*" (Robertson, 1988). The relative instability of

Al-Anon's philosophy in its first few decades was probably inevitable given the shifting ground of gender relations in western countries (Haaken, 1993; Rosenqvist, 1992). Al-Anon's membership has always been composed primarily of wives of alcoholics, and the vision of the proper relationship between a husband and wife was changing rapidly over the organization's development. For example, in the 1950s Al-Anon emphasized the importance of a wife being patient and understanding of her alcoholic husband, and of not "usurping his role as head of the family" (Haaken, 1993). With the coming of the modern women's movement, the organization began to acknowledge a wife's need for personal control, respect, and independence. By the time the organization revised its basic text in 1985, it had achieved more philosophical certitude and coherence, at least if such a judgement can be made from the fact that the second edition much more consistently presents an organized perspective about the meaning of recovery for its members (Martin, 1992).

In addition to negotiating changing gender relationships, Al-Anon Family Groups faced a novel challenge in the late 1970s and 1980s, when US popular culture experienced a boomlet of interest in adults who had been children of alcoholic and other "dysfunctional" families. Claudia Black (1981), John Bradshaw (1988) Stephanie Brown (1991), Sharon Wegscheider-Cruse (1985), and Janet Woititz (1983) were among the professional psychotherapists who popularized interest in "adult children," and the related phenomenon of "co-dependent relationships" (Beattie, 1987; Rice, 1992; Schaef, 1986). Hollywood celebrities went public – to accolades and excellent book sales – with their status as adult children (Denzin, 1990), and the mass media gave alcoholic families unprecedented attention. A few enterprising individuals packaged themselves as experts on dysfunctional families and set up lucrative networks of television appearances, book sales, workshops, conventions, and even specialty "recovering" vacation tour packages. The distinguished self-help scholar Frank Riessman (Riessman & Carroll, 1995) has argued that this naked commercialism, though independent of self-help organizations per se, was damaging to the spiritual aspects of self-help groups, as well as to their image.

The publicity generated by the adult-children movement helped Al-Anon to increase its number of adult-children-focused meetings from 14 groups in 1981 to 1100 groups in 1986. However, the movement also presented a challenge to Al-Anon in two respects. First, the average citizen in search of help had difficulty in differentiating a non-profit mutual-help organization from similarly named, often quite expensive, professionally developed treatments. Second, there were disagreements within Al-Anon over how influenced the organization should be by the language, writings, and concepts of the professionals in the adult-children movement. Al-Anon had had adult children of alcoholics as members and had held "adult-children-focused" meetings for decades prior to the adult-children movement, but such meetings closely followed the general outline provided by the 12 steps and 12 traditions and official Al-Anon literature. In the late 1970s, some adult children of alcoholics, wishing to break away from these aspects of Al-Anon, formed their own organization in Torrance, California (Adult Children of Alcoholics World Service Organization, 1997). This organization called itself "Adult Children of Alcoholics" (ACA), whereas Al-Anon continued to hold adult-children-focused meetings under its overall umbrella, which approximately 20% of its members were attending in 1990 (Wolf/Altschul/Callahan Inc., 1990).

The unflattering stereotypes that emerged were that independent ACA meetings relied more on psychotherapeutic writings, operated their meetings more like psychotherapy sessions (e.g., with cross-talk, advice giving, and psychobabble), and ignored the 12 steps, whereas Al-Anon-affiliated adult-children-focused meetings were stodgy, rigid, and out of touch with members' psychological issues. The author's experience over several years of studying these organizations is that both are too decentralized and diverse for the stereotypes to hold beyond a general level (Humphreys, 1993b). Some members of independent ACA groups are devoted to the 12 steps, some members of Al-Anon-affiliated adult-children-focused groups greatly value the writings of professional therapists, and some members of both organizations have no interest in whether their home group officially belongs to one organization or the other.

Consistent with its traditions, Al-Anon never made any official effort to differentiate itself from the professionalized adult-children movement. This became less of a concern in the 1990s as the popular psychology/consumerist aspects of the adult-children movement receded significantly. In contrast, Al-Anon has continued to grow in size and to diffuse internationally, and, with the exception of AA, is today the most prevalent addiction-related mutual-help organization in the world.

Philosophy and approach

Al-Anon's approach reflects its status as the first offshoot of AA. Al-Anon endorses the AA concepts that alcoholism is a disease that can only be arrested through abstinence, and that recovery is a spiritual process. Al-Anon uses the steps of AA verbatim, but interprets step 1 somewhat differently. In AA, powerlessness in step 1 refers to one's own alcohol use, whereas in Al-Anon it refers to powerlessness over the alcoholic's behavior. Accepting one's lack of control over the alcoholic reduces feelings of self-blame and efforts at manipulation. Similarly, accepting that one's alcoholic loved one is powerless over alcohol eases resentment and anger (Martin, 1992).

Although much of Al-Anon's approach is drawn from AA, the organization places unique emphasis on two concepts: "enabling" and "loving detachment." Enabling behaviors facilitate continued drinking by the alcoholic, for example making excuses for him, taking over the responsibilities he is avoiding, forgiving him too easily, etc. Al-Anon encourages members to identify and then to stop such behaviors. In this sense, Al-Anon philosophy holds that members may contribute to their loved one's alcoholism despite also being victimized by it.

Loving detachment in Al-Anon is not the same as coldness or punitive emotional withdrawal. Rather, it is a specific application of the general spiritual principle in Al-Anon that members should surrender responsibility for what they cannot change to their Higher Power (Ablon, 1974). Most obviously, this implies giving up efforts to control the alcoholic's behavior, or to change the fact that he is alcoholic, while at the same time maintaining a loving attitude toward him (L. F. Kurtz, 1994). This allows the member to release resentments about a loved one's involvement in alcoholism, and, when applicable, over-involvement in AA. The potential for Al-Anon members to resent their loved one's new AA friends, AA lifestyle, and AA meetings is highlighted in Al-Anon meetings through the occasional telling of the "legend of Lois's shoe" (Robertson, 1988). After years of resenting her husband's drinking, Lois reputedly began to resent his intense focus on starting AA, and threw her shoe at him, yelling, "Damn your old meetings" (Wilson, 1979).

As members cease spending energy enabling the alcoholic's behavior and trying to change the fact of his alcoholism, Al-Anon encourages them to redirect their efforts to taking care of their own well-being (Ablon, 1974). Al-Anon's literature promises that, through loving detachment, members can live a serene existence independent of an alcoholic's behavior (Martin, 1992), and focus instead on activities that enhance their own self-esteem and independence (Ablon, 1974). Relative to AA's focus on minimizing self-centeredness, attaining humility, and increasing sensitivity to others, this is a relatively selfish goal (Ablon, 1974, 1982). This should be understood like all self-help philosophies as an effort to compensate for the problems members bring to the organization, which in Al-Anon are believed to be low self-worth and excessive self-abnegation rather than the arrogance and selfishness AA believes characterizes its new members (Humphreys & Kaskutas, 1995).

Group process in Al-Anon meetings varies from place to place, but, as in AA there are typically opening and closing rituals bracketing a discussion of issues surrounding recovery (e.g., anger, gratitude, acceptance, criticism; see Rosovsky *et al.*, 1992). The author could not find a description of the group process of Alateen meetings, which may be symptomatic of the more general problem in addiction research of minimal attention to adolescents.

Membership

Al-Anon had approximately 390 000 members and 29 800 groups in 1999 (Al-Anon/Alateen World Service Organization, 2000). Just over half of its groups are based in the USA, and about 6% are based in Canada. Al-Anon's 1999 survey of members in these two countries found that the average Al-Anon member was 51 years old, was a woman (85%), had been attending Al-Anon for 5 or more years (53%), and had an alcoholic husband (78%). The average Alateen member was 14 years old, female (62%), and had been in Alateen for a year or more (56%). Almost all (90%) Alateen members had an alcoholic parent. Many members of Al-Anon and Alateen had multiple alcoholic relatives, and other studies have found that a history of alcohol-related family violence is prevalent among members (L. F. Kurtz, 1994; Rosovsky *et al.*, 1992). The 1999 survey did not report race, but in the 1990 survey, most members of Al-Anon (95%) and Alateen (91%) were non-Hispanic Caucasians (Wolf/Altschul/Callahan Inc., 1990).

Al-Anon has chapters throughout Europe, South America, and Australia, as well as in India and Japan. However, information on Al-Anon outside the USA is scarce. In a study conducted in Mexico City, Haydée Rosovsky *et al.* (1992) described Al-Anon members as women (96%), married (78%), and over 35 years of age (73%). An almost completely female membership was also reported for Al-Anon in Finland (Rosenqvist, 1992). Even outdated gender breakdowns for other countries could not be found.

One basic unanswered question about Al-Anon's members is what proportion have an alcoholic spouse or relative who participates concurrently in another 12-step self-help organization. Studies conducted in Canada, Finland, Mexico, and the USA suggest that the majority of women in Al-Anon are married to an alcoholic who attends AA (Al-Anon/Alateen World Service Organization, 2000; Bailey, 1965; Corenblum & Fischer, 1975; Gorman & Rooney, 1979; Rosenqvist, 1992; Rosovsky *et al.*, 1992). In the USA and, to a lesser extent, in other countries, this phenomenon is supported by professional alcoholism treatment agencies referring husband–wife pairs to AA and Al-Anon, respectively (Asher, 1992).

All Nippon Sobriety Association/the Sobriety Friends Society (Danshukai)

Origins and history

As exemplified in writings such as those of the eighteenth century moral philosopher Baigan Ishida, Japanese culture has long emphasized the importance of the collective good, loyalty to one's circle, and reliance upon within-group resources rather than external help. This cultural heritage was a fertile soil in which some self-help-oriented writings from the West took root in the years of increased contact following the Meiji Restoration (Oka, 1994a). Japanese people created a few mutual-help organizations in the early decades of the twentieth century, but these were swept away by the war and the political oppression of the 1930s and 1940s. It was not until after World War II that a number of enduring mutual-help organizations took hold, including some for alcohol problems (Oka, 1994a, b).

Again because of western contact during the Meiji period, an alcohol temperance movement had emerged in Japan in the late 1800s (Smith, 1997). Members of this temperance movement and supportive medical professionals learned of AA in the early 1950s and encouraged Japanese alcoholics to establish AA groups. Initial efforts were made, but AA principles were simply too culturally inappropriate to transfer (Oka, 1994b). AA's peer-oriented model was anathema to Japanese professionals accustomed to hierarchical relationships with "their patients." These professionals wanted to control AA groups themselves rather than promote indigenous peer leadership (Smith, 1998). AA's Christian overtones also limited its transferability to a country with quite different dominant spiritual traditions. Finally, AA's focus upon the individual alcoholic conflicted with the Japanese perspective of viewing couples and families as inseparable units. For one alcoholic member to attend meetings alone and anonymously therefore seemed overly individualistic (Smith, 1997). A few decades later, as traditional religions became less influential and Japanese culture became more individualistic, AA did eventually establish itself in Japan; however, the 1950s were another time.

The Sobriety Friends Society (Danshu-Tomo-no-Kai), founded in 1953, represented a compromise between Japanese cultural values and AA's approach. Several similar societies formed in other parts of Japan, including some that splintered from The Sobriety Friends Society (Oka, 1994b). In 1963, several of these societies joined to form the All Nippon Sobriety Association (Zenkoku Danshu Renmei).

Despite their different histories and founding dates, clearly distinguishing Danshu-Tomo-no-Kai and Zenkoku Danshu Renmei is difficult, so many individuals refer to them collectively as "Danshukai." The ineluctability of such blending stems from several factors. First, "Danshu-tomo-no-Kai" is officially abbreviated in Japanese as "Danshukai," but this same word is sometimes used by Japanese people to refer to all alcohol-related self-help organizations collectively (i.e., in the same way that many people use "Coke" to refer to all brands of cola-flavored soda). Second, the organizations themselves have little concern about whether their names are used precisely. Some groups that call themselves "Danshu-tomo-no-Kai" have no connection to the original organization, and neither the Sobriety Friends Society nor the All Nippon Sobriety Society has shown any official interest in policing such matters. Finally, as an empirical matter, studies that have attempted to delineate individuals belonging to one organization or the other have found that the populations are similar on demographic and alcohol problem variables (Shido *et al.*, 1986). The term "Danshukai" will be used in this book as an umbrella term for groups belonging to either organization, but where known, differences between the All Nippon Sobriety Association and the Sobriety Friends Society will be noted.

Philosophy and approach

Danshukai meetings are arranged by local branches (shibu) of the society. Branches usually hold meetings once a week in the evenings (Smith, 1998). Individuals attend branches based on their place of residence and do not "shop around" for meetings in different locales. The following description of meeting process and organizational philosophy is taken mainly from the writings of Hiroshi Suwaki (1979, 1980, 1988), Tomofumi Oka (1994a, b) and Stephen Smith (1997, 1998). Meetings of The Sobriety Friends Society have the reputation of being somewhat more formal and traditional than those of the All Nippon Sobriety Association, but otherwise the following description applies to both.

Danshukai is a family organization in which spouses, and sometimes children, of the alcoholic member attend. Meetings may open with a silent prayer, a linking of hands and chanting of slogans (e.g., "Wiser!" "Stronger!" "More serious!" "Let's go!" "Let's go!"), or the singing of a sobriety song. Members sign in at the beginning of the meeting, and then a moderator offers a brief greeting and begins calling upon individuals from this list to speak. Unlike in AA, the moderator may put some social pressure on reticent members to talk even when they are hesitant to do so.

Members are supposed to tell stories related to alcohol and to the organization, but in reality contributions range over many topics. The scarcity of available space in Japanese cities constrains the number of meetings that can be held. This results in available meetings being very well attended, which puts some pressure on members to speak only for a few minutes each. The association appears to have only two strict rules of talk during meetings. First, to maintain an egalitarian ethos, members are forbidden from mentioning their social position (Kurube, 1992b). Second, when couples are called upon, the husband always speaks first, followed by the wife. Smith (1998) points out that this and other traditional gender role features of meetings may be a compensation to alcoholic males who are now abstinent, which in Japan is often viewed as unmanly.

Danshukai's philosophy insists on abstinence, emphasizing its essential role in meeting responsibilities to one's spouse and children. Drawing directly from AA, Danshukai asserts that abstinence is necessary to arrest alcoholism, which is viewed as a disease. Danshukai also shares with AA the expectation that members not only stop drinking, but also reform their moral character. Humility, charity, and generosity are celebrated as character traits which members should try to develop. The spiritual aspect of recovery is interpreted mainly in terms of the shared fate and interdependence of all members rather than with reference to a Christian-style deity. Because individuals attend with their families and because most meetings are open to interested professionals and to the public, there is no tradition of anonymity in Danshukai.

Danshukai enjoys positive relationships with treatment professionals, who sometimes visit meetings or provide meeting space (Poshyachinda, *et al.*, 1982). Another key tie to professionals is financial: the All Nippon Sobriety Association (but not The Sobriety Friends Society) accepts sizable, direct grants from the government (Oka, 1994b). Kurube (1992b) made the piquant observation that positive relationships with professionals may be less in evidence among young doctors, who sometimes view AA as of higher status than Danshukai and hence more worthy of receiving referrals.

Membership

Danshukai is well disseminated throughout Japan, but does not appear to have chapters in any other country. A consensus estimate of membership size based on the work of the above scholars and a recent World Health Organization (1999) report would be in the range of 30 000–40 000 in the 1970s, increasing to the 40 000s in the 1980s, and stabilizing around 50 000 through the 1990s. Because of the careful organizational procedures of Danshukai (e.g., regional membership, sign-in procedures, lack of anonymity), these membership numbers stand out as probably the most reliable of all alcohol self-help organizations.

Although, as mentioned, many groups disregard the distinction between the All Nippon Sobriety Society and the Sobriety Friends Society, far more groups that claim an official allegiance do so to the former society. Danshukai members outnumber AA members in Japan by about 10 to 1 (Oka, 1994b; World Health Organization, 1999).

Some descriptive studies of Danshukai participants have been conducted, including a survey of 366 members in Shizuoaka prefecture (Sugita *et al.*, 1985). Although the organization is not explicitly solely for men, a striking 98% of its members were male. The average member was 51 years old, and reported the onset of habitual drinking at 27 years of age, and of problem drinking at 36 years of age. Only 7.4% had a college-level education. Virtually all respondents reported being in a period of abstinence at the time of study. However, median length of membership was 5–10 years and mean length of abstinence was 3–5 years, indicating that members had not necessarily attained abstinence immediately or consistently throughout involvement. Similar lengths of abstinence were found among Danshukai members in Kanagawa prefecture (Shido *et al.*, 1986).

In terms of involvement patterns, over a third of members came to the organization through a medical facility and another third through relatives or acquaintances (Sugita *et al.*, 1985). The vast majority of members are married, and remarkably, nearly 80% were accompanied to their first meeting, usually by a spouse (Shido *et al.*, 1986; Sugita *et al.*, 1985). Oka (1994b) notes that one of the key differences between AA and Danshukai in Japan is that the latter organization has no Al-Anon-style organization for spouses because the wife's expected role is to attend meetings with the alcoholic husband. Most members attended meetings once a week and reported that physical health and desire to support their family were their main motivations for continuing. A separate study indicated that Danshukai members value both attending group meetings and thinking about them as strategies for reducing craving (Maruyama *et al.*, 1994).

Blue Cross (Croix Bleue)

Origins and history

Blue Cross was founded by a Protestant pastor named L. L. Rochat in Geneva in 1877, and spread to France by 1880 (Barrucand, 1984). It became established over the next several decades in German-speaking Switzerland, Germany, Austria (Eisenbach-Stangl, 1996), and Denmark (Steffen, 1994), and later expanded its reach to 40 countries around the world (Fédération Internationale de la Croix Bleue, 2002). The impetus for Blue Cross and its official sanction came from the Reformed Church (Bénichou, 1980). Blue Cross has also had a synergistic relationship with temperance organizations for much of its existence (Eisenbach-Stangl, 1998). In addition to mutual-help groups, the Blue Cross organization operates other alcohol services, including rehabilitation centers, halfway houses, and outpatient counseling programs (Fédération Internationale de la Croix Bleue, 2002).

Each national association of Blue Cross has evolved its own somewhat culturally specific character and a large measure of independence, but national associations do provide consultation and assistance for each other. For example, in Catholic Austria the Blue Cross does not receive enough donations to survive, so the Blue Cross organizations in Switzerland and Germany send it financial aid (Eisenbach-Stangl, 1996).

Blue Cross is one of the few alcohol-related mutual-help organizations that did not adapt any part of its program or approach from AA. However, the history of the organizations is linked in a different respect. Blue Cross members were among those who helped bring AA to each region of Switzerland (Rehm & Mariolini, 1998). Ironically, AA subsequently became very popular and Blue Cross membership in Switzerland plummeted as a result (Rehm, 1996). Blue Cross' other important contribution to the development of alcohol-related mutual-help organizations in Europe was to inspire the Catholic Church to create its own, similar, organization, called "Gold Cross" (see Bénichou, 1980; Kurube, 1992b; Lhermitte, 1975).

Philosophy and approach

The influence of organized religion and the temperance movement has obviously diminished in Europe since Blue Cross was founded. Nevertheless, the stamp of both these institutions is clearly evident in the philosophy and methods of Blue Cross. The spirit of the Protestant Reformation is reflected both in the organization's language and in its defined mission, namely to "liberate the individual from the oppressive bonds of alcoholism" (Barrucand, 1984;Bénichou, 1980). Blue Cross considers alcoholism to be a disease of the body and the soul, requiring salvation by God (Cerclé, 1984), and makes direct references to biblical scripture and to Jesus Christ in its literature (Fédération Internationale de la Croix Bleue, 2002). Religious hymns are sung at some group meetings and national conventions (Barrucand, 1984). An evangelical spirit of outreach to other alcoholics is also prominent in Blue Cross. To avoid overstatement of its religious nature, two caveats should be offered. First, many Blue Cross members may of course value the fellowship provided by the organization more than its religious aspects per se (B. L., 1978). Second, many Blue Cross members today are not involved in the Protestant Church (i.e., they are non-religious, Catholic, or of other faiths).

Just as in many temperance movements, Blue Cross members write and sign pledges to abstain from alcohol. Status and markers of achievement (e.g., being recognized as a full member, earning a Blue Cross medal) are awarded based on the time an individual has been abstinent (Cerclé, 1984). In some Blue Cross groups, success or failure at keeping to pledges and attendant status in the organization is explicitly stated at the beginning of the meeting during a formal roll-call. Unlike in mutual-help organizations that have a tradition of anonymity, public displays and testimonies of the value of abstinence and of the organization are highly valued in Blue Cross. For example, at a national conference of the French Blue Cross, members organized a parade through the streets of the city (B. L., 1978).

The only requirement for membership in Blue Cross is a commitment to its goals. One need not be a Protestant nor have a drinking problem. Many individuals join the organization to support a family member or friend, or simply to live out religious or temperance ideals. Other members currently have drinking problems and have yet to maintain an extended period of abstinence successfully. The influence and prevalence of former problem drinkers appears to be greater in the French incarnation of Blue Cross than in its cousins in Austria and German-speaking Switzerland (see, e.g., Bénichou, 1980; Eisenbach-Stangl, 1997; Rehm, 1996), although this must remain a tentative observation because each national association varies in how it defines and tracks membership.

Historically, the French Blue Cross was openly suspicious of the medical profession's role in the treatment of alcoholism and put substantial effort toward not having Blue Cross suborned to it (Cerclé, 1984). The origin of this stance is not clear, but in some locales it may have derived from tensions between Protestants and the Catholic Church, which operates many medical institutions in areas where Blue Cross is based. A non-competing explanation is that a number of members have had negative experiences with aversion therapies, which made them resent the treatment system (Bénichou, 1980). Some commentators writing in the 1980s (e.g., Barrucand, 1984) felt that the French Blue Cross would eventually become more open to cooperation with medical professionals. In contrast, according to Irmgard Eisenbach-Stangl (1996), the Austrian Blue Cross has always had a close, positive relationship with treatment professionals.

Membership

Assessing Blue Cross' membership in specific nations is challenging because data are often lacking or do not distinguish former alcohol abusers from other organizational affiliates. France appears to have the healthiest Blue Cross organization, or at least one that is growing. Estimates made by scholars specifically of problem drinkers in the French Blue Cross were around 4000–5000 in the 1970s and 1980s, compared with a 1993 estimate of 6000 members (Mäkelä *et al.*, 1996). About half of all French Blue Cross members are former problem drinkers (Bénichou, 1980), implying a total membership of 12 000 people in 1993. A survey conducted over a quarter-century ago found that 90% of former problem drinkers in the French Blue Cross were male, but this pattern may not have been maintained to the present day (Bénichou & Orsel, cited in Room, 1998).

In contrast to its growth in France, Blue Cross membership has been dropping precipitously in German-speaking Switzerland since the arrival of AA in the early 1960s (Rehm, 1996). Extrapolation from data provided by Jürgen Rehm (1996) yields a current estimate of 3000–5000 Blue Cross members in that region today, about two-thirds of whom are male. Alcoholism-treatment-center patients are much more likely to indicate an intention to attend AA than Blue Cross, indicating that the organization may continue to decline in German-speaking Switzerland in the future (Rehm, 1996).

The author was unable to find recent estimates of the number of Blue Cross members in French-speaking Switzerland, Denmark, or in Germany. Turning to Austria, Eisenbach-Stangl (1996, 1997) identified 12 Blue Cross groups in that country. These groups are officially open to supportive family members and others, but are composed almost entirely (75%) of alcoholics. Austrian Blue Cross groups stand out as attracting a high proportion (43%) of women members. Eisenbach-Stangl (1997) suggests that this is because the Protestant theology of the organization promotes greater gender equality than is found in other alcohol intervention options.

Clubs of Treated Alcoholics

Origins and history

The precursors of today's "Clubs of Treated Alcoholics" (CTAs) came into being prior to World War II, as one of the anti-alcoholism programs initiated by the public health pioneer Andrija Stampar, who later was involved in the creation of the WHO (Lang & Srdar, 1992). Stampar founded a School of Public

Health in Zagreb, and in the 1930s he and his colleagues created some clubs for abstainers. Although these specific organizations collapsed during the war, the concept of bringing alcoholics together for mutual support survived.

The psychiatrist Vladmir Hudolin (1984) developed an array of new alcoholism treatment programs in Zagreb, including Clubs of Treated Alcoholics in 1964. Hudolin was aware of AA's 12-step model, but laws at the time forbade adoption of its spiritual elements and traditions of anonymity (Lang & Srdar, 1992). Under Hudolin's guidance, CTAs such as exist today spread from Zagreb into surrounding Croatia and then into other parts of Yugoslavia.

After CTAs were well established in Yugoslavia, Hudolin (1984) and his colleagues collaborated with innovation-minded treatment professionals from the Italian provinces of Friuli-Venezia Giulia and Veneto to extend the program abroad. CTAs spread across the border to Italy in 1979 and subsequently became quite popular (Allamani *et al.*, 1994). Indeed, despite arriving in Italy 7 years after AA, CTAs now have more members (Allamani & Petrikin, 1996).

Most articles about CTAs were published prior to the Balkan wars of the 1990s; indeed many were written before the break-up of Yugoslavia. Hence, the current status and future of CTAs in that region are difficult to assess. Many CTA meeting places have been destroyed, the supportive professionals assigned to different tasks (e.g., dealing with post-traumatic stress disorders), and many members and professionals have fled the area or been killed. These changes forced (or allowed, depending on one's point of view) CTAs to act more independently of professionals (Thaller *et al.*, 1996). This trend for CTAs to become truly autonomous self-help groups may continue in the future (Room, 1998), especially because AA's presence in the region demonstrates to interested parties that self-help groups for alcoholics can operate without professional control. Italian CTAs may also eventually experience greater independence from professionals in the future if the country's public sector contracts for fiscal or political reasons (Allamani *et al.*, 1994).

Philosophy and approach

CTAs in the Adriatic countries raise the same question as Poland's Abstainers Clubs, namely, "Are these really self-help groups, or are they professionally operated support groups"? The fact that CTAs were initially designed and operated by professionals differentiates them from the many self-help organizations in which professionals played a supportive, but non-central, role in founding the organization. Across the former Socialist countries of eastern Europe, full autonomy has not been the norm for self-help organizations, and CTAs and

Poland's Abstainers Clubs follow in that mold (Barath, 1991). Yet even in the context of that general principle, Bennett (1985) observed wide variation in the extent of authoritarianism among professionals who work with CTAs. Some controlled all aspects of the organization and group process, making it more like group psychotherapy. Others intentionally stayed in the background, and encouraged members to take full responsibility for the group. Beyond questions of personality and leadership style, other variations are created by local traditions and by the availability of professionals in different regions. Thus, like "Abstainers Clubs," the term "CTAs" comprises professional treatment efforts, peer-led self-help groups, and gradations between these poles. Some forces may be leading more clubs toward a true self-help orientation, but that is speculation in advance of firm data from the post Balkan War period.

CTAs meet at least one evening a week, and may be open all day at weekends (Matijevic & Paunovic, 1973; Sikic *et al.*, 1973). In addition to supportive group meetings, they also often arrange social and recreational events. Clubs usually have medical professionals available for counseling, education, and the prescription of disulfiram (Bennett, 1985; Hudolin, 1984). A number of clubs include paraprofessional workers who are recovered alcoholics (Bennett, 1985). The time that professionals spend on CTAs is typically paid for from public funds.

Both alcoholics and their family members attend CTAs, and in most clubs they are asked to make a 5-year commitment to participation. To avoid growing to an unwieldy size, CTAs split into two when membership exceeds some standard. The standard varies from place to place, and can be some number of families (e.g., 13–15; Allamani & Petrikin, 1996; Patussi *et al.*, 1996) or people (e.g., more than 25 or 30; Hudolin, 1984; Lang & Srdar, 1992). Hudolin (1984) established the splitting rule to prevent diffusion of responsibility for abstinence within clubs, and recommended that clubs split in such a fashion that each new club has an equal share of experienced members. Yet he was cognizant that clubs often would not wish to split even when they attain a large size, and that his guidelines in this area would thus sometimes be ignored.

CTAs address alcoholism through long-term social support, social pressure, education, and medication. Hudolin (1984) conceptualized alcoholism as both "a chronic illness" and "a social disturbance," which suggests that he was much more strongly oriented to social psychiatric concepts of "disease" than to AA's. Accordingly, CTAs neither have a spiritual change component nor see a need for broader sobriety (e.g., moral reconstruction) beyond abstinence from alcohol (Pini *et al.*, 1996). They emphasize the role of the social environment in drinking problems, and as part of this concept expect non-alcoholic family members to abstain as well (Hudolin, 1984).

Membership

Membership in CTAs is broader than that name implies. Non-alcoholic family members and alcoholics who have never been treated also attend CTAs. Neither of these populations has been researched extensively, other than an early study indicating that 5–10% of alcoholic CTA members were in fact untreated (Sikic, Walker, & Peterson, 1973).

Assessing prevalence in the former Yugoslavia is hampered by the lack of post-war data. Just prior to the war, there were perhaps 200 CTAs in the Zagreb area, 500 in Croatia, and 800–900 in all of the former Yugoslavia (Lang & Srdar, 1992; see also Hudolin, 1984). Given the influence and energy of the Zagreb alcohol group, CTAs probably continue to be strongest in that city, even if the number of clubs has declined in absolute terms due to warfare. An early description of a CTA in Vinckovci provides some limited information on alcoholic members only (Matijevic & Paunovic, 1973). The modal age was 30–50 years, and the modal socioeconomic status was working class. Almost all alcoholic members were married and attended with their spouses. In this study, alcoholics composed 40% of all club members, whereas a different study conducted in Croatia, Bosnia-Herzegovina, and Slovenia found that alcoholics slightly outnumbered family members in CTAs.

In the mid-1990s, 2163 CTAs serving 15 000 alcoholics existed in Italy, and were heavily concentrated in the northern regions that have the strongest cultural and ethnic ties to Slav populations (Allamani & Petrikin, 1996; Patussi, Tumino, & Poldrugo, 1996). If the proportion of alcoholics and family members are similar in Italian and Yugoslavian-based CTAs, this would imply a total Italian membership of 25 000–40 000 people. The author could not find a description of the characteristics of Italian CTA members.

Double Trouble in Recovery

Origins and history

Double Trouble in Recovery is easily confused with another organization – Double Trouble – with which it shares part of its name and its history. This latter organization was founded in Philadelphia, Pennsylvania, in 1987 by a substance-dependent man who also had co-occurring psychiatric problems.

Mental health professionals advised on the establishment of the organization, which was initially operated by peer members. However, professionals increased their control of the organization over time to the point that they were running a large number of Double Trouble's meetings (Caldwell & White, 1991; Zaslav, 1993). Double Trouble increased in size to perhaps 50 groups spread throughout eastern Pennsylvania and into the neighboring state of New Jersey, but in the process generally lost the character of a true self-help organization under the control of peer members. Professionals' published writings about Double Trouble do mention self-help concepts such as the 12 steps, but refer to group participants as "patients" rather than as "members," reduce members' lives to psychiatric diagnostic categories, and emphasize participants' problems rather than their strengths. Such writings explicitly and implicitly conceptualize Double Trouble as a component of professional treatment services rather than as an autonomous alternative. Some mental health professionals clearly envisioned a shared leadership model for Double Trouble (e.g., Caldwell & White, 1991), but it nonetheless evolved into a primarily professionally controlled organization providing psychiatric services – a worthy mission but largely distinguishable from a mutual-help organization. That some professional writings about Double Trouble seem not to appreciate this difference is not completely surprising. As has been demonstrated empirically many times, psychiatric treatment professionals' perceptions of how much control they exert are almost always lower than patients' perceptions, and patients' perceptions of how much autonomy they have are almost always lower than what professionals imagine patients to be experiencing (Moos, 1997b).

The professional usurpation of Double Trouble, ironically enough, was partially responsible for the creation of a true self-help organization for persons with substance abuse and psychiatric problems. Howard Vogel began attending Double Trouble groups to help address his comorbid drug and psychiatric problems in 1989. He became disillusioned with the professional control of the organization and the focus in meetings on professional-treatment-oriented topics such as psychiatric medication compliance (Laudet, personal communication, 2001). He also felt that addiction-specific self-help organizations like NA did not fully meet the needs of members who had co-occurring psychiatric disorders (Vogel *et al.*, 1998). Vogel's dissatisfactions with other approaches led him to create an independent self-help organization known as "Double Trouble in Recovery" (DTR). He was supported in this effort by the Mental Health Empowerment Project of the New York State Office of Mental Health (especially Edward Knight), which, among other activities, fosters greater control by consumers of the mental health system. A key aspect of the support provided to

DTR was a grant to train peer group leaders, which has helped the organization expand rapidly within New York State.

Philosophy and approach

Unlike in Double Trouble, all DTR groups are led by individuals with dual disorders, even those groups that meet in institutional settings (Vogel *et al.*, 1998). The organization believes strongly that its members – most of whom have been marginalized and powerless within and without the healthcare system – benefit from being able to participate fully and operate the organization themselves.

DTR resembles AA in many respects. Addiction and psychiatric problems are conceptualized as diseases that cannot be eliminated or controlled through self-will, and spiritual change is considered essential to recovery. DTR uses AA's 12 steps with little modification, other than replacing references to alcohol and alcoholics with equivalent terms for dual disorders. DTR differs from AA mainly in acknowledging psychiatric disorders as a distinct, important focus of recovery, rather than as an issue secondary to addiction. As a consequence, in DTR meetings members speak much more openly about their psychiatric problems, psychiatric medication, and related issues than they do in addiction-specific, 12-step self-help groups. This helps to explain why DTR members who concurrently attend other 12-step fellowships report feeling more comfortable and accepted within DTR (Vogel *et al.*, 1998).

DTR operates a small non-profit organization staffed by experienced members who provide assistance to dually diagnosed individuals wishing to start or maintain DTR groups. Given the many challenges faced by dually diagnosed people, DTR believes its organizational growth depends on training being offered to potential group leaders (e.g., on how to advertise a meeting, what the program offers, etc.). If DTR becomes a larger organization with many long-term members, such knowledge may eventually be transmitted informally as needed without any centralized consultation service, as usually happens in AA.

Membership

Extrapolating from recent prevalence and growth data in Vogel *et al.*'s (1998) study yields a current estimate of 150 DTR groups in existence. All DTR groups are in the USA, and most are in New York City. Hence, a recent interview survey of 310 members attending one of 25 DTR meetings in the New York metropolitan area can be considered a representative snapshot of members (Laudet *et al.*, 2000b).

DTR participants are predominantly (72%) male and African-American (58%). Almost all (95%) members report disability insurance as their primary source of income, and only 21% live in their own house or apartment. The median age of members is 39 years, the median age of initiation of substance use is 14, and the median age of first serious psychiatric symptoms is 18. The most common primary substances of abuse of DTR members are cocaine/crack (42% of respondents), alcohol (34%), and heroin (11%). Schizophrenia (43%), bipolar disorder (25%), and unipolar major depression (26%) are the most common psychiatric diagnoses among members. The vast majority of members have received inpatient substance-abuse treatment as well as psychiatric hospitalization, and 91% are currently receiving outpatient mental health services. In summary, even relative to the other addiction-related self-help organizations described in this book, DTR attracts a population that faces serious challenges.

In terms of participation patterns, 37% of members attend DTR meetings twice a week and 60% on a weekly basis. Two-thirds of members have been attending for a year or more. These survey findings on frequency and length of attendance probably do not generalize outside the New York City area to those parts of the country where DTR is newer and less prevalent. Even though part of the rationale of DTR is to provide support not available in addiction-specific 12-step fellowships, 75% of DTR members concurrently attend AA and/or NA meetings. Comfort with other 12-step organizations is also suggested by findings that, of a list of 29 challenges in recovery (e.g., overcoming isolation, being bored, dealing with medications), DTR participants rated as the three *least* difficult challenges: "not being accepted at other 12-step groups," "following a program such as the 12 steps," and "accepting a Higher Power" (see Laudet *et al.*, 2000a).

Free Life (Vie Libre)

Origins and history

As mentioned in the description of the history of the Protestant-supported Blue Cross, the Catholic Church in France created a parallel alcohol-related mutual-help organization called Gold Cross (Croix d'Or) in 1910. Gold Cross attracted many members, some of whom eventually became dissatisfied with its Catholic-derived religious and moralistic aspects. Chief among these apostates was a priest named Father Talvas, who decided to start a new, secular mutual-help organization (Fainzang, 1994). "Free Life" was created in 1953 through the efforts of Talvas and other individuals disaffected by Gold Cross, including a

disulfiram-prescribing physician and his patients (Cerclé, 1984). They intentionally modeled their new, alcohol-based mutual-help organization more on a
trade union than on a church (with some respectful nods toward AA, of which
some of the founders were aware; Cerclé, 1984).

Free Life has been one of the most politically involved addiction-related
mutual-help organizations. It reached out specifically to the working classes by
emphasizing how social and economic inequality makes workers particularly
vulnerable to alcoholism (Barrucand, 1984; Cerclé; 1984; Fainzang, 1994). Free
Life has also advocated the rights of alcoholic patients to receive high-quality,
specialized care from the healthcare system (Barrucand, 1984; Bénichou, 1980).
Further, its national congress has adopted resolutions condemning gambling and
endorsing increases in the health budget (Cerclé, 1984).

Philosophy and approach

Free Life describes alcoholism as a "disease," but does not use this term in the
same fashion as 12-step organizations (Cerclé, 1984). Free Life instead views
alcoholism as a social disease caused, in part, by economic and political forces
(e.g., "society makes us drink;" Fainzang, 1994). In Free Life's philosophy, the
disease can be cured, and this occurs entirely due to secular forces: high-quality
medical care (conceived as the political right of every alcoholic), solidarity
among the membership, and abstinence from alcohol.

Free Life has a national committee with local, departmental, and regional
sections. Public education campaigns and advocacy efforts are usually coordinated at the higher levels of the organization, as is the operation of a small
number of sobriety homes (Barrucand, 1984). The smallest unit of organization in Free Life is a cell of 5–6 members who contact alcoholic patients in
the hospital, encourage them to join the movement, and attempt to help them
abstain (Bénichou, 1980). Free Life mutual-help group meetings are open both
to alcoholics and their families. In addition to former drinkers and their "supporters," who are not problem drinkers but nonetheless abstain from alcohol,
the organization also has a broader cadre of "sympathizers," who support the
movement's general goals even though they do not personally abstain.

The following description of the process of Free Life mutual-help meetings
is drawn entirely from Sylvie Fainzang's (1994) ethnographic research in Paris.
The meeting begins with an embrace of each member by each other member,
which reaffirms solidarity among those who suffer from alcohol problems. This
ritual also has the practical function of making it difficult to come to meetings
intoxicated, which would be detected through the smell of alcohol on the breath.
After the ritual embraces, everyone present speaks in turn about a particular

theme or question. Typical topics include how drinking began, the damaging effects of alcohol, relapses, and the benefits of abstinence. After this discussion period, members have a social period where they collectively consume non-alcoholic beverages.

Free Life is one of the many mutual-help organizations that gives awards for the achievement of abstinence. After 6 months of abstinence, a pink card symbolizing full membership in the organization is presented with great ceremony and celebration to the former problem drinker (Fainzang, 1994). Like other events of the organizations, these ceremonies are typically attended by supporting family and friends of the problem drinker.

Membership

Free Life is based almost entirely in France, but has some group meetings in neighboring Belgium. Free Life shares with Blue Cross a tripartite classification of its membership (i.e., former drinkers, their abstaining supporters, and movement sympathizers), which complicates assessment of the number of problem drinkers in the organization. In the 1980s, several researchers estimated that Free Life had 15 000 members, but did not specify if this number was restricted to former problem drinkers or also included supporters and sympathizers (Barrucand, 1984; Bénichou, 1980). Regardless of what assumptions are made about those data, Free Life must have grown in the ensuing decade because it had 20 000 former problem-drinking members by 1993 (Mäkelä *et al.*, 1996). The modal membership situation in Free Life, as in Danshukai, is of a formerly problem-drinking man attending with his wife as a supporter. Other details on members' characteristics could not be found.

Jewish Alcoholics, Chemically Dependent Persons, and Significant Others

Origins and history

Jewish Americans are stereotyped as uniformly abstemious, but no ethnic group is completely free of substance-abuse problems (Vex & Blume, 2001). Few specialty helping resources are targeted toward Jewish Americans because of stigma and the unwillingness of some alcohol-dependent Jews to seek help for a "Gentile problem" (Bayer & Levy, 1980; Trainin, 1986). As a result, Jewish American alcoholics have historically availed themselves of existing resources, including AA (Bayer & Levy, 1980; O'Connell, 1989). Although many Jews report positive experiences with AA, some feel a conflict between their Judaism and the Christian overtones of some AA meetings and writings

(Master, 1989). Others do not view AA as Christian in outlook, but nonetheless desire a recovery resource that makes Jewish identity and teachings central to the recovery process (O'Connell, 1989; Rabinowitz, 1986).

Several task forces and retreats organized in the USA in the 1970s concluded that a Jewish-specific recovery resource was needed (Bayer & Levy, 1980; Rabinowitz, 1986; Vex & Blume, 2001). A group of concerned Jewish leaders and Jewish members of addiction-related 12-step fellowships formed "Jewish Alcoholics, Chemically Dependent Persons, and Significant Others" (JACS) in New York City in 1979. JACS' founding date is sometimes reported as 1980, which is the year in which the JACS foundation was formally incorporated (JACS, personal communication, August 15, 2002).

JACS-related activities as a whole, including the founding of self-help groups, were initially varied and uncoordinated, with committed individuals in different parts of the USA operating fairly independently. The organization became more cohesive after a national conference in 1985 in Philadelphia, during which its affiliates developed and endorsed a mission statement (reproduced in its entirety in Rabinowitz, 1986). The mission statement clarified that the purposes of JACS are to provide spiritual and communal support to addicted Jews and their families, to serve as a resource center and information exchange point, and to conduct community outreach. The statement specifically endorses the value of 12-step organizations such as AA and NA, and makes clear that JACS complements, rather than competes with, such programs by adding a Jewish-specific aspect to 12-step recovery.

An intriguing aspect of the organization's subsequent history was the unsuccessful effort of some JACS members to bring the program to Israel, where it might be presumed to have appeal. As described by Natti Ronel, Israeli Jews found it difficult to accept the idea that an additional program was needed to connect their recovery from addiction specifically to their Jewishness (Ronel & Humphreys, 1999). Israeli Jews involved in 12-step groups considered Judaism to be an ineffable, secure aspect of their identities that required no specific validation by another organization. This implies that JACS reflects the needs of Jews who are a small minority in a national population, which may make questions of maintaining Jewish identity more salient.

Philosophy and approach

JACS sees no contradiction between 12-step programs and Jewishness per se and fully endorses the 12-step model. Indeed, the organization works to have more synagogues host AA and NA meetings, and encourages its members to use

JACS groups as a supplement to 12-step self-help groups (O'Connell, 1989). The unique philosophical aspect of JACS relates not to addiction per se, but to Jewish identity. The organization believes that a certain number of Jewish alcoholics will benefit from mutual-help groups that explicitly tie Jewishness to 12-step recovery, for example by discussing connections between traditional Jewish values and traditions with those expressed in the 12 steps.

In addition to supporting mutual-help groups, JACS conducts retreats for recovering Jews and their families. It also operates community education programs that are designed to raise awareness of alcoholism and drug addiction within Jewish communities (Rabinowitz, 1986).

Membership

JACS is a small organization catering for the specialized needs of a minority population, but it has grown significantly since its founding. As of 2002, the organization's website listed about 50 JACS meetings. Almost all JACS meetings are held in the USA, with a few occurring in Australia, Brazil, Canada, and Mexico. In terms of number of members, in 1998 JACS' mailing list included 1100–1300 chemically dependent members, most of whom were concurrently involved in AA, NA, or a related 12-step organization (Vex & Blume, 2001).

A recent survey of 379 substance-dependent members provided the first data on the characteristics of JACS affiliates (Vex & Blume, 2001). Relative to general population samples of substance-dependent people, JACS' membership was notable for its high proportion of women (almost half) and people with graduate-level education (47%), although these findings may be partly attributable to gender and educational differences in willingness to complete research surveys. About 45% of members were currently married, about 25% were divorced, and the average member was 49 years of age. In terms of Jewish religious identification, 10% were Orthodox, 28% Conservative, 32% Reform, and 30% Non-Affiliated. Alcohol was the most common substance upon which members were dependent. Members reported very positive views of AA, NA, and CA, rating them more helpful than all types of treatment and counseling (including rabbinical) in promoting recovery.

The Links

Origins and history

The history of The Links begins with a Swedish temperance board worker named Axel Sällqvist and a group of recovered alcoholics who, in 1939, began initial efforts to start a self-help organization (Helmersson Bergmark, 1998). They were influenced by their perceptions of temperance organizations, the Oxford Group Movement, and AA, which then had no meetings in Sweden but had been the subject of a positive story in a widely read magazine (Kurube, 1992a, b). Their organization was formalized as the "Society of Links" in 1945 (Kurube, 1992a). It attracted more members over time, particularly in 1955 and 1956, when an alcohol-related exhibition called "The Bottle and the Jester" toured Sweden and spread word about "The Links" (Helmersson Bergmark, 1998).

The Links went through many years of internal and external discussions concerning whether the organization was part of AA, which began groups in Sweden in the early 1950s. AA co-founder Bill Wilson and his wife Lois Wilson visited Sweden in 1950 and debated with Links' members their departures from the traditional AA program (Helmersson Bergmark, 1998). Comparing AA with "The" Swedish Links became increasingly complex as the latter organization splintered with regularity in the decades following its founding into separate societies with somewhat different approaches and attitudes (Kurube, 1992a). Because they did not adapt many aspects of AA's program, including its steps and emphasis on spiritual change, the relationship between AA and The Swedish Links was, at times, frosty in the 1960s and 1970s (Helmersson Bergmark, 1998). Today, AA and the various incarnations of The Swedish Links are clearly different organizations in Sweden, as the arrival of Minnesota Model treatment has put a distinctive stamp on Swedish AA (Blomqvist, 1998; Kurube, 1992a; Mäkelä et al., 1996).

Sweden is not the only Scandanavian country with a Links organization. The Danish Links (originally called "Ring in Ring") was created in 1948 by alcoholic working-class individuals and supportive treatment professionals who had heard about AA. The Links did not start in Norway until 1979, when it was initiated by members of The Swedish Links.

The Links in each of the above countries created a larger federation of non-12-step mutual-help organizations called "Sobriety International," which includes the All Nippon Sobriety Association and Abstainers Clubs as member organizations (Kurube, 1992b). Sobriety International was organized as a religiously and politically independent advocate for better understanding of, and policy toward, alcohol problems. The Links have meanwhile been experiencing some competition for members with AA, which has been buoyed by the expansion of Minnesota Model treatment across Scandanavia (Blomqvist, 1998; Mäkelä et al., 1996; Steffen, 1994).

Table 3. *The "Seven Points" philosophy of The Links*

1. Admit that you are powerless over alcohol.
2. You must believe in a power that is greater than your own.
3. Do not demand anything from your fellow beings.
4. We aim for absolute honesty, purity, love for our fellow beings, and unselfishness.
5. Admit your faults and imperfections to some other human beings.
6. Resolve all conflicts with others and try to make up for your mistakes.
7. As you were helped, you shall help others.

Source: Kurube (1992a)

Philosophy and approach

Because it is newer, smaller, and a direct offshoot of The Swedish Links, The Norwegian Links and The Swedish Links are more similar than either is to The Danish Links. Most Links groups in Sweden and Norway base their philosophy on "Seven Points" (Table 3), adapted from the 12 steps of AA. The Links' points differ from AA's steps primarily in their de-emphasis of spiritual forces and God (Blomqvist, 1998; Helmersson Bergmark, 1998; Kurube, 1992a). The power greater than the drinker is typically conceived in terms of solidarity rather than divinity, which is one of several similarities between The Links and the Free Life organization. Replacing "steps" with "points" would also seem to rule out any analogies to a "Pilgrim's Progress." In contrast, point 4 of The Links harkens back to the perfectionistic religious language of the Oxford Group (cf. its "absolutes"), which AA specifically sought to eliminate from its argot.

The Danish Links' groups usually don't use the seven points, relying instead on a professionally influenced program of change that emphasizes the role of psychological factors in recovery (e.g., self-knowledge, psychological insight, rationality; see Kurube, 1992b). The Danish Links' view of alcoholism is more similar to Free Life's than to its Norwegian and Swedish cousins, in that alcoholism is considered as a cultural and social problem rather than an incurable, progressive disease (Helmersson Bergmark, 1998; Kurube, 1992b). At the same time, The Danish, Swedish, and Norwegian Links all agree on the importance of abstinence in recovery from alcohol problems.

Mutual-help group meetings are only a small part of the activities of The Links in all of its host countries. Members openly (i.e., non-anonymously) engage in advocacy around alcohol problems, actively recruit members, obtain external funding, and arrange social activities (Helmersson Bergmark, 1998; Kurube, 1992b). Membership in The Links is open to supporting members as well as to problem drinkers, with family participation being most strongly emphasized in The Danish Links (Kurube, 1992b).

Membership

The Links organization is strongest in its country of origin. Counting both former problem drinkers and their supporters, Kurube (1992b) reports 1990 figures of 17 500 in Sweden, 5000 in Denmark, and only 300 in Norway. The only data the author could find on the characteristics of Links' members comes from a study of Swedish members, which reported that 82% were male, 47% were married or cohabiting, and 60% were employed. Average duration of education was only 9 years – one of several indicators that, relative to AA in Sweden, The Links attracts problem drinkers of lower socioeconomic status (Helmersson Bergmark, 1998).

Moderation Management

Origins and history

Moderation Management's history began in Michigan with a female problem drinker named Audrey Kishline. During Minnesota-Model-style alcoholism treatment episodes, Kishline was aggressively confronted with the idea that she had an incurable disease over which she was powerless, which undermined her confidence and self-esteem and did not match her subjective experience of alcohol abuse (Kishline, 1994). She also had difficulty in relating to other patients in treatment because, relative to them, her drinking problem was of much lower severity (e.g., she never experienced withdrawal symptoms and she continued to work and attend school). As an example of how different she was from the typical alcoholic inpatient, when Ms. Kishline's group therapist left the room for a moment, the rest of the inpatients voted her "least likely to really be an alcoholic" (Kishline, 1998, personal communication).

Although 12-step-influenced interventions were not helpful to Kishline, she returned to moderate drinking when she got married, had children, and took on other responsibilities. She retained a negative view of the US alcohol treatment system and resolved to create a new option for problem drinkers. Drawing on the work of cognitive–behavioral researchers (e.g., Sanchez-Craig *et al.*, 1995), Kishline created Moderation Management (MM) in 1994 to serve non-dependent problem drinkers for whom traditional 12-step treatments might be ineffective.

MM famously departed from all other existing alcohol mutual-help organizations by allowing members to attempt a return to moderate drinking. The organization never denied that some individuals were alcohol-dependent and could not control their drinking, and further stated that it was not intended for such individuals (Kishline, 1994), but it was still widely criticized for "encouraging alcoholics to drink." The UK organization "Drinkwatchers" handled this concern by allowing treatment professionals to decide who was appropriate for its groups, a policy which blunted criticism but which also prevented UK Drinkwatchers from becoming a true peer-controlled mutual-help organization (Josef Ruzek, personal communication, May 29, 2001). MM left judgements about the appropriateness of a moderate drinking goal to individual members and their groups, which further exacerbated some treatment professionals' worry about the organization. Yet, the organization also attracted some positive media attention and the support of some well-known individuals within the alcohol field.

MM was also unique in its unprecedented use of computer-based communication technology to establish a mutual-help organization. Almost all self-help organizations have a website and some online meetings, but MM was remarkable in launching itself heavily over the Internet. Indeed, even though MM face-to-face mutual-help groups spread in the organization's early years, very soon the majority of MM members were meeting in online MM discussion groups.

In January 2000, Kishline announced publically to the membership of MM that she had concluded that the best drinking goal for her was abstinence. She began attending AA meetings instead, while continuing to support the value of MM for others. Eight months later, Kishline relapsed and drove her truck the wrong way on a highway, eventually hitting another vehicle head-on and killing two passengers. This tragedy led to a storm of controversy in the USA that, in many respects, paralleled the controlled-drinking debates of the 1970s. Both MM and Kishline were widely condemned in the mass media and within the alcohol treatment field. Some of these critiques were well founded, but many drew conclusions that simply did not follow from the facts of the case (i.e., that the tragedy proved AA's superiority to MM even though Kishline was in AA and not MM when the accident happened). Interested readers are referred to an outstanding compilation by Alexander DeLuca of the opinion columns and public statements about the case, available on the World Wide Web (http://doctordeluca.com/Documents/PrimaryDocuments.htm).

Ms. Kishline is currently imprisoned for vehicular manslaughter. Perhaps surprisingly, MM has continued to grow in her absence and appears to have a stable organizational footing. As of this writing, to the author's knowledge it is the only addiction-related mutual-help organization in existence that supports moderate use as a goal for members.

Philosophy and approach

MM explicitly targets non-dependent problem drinkers rather than alcohol-dependent individuals. By making such a distinction, it rejects the idea that all alcohol problems should be viewed as an uncontrollable, incurable disease (Rotgers & Kishline, 2000). Rather, MM views non-dependent problem drinking as a controllable bad habit. MM does not believe that surrender to a Higher Power or any other spiritual change is required to resolve alcohol problems.

MM members are encouraged to follow a nine-step cognitive–behavioral change program. Like all aspects of the group's philosophy and approach, the nine steps are described in a basic text that many members read (Kishline, 1994). The steps ask members to complete a 30-day abstinence period, during which time members are to appraise the positive and negative effects of drinking in their life. If a member cannot complete the 30-day abstinence period, it is taken as an indication that the member's drinking problem may be too severe to be ameliorated by the MM approach (Rotgers & Kishline, 2000). After the abstinence period, members are encouraged to limit their drinking to what the MM program considers to be a safe limit, based on research (e.g., Sanchez-Craig, Wilkinson, & Davila, 1995): no more than 3 drinks on any day or 9 drinks in any week for women, and no more than 4 drinks on any day or more than 14 drinks in any week for men. In addition, both men and women are to have three to four non-drinking days each week. MM does not mandate that members drink as much as these limits, or even that they consume alcohol at all; MM simply presents a return to moderate drinking as an option. After alcohol consumption has been moderated, members are also encouraged to make other healthy lifestyle changes, such as improving quality of diet and increasing exercise.

Member-led self-help groups are the core of the MM program. Treatment professionals are allowed to help start MM groups, but, as with all self-help organizations, ultimate control rests with the participants (Gartner & Riessman, 1977; Humphreys & Rappaport, 1994). Whether conducted face-to-face or over the Internet, MM self-help groups are intended to give members the opportunity to identify with each other, learn from other members who have successfully controlled their drinking problem, and provide support and encouragement

(Kishline, 1994). Face-to-face MM meetings typically last an hour, whereas online "meetings" are ongoing, with members able to write and receive messages electronically at any time. There is no "cross talk" prohibition in MM meetings; rather, exchanges of direct advice are considered appropriate (Klaw & Humphreys, 2000).

A formal context analysis of Internet-based MM meetings indicated that the most common types of communication by members are self-disclosure, provision of information and advice, and provision of emotional support (Klaw, Huebsch, & Humphreys, 2000; Klaw & Humphreys, 2000). Interestingly, parallel analyses of online self-help groups for depression (Salem, *et al.*, 1997) and eating disorders (Winzelberg, 1997) have found the same rank ordering of communication types.

Membership

All MM face-to-face groups are based in the USA, but individuals in other countries access MM over the Internet. MM membership is probably around 500 individuals at any one given moment, with several times that many people having contact with the organization each year. Most contact with MM occurs over the Internet rather than in face-to-face groups (Humphreys & Klaw, 2001). A final indicator of the organization's prevalence is that its primary text has sold more than 50 000 copies.

A recent survey (Humphreys & Klaw, 2001) indicated that MM members are Caucasian (96%), employed (81%), and well educated (72% college education or post-graduate degree). Relative to the US population, which is among the most religious in the developed world, MM members are secular in outlook: 32% describe themselves as atheist or agnostic and only 16% attend religious services once a week or more. MM attracts unusually high proportions of women (49%) and people under the age of 35 years (24%). Both of these populations are particularly likely to access MM over the Internet, and may feel that the organization's description of, and approach to, alcohol problems is a good match to their own experience.

The level of pre-existent substance-abuse problems among members appears lower in MM than in any other addiction-related self-help organization. Prior to MM involvement, 40% of members consumed 4 or less drinks per drinking day, and less than 10% experienced serious alcohol-dependence symptoms or comorbid drug abuse. Fears to the contrary notwithstanding, MM thus primarily attracts the high-functioning, non-dependent problem drinkers it was intended to serve (Humphreys & Klaw, 2001).

Narcotics Anonymous

Origins and history

NA has a complex history involving several cul-de-sacs and resurrections. The idea that Alcoholics Anonymous' approach could be applied to other substances was raised early in AA's development, but AA co-founder Bill Wilson was against non-alcoholic individuals attending AA (White, 1998). Beginning in the 1940s, numerous individuals in different parts of the USA (sometimes in concert, sometimes independently) attempted to found a parallel organization for individuals who were dependent on drugs other than alcohol. The earliest attempt appears to have been made at the famous US Public Health Service Hospital in Lexington, Kentucky (Ellison, 1954; Peyrot, 1985). The Lexington facility, which was a cross between a medical center and a prison, was the first effort of the US federal government to treat narcotic addiction. The facility's culture of innovation flourished under medical director Victor Vogel, who accepted an offer by an experienced AA member named Houston Smith to start an AA-style meeting for drug addicts in 1947 (Sewell, 1998; White, 1998).

The Lexington-based group was originally called "Addicts Anonymous," and news of it spread as discharged residents returned to their communities or to other correctional facilities. A former Lexington patient named Danny Carlson organized addicts to start meetings in New York City in 1949. Carlson changed the group's name to "Narcotics Anonymous" to avoid the potential confusion of having two organizations called "AA" (White, 1998). Like Alcoholics Anonymous, NA in New York City got a strong membership boost when it was the subject of a positive story in the *Saturday Evening Post* (Ellison, 1954). NA continued in New York City for several decades, going through periods of greater and lesser stability before finally withering away by the 1970s (White, 1998).

The second "origin story" of NA begins in California, and is the one more commonly reported in official NA literature (see, e.g., Narcotics Anonymous, 1995a, b). This history begins with southern California AA members who were also dependent on drugs other than alcohol. Such individuals started several AA-style organizations for drug addiction in the 1950s, most of which had difficulty catching on. However, in 1953 in Sun Valley, California (Part of the Greater Los Angeles Area), a stable NA group became firmly established. This group included an addict named Jimmy Kinnon, who is today widely regarded in NA as the organization's founder (the New York City history notwithstanding) in the same way that Bill Wilson and Robert Smith are in AA. Kinnon, a skilled and diligent organizer, helped start other NA groups and spread the organization's message.

The post-Kinnon history of NA could be characterized as "two steps forward, one step back." NA groups and NA's presence in different cities were unstable, with many false starts. The illegality of drugs led to problems such as narcotics' officers waiting at meetings to arrest members (Sewell, 1998). Furtive "rabbit meetings" that rotated from location to location helped members avoid police officers, but also made it difficult for newcomers to find an NA group (Narcotics Anonymous, 2000). NA's progress was also inhibited by an unusually high prevalence of personality and philosophical clashes within the organization. The West Coast NA was frequently at risk of dying out throughout the 1950s. The arrival of a non-addict, master bureaucrat – Robert Stone (1997) – as executive director seemed to help stabilize NA. Stone's prudent management style and Kinnon's entrepreneurial zeal (a rough analogy to Dr. Bob and Bill W. may be warranted here) helped the organization come back to life in the 1960s, and its future has not been in doubt since. NA created a World Service Office in 1977 and saw its greatest growth in the following years. During this period, a charismatic NA member named Bo S. organized a series of conferences around the country devoted to writing collectively the organization's basic text (James Awbrey, personal communication, April 7, 2001). Both the conferences themselves and the publication of this text – which has sold four million copies – helped fuel interest in NA, and its number of groups exploded 100-fold from 1978 to 1994. The organization also expanded to a truly international scope, spreading from three countries to 70 by 1994 (Narcotics Anonymous, 1995b). Since that time, the organization has continued to grow, though at a slower pace (Narcotics Anonymous, 2000).

Philosophy and approach

NA's philosophy and approach are quite similar to AA's in most respects. Like AA, NA has 12 steps and 12 traditions, endorses the view that addiction is a disease, views recovery as a spiritual and moral process, and insists on lifetime abstinence for members (Narcotics Anonymous, 1995b; Peyrot, 1985). Yet NA made two intriguing modifications to the 12 steps.

First, it replaced the word "alcohol" with "addiction" rather than "drugs" (Narcotics Anonymous, 1992). This change explicitly opens the organization to individuals with problems with any drugs as well as with alcohol. The implicit effect of shifting focus to a trait from the substance itself may be to center attention on the personality problems of members. Second, the organization added the word "We" at the beginning of all of the steps, a word members sometimes say aloud together when the steps are read in meetings, which builds group cohesion (James Awbrey, personal communication, July 16, 2001).

The second key difference between AA and NA concerns sponsorship. Members in both organizations often remark that "the sobriety is better in AA." This complaint reflects NA's long-standing trouble retaining a large cadre of senior, recovering members (Duncan, 1965). This may be why NA's literature gives relatively more attention to sponsorship than do AA's primary texts, which do not even use the term. For example, the organization's introductory guide includes sections on how to find a sponsor, what qualifications sponsors should have, and how to sponsor other members (Narcotics Anonymous, 1992).

Membership

A 1996 NA publication reported 21 500 groups in 77 countries (NA, 1996); the organization's website (www.na.org/) gives a 2001 estimate of 19 192 groups in 113 countries. About 80% of NA groups are based in the USA, and 5% are based in Canada. Within Europe, NA appears strongest in the UK, Germany, Portugal, Switzerland, and Sweden; no other European nation has more than 100 groups (Narcotics Anonymous, 1995b, 2000). NA has a significant presence in Australia and Brazil, and is growing in other parts of Asia and South America, respectively (Narcotics Anonymous, 1995b, 2000). As mentioned in the section on AA above, NA also has chapters in a number of Middle Eastern countries. Accounts of NA's spread from the USA to other countries are available for Australia (O'Brien, 1996), Germany (Appel, 1996), Israel (Ronel, 1998), and the UK (Wells, 1994). Although data are limited, in these countries NA seems to maintain much of the character it developed in the USA (O'Brien, 1996; Ronel, 1997; Ronel & Humphreys, 1999).

In terms of member characteristics, a number of NA documents (Narcotics Anonymous, 1995a) mention an "informal poll of 5000 NA members" conducted in 1989. The survey found that NA members were young, with 11% being under 20 years old, 37% being 20–30 years old, and only 4% being over 45. About two-thirds (64%) of respondents were male. The survey write-up typically mentions a diversity of social classes and religious backgrounds, but gives no specific figures. Where and how this survey was conducted are not described, so its generalizability and validity cannot be assessed. NA itself has been admirably candid about the precise characteristics of current members being unknown (NA, personal communication, 1996).

Nicotine Anonymous

Origins and history

Californian AA members of AA began applying the 12-step approach to their nicotine addiction in the 1980s, calling their groups "Smokers Anonymous" meetings. Members of these groups held a state-wide conference in Bakersfield in 1986 and joined under an umbrella organization shortly thereafter (Lichtenstein, 1999). The organization changed its name to "Nicotine Anonymous" in 1989 to avoid a trademark conflict with a for-profit smoking cessation company (Lichtenstein, 1999) and to indicate openness to members who had used nicotine in forms other than cigarettes and cigars.

Approach and philosophy

Nicotine Anonymous closely follows AA's approach, including adapting some of AA's writings (with permission) directly into their own. The organization relies on the 12 steps and believes that total abstinence from nicotine is necessary for recovery. Although no ethnographic research appears to have been conducted on Nicotine Anonymous meetings, they are probably similar to those of AA – minus the tobacco smoke.

Membership

Nicotine Anonymous has about 500 groups with perhaps 5000–10000 members. About 90% of these meetings occur in the USA, with Canada, Brazil, Australia, and England, respectively, being the countries with the next most common meeting places. The organization has chapters in 23 countries, and some evidence indicates that it continues to spread internationally. For example, in 1990 there were no Nicotine Anonymous groups in Austria or Poland (Mäkelä *et al.*, 1996), but a World Wide Web search conducted by the author in early 2002 identified meetings in both of these countries. However, other countries that had no groups in 1990 (e.g., Switzerland, Finland, and Iceland; see Mäkelä *et al.*, 1996) still appear to have no Nicotine Anonymous chapters, suggesting that diffusion has neither been rapid nor inevitable.

A scientific survey of Nicotine Anonymous members has not been conducted and hence membership characteristics cannot be described. However, Edward

Lichtenstein's (1999) conjecture that the organization attracts a disproportionate number of individuals who are involved in other addiction-related 12-step organizations seems plausible on two grounds. First, recovering alcoholics who smoke are usually highly dependent on nicotine (Kozlowski, Jelinek, & Pope, 1986) and hence might be more amenable to conceptualizing tobacco use as an uncontrollable, disruptive disease. Second, individuals who have recovered through AA would already be comfortable with the 12-step approach used in Nicotine Anonymous.

Oxford Houses

Origins and history

The origins of Oxford Houses can be traced to an alcoholic US Senate staff member named Paul Molloy. Molloy left his government position in 1975 and sought help from AA and treatment professionals (Jason *et al.*, 2001). While staying in a halfway house, Molloy noticed that the substance-dependent residents often relapsed when they reached the maximum length of stay and were discharged. When the halfway house lost its funding and was on the verge of closure, Molloy and a group of other recovering alcoholics decided to convert it into a member-run sober community (Jason *et al.*, 2001). They named their house after the Oxford Group, the quasi-religious organization that influenced the founders of AA and The Links.

The initial Oxford House was located in Silver Spring, Maryland, a community adjacent to Washington DC (Oxford House, 2001). The residents paid for the lease and maintenance, and could stay as long as they remained sober. When the residents eventually accumulated sufficient funds, they started another Oxford House. Oxford Houses spread in this fashion throughout the Washington DC area, with 18 established by 1988 (Oxford House, 2001).

In 1988, the US Congress was developing legislation concerned with drug and alcohol abuse, which presented an opportunity, given Molloy's excellent contacts with federal law makers. The organization had an internal debate over whether to lobby that the legislation should include funds for more Oxford Houses, recognizing that such monies would increase growth but also pose risks of bureaucratization and distraction. The organization ultimately decided to ask for federal support, which was granted in the 1988 Federal Anti-Drug Abuse Act (Oxford House, 2001). Under the legislation, each of the 50 US states established a revolving loan fund to help recovering individuals start new Oxford Houses. This new funding greatly accelerated the organization's growth. Hundreds of new Oxford Houses were created, including specialty homes for women and for women with children.

Philosophy and approach

The Oxford House group is the only entirely residential mutual-help organization discussed in this chapter. In most other respects, it has parallels with AA even though the organizations are not officially connected (Oxford House, 2001). Almost all Oxford House residents have been involved in AA/NA and carry that perspective into their interactions with other residents (Oxford House, 2001). The organization's 10 traditions also adapt many AA/NA ideas.

Oxford Houses must be completely peer-run and must operate on democratic principles, which the organization believes promotes responsibility in the residents (Oxford House, 2001). Members can maintain residence indefinitely provided that they abstain from alcohol and drugs, pay an equal share of house expenses, and refrain from highly disruptive behavior (e.g., violence toward other residents). Lack of continued involvement in AA and NA is not grounds for dismissal unless the individual relapses. Membership requirements are minimal beyond these clear rules, which reflects the influence of AA's slogan, "Keep it simple," on the founders of the Oxford House group.

New Oxford House members typically come directly from a treatment program or from self-help organizations, and apply for membership at a house that has an opening. After meeting the prospective resident, members vote on whether to accept him/her, with 80% agreement being required for entry (Oxford House, 2001). Most houses have 6–15 members at any given time, with all adults being of the same sex. Length of stay in an Oxford House is not pre-determined, but some residents choose to move on, at which time they can become an "associate member" who continues to help less experienced house members.

Each Oxford House has regular business meetings to ensure the smooth operation of the community. House leaders are elected by members and may not serve for more than 6 months. Oxford Houses within the same geographic area are organized as chapters, and a national office grants charters to new houses that agree to the minimal rule structure described above. The organization's leaders construe themselves as "trusted servants who do not govern," and, as with AA groups, each house is autonomous in decisions about its own setting (Oxford House, 2001).

Membership

At this writing, there are about 600 Oxford Houses with space for about 5000 residents. All of these are based in the USA, with the exception of 13 houses in the Canadian Province of Alberta and one house in Victoria, Australia. About one out of five Oxford Houses are dedicated to women (with or without children). The organization does not provide data on associate members, but given that the average length of stay is a little over a year, it seems likely that they are nearly as numerous as current residents. This would place the organization's overall membership in the region of 9000–10 000 people.

Member characteristics were delineated by a national survey of 858 Oxford House residents in the USA (Jason *et al.*, 1997a). About 80% were male and about 60% were Caucasian. Most members were young (usually in their early to mid-30s), had at least a high-school education, and were employed, which is to be expected given that Oxford House members must contribute to household expenses. Most residents have a history of using illicit drugs in addition to alcohol, and 10% were homeless prior to joining a house. A history of criminal and antisocial behavior (especially property crime) was common among residents.

Pui Hong Self-Help Association

Origins and history

Hong Kong is one of the few Asian societies with a rich tradition of western-style, health-related self-help groups, including organizations that address arthritis, chronic pain, psychiatric problems, and stroke (Chow, 1997). Many of these associations are supported by the mutual-help network of the Hong Kong Society for Rehabilitation. Alcoholics Anonymous meetings for British expatriates and Chinese members are also available in Hong Kong.

Hong Kong's opiate-addiction-related mutual-help organizations have a distinct history. Opiate dependence had always existed in Hong Kong, but did not become a major social problem until the Chinese Civil War of 1945–1949. As described by James Ch'ien (1980), the countless Chinese refugees who entered Hong Kong during and after the war included many smokers of opium, some of whom switched to heroin after their arrival. Hong Kong experienced rapid urbanization and explosive population growth over the 1950s, with attendant social and economic strains for the population. In this context, opiate dependence became widespread and an object of great public concern (Ch'ien cites a 1959 government report indicating 5–6% population prevalence). This led to the establishment of the first drug treatment agencies in Hong Kong in the late 1950s and early 1960s, including the Society for the Aid and Rehabilitation of Drug Addicts (SARDA).

SARDA itself is not a mutual-help organization, but a network of professional treatments, comprising detoxification services, inpatient facilities, and halfway houses (Ch'ien, 1980). Some former SARDA patients founded an alumni association in 1968 to provide ongoing recovery support after treatment. This organization has evolved into a self-help organization of drug-dependent individuals who are dedicated to maintaining members' abstinence and to serving the larger community. It re-named itself as the "Pui Hong Self-Help Association," but still draws members from SARDA treatment programs (Porter *et al.*, 1999).

Philosophy and approach

Pui Hong Self-Help Association members invite SARDA patients to join the mutual-help organization at the conclusion of treatment. Other members may come to the organization directly on their own, but data on how often this occurs are lacking. The association provides those accepting its invitation with emotional support, advice, and practical assistance (e.g., help in finding a job or housing). It also encourages members to do voluntary service work for other addicts and for the broader community, consistent with the dominant cultural belief that rehabilitation from addiction involves moral as well as physical reformation (Ch'ien, 1980; Poshyachinda *et al.*, 1982). Although the association makes contact with all former SARDA patients, formal membership has to be earned. Individuals must attain 6 months of crime and drug-free living to become an associate member, and 2 years of productive community living to become a full member (Poshyachinda *et al.*, 1982). At association gatherings, members are awarded colored badges indicating their length of maintained abstinence.

The Pui Hong Self-Help Association organizes a large amount of service projects, including outreach to current addicts, AIDS education, drug-use prevention programs, and charitable fund-raisers (e.g., through shows of their Lion's Dance Troupe; Ch'ien, 1980). As likely goes without saying, the organization has no tradition of anonymity for members.

Membership

Association membership was estimated at 1200–1800 in the early 1980s (e.g., Ch'ien, 1980; Poshyachinda *et al.*, 1982). Higher estimates of 1900–2450 members were reported in the late 1990s, suggesting modest organizational growth over time (Cheung & Ch'ien, 1997; Porter *et al.*, 1999). The association is organized into five comparably sized chapters for men and one for women (Poshyachinda *et al.*, 1982). Other than this gender breakdown, descriptive data on members are lacking in the available scientific literature. Whether the association has members from outside the Chinese community is a particularly interesting unanswered question. A published photo of an association ceremony (Poshyachinda *et al.*, 1982) shows Caucasians in attendance, but it is not clear in what capacity.

Rational Recovery

Origins and history

Rational Recovery's origins can be traced to the publication of *The Small Book* by Jack Trimpey (1988), a licensed social worker who had personally overcome an alcohol problem. This book sharply criticized AA and argued that addiction could be better addressed using principles of cognitive self-examination, rational analysis, and self-control drawn in part from the rational–emotive therapy of Albert Ellis. Trimpey founded a for-profit corporation to provide professional addiction services, and a non-profit organization known as the "Rational Recovery Self-Help Network" to coordinate a network of free self-help groups.

The Rational Recovery (RR) Self-Help Network separated from RR's for-profit ventures in 1994 after a series of disagreements with Trimpey, and changed its name to "SMART Recovery" (described below). Each individual RR self-help group then decided whether to stay affiliated with RR or to become affiliated with SMART Recovery. Trimpey publically repudiated all addiction-related self-help groups in 1999, including RR groups (see his statement at http://rational.org//RRSN.html). In the wake of this announcement it is unclear if the remaining RR self-help groups will begin to call themselves SMART Recovery groups, will continue as independent groups without the recognition of the national organization, or will die out.

Philosophy and approach

As might be inferred from the satirical title of their primary text (*The "Small" Book*), much of RR's philosophy is put forward by the organization in direct contrast with AA's philosophy. RR rejects the concepts that spiritual factors are involved in recovery, that addiction is a disease, that individuals should acknowledge powerlessness over addiction, and that sponsorship is valuable. These and other criticisms of AA are put forward so often and with such force that it would be reasonable to say that part of the official philosophy of RR is that AA is a pernicious organization.

RR adopts a cognitive–behavioral approach to alcohol problems, which includes the "Addictive Voice Recognition Technique." This technique is designed to help members recognize and control compulsive thoughts and primitive desires that lead to alcohol abuse. In RR's terminology, the primal and irrational parts of human nature are called "The Beast," and are believed to originate in the "old" midbrain that humans share with animals (Schmidt, 1996). RR members try to monitor and master "The Beast" using the rational resources of the "new" brain or "neocortex" (Schmidt, 1996). Although the organization does not make the connection itself, observers who are familiar with Sigmund Freud's writings on the id and the superego would note parallels here both in RR's concepts and in its mechanistic analysis of the human psyche.

In RR's framework, defeating addiction is an exercise in rational, individualistic self-control rather than a process of spiritual change or mutual support. Despite this emphasis on the power of self-control and personal mastery, the organization does not view controlled drinking as a legitimate goal. Lifetime abstinence is believed by RR to progressively weaken the power of "The Beast" (Schmidt, 1996).

RR self-help groups typically meet once a week and have 5–10 members (Galanter *et al.*, 1993). Each group has a coordinator who maintains contact between meetings with a mental health professional familiar with the organization's approach. Meetings are not highly structured (Horvath, 1997). During meetings, members discuss how to control irrational beliefs, relying at times on a "Sobriety spreadsheet" on which they record cognitions that increase their desire to drink. RR meetings do not forbid cross-talk; rather, members directly speak to each other in meetings and exchange ideas, comments, and advice. To encourage self-reliance, the organization frowns upon members having supportive exchanges between meetings, and discourages lifelong affiliation.

Membership

RR self-help groups were founded in California and are based almost entirely within the USA. The size of the organization is almost impossible to gauge currently for reasons mentioned above. Just prior to Trimpey's public rejection of the value of self-help groups, the organization had as many as 800 groups with perhaps 5000 members in total (White & Madara, 1998).

Marc Galanter *et al.* (1993) conducted a survey of 70 RR groups. The high response rate (63 out of 70 groups contacted and 97% of members in those groups) increases confidence that their findings provide a representative picture of members. Most (72%) were male and employed full-time (60%). The sample was remarkably educated (e.g., 81% had attended college) and non-religious (e.g., 47% atheist) relative to the US population. Although the survey did not assess race, the author's informal observation is that almost all RR members are Caucasian. Like other AA alternatives in the USA (e.g., MM, SMART Recovery, Women for Sobriety), RR draws its membership mainly from the achieving, educated, individualistic, Caucasian-American middle class.

The typical member reported that their substance-abuse problems began 25 years ago. A history of alcohol abuse was nearly universal, with the next most common drugs of abuse being marijuana (51% of respondents) and cocaine (41% of respondents). Most members learned of the organization through the media, which covered RR extensively when it was first created. Active members of the organization attended about four meetings per month. Perhaps because of its novelty, the ratio of new members (those with less than 1 month of involvement) to experienced members was large – almost 1:2. Many RR members concurrently attended AA meetings, the organization's strong anti-AA rhetoric notwithstanding.

SMART Recovery

Origins and history

SMART is an acronym for "Self-Management and Recovery Training." As described above, SMART originated as the result of the splintering of RR in 1994. SMART (also known as "SMART Recovery") has grown since that time as an independent, non-profit mutual help organization. It was helped in this process by a grant from a foundation to train group leaders.

Philosophy and approach

SMART intends to provide an alternative to AA, but the near-evangelical anti-AA rhetoric of RR is not evident in its literature. For example, the SMART program does not include spiritual change, but the organization acknowledges that spiritual beliefs and practices may be helpful to some members (Orr, 1996), and about half of members report belief in a Higher Power (Li, Strohm, & Feifer, 1998). The organization conceptualizes addiction as a learned behavior that can be changed using cognitive–behavioral principles. The main professional sources of knowledge upon which SMART's approach relies are research and theory concerning rational–emotive behavior therapy, relapse prevention training, motivational enhancement interventions, mood management, communication skills, and stress management (Horvath, 1997; Orr, 1996).

SMART Recovery is the only addiction-related self-help organization that explicitly acknowledges science as the ultimate authority, and states that its approach may change over time depending on what science discovers (Horvath, 1997). This perspective reflects the composition of its advisory board being primarily professionals in the addictive behavior field.

SMART Recovery acknowledges that some individuals may wish to moderate addictive behaviors and may succeed in so doing (Horvath, 2000). SMART recommends abstinence for its members, but does so in a non-dogmatic fashion, for example by encouraging individuals unwilling to make a lifetime commitment to abstinence to consider a "trial period" (Horvath, 1997).

SMART has a "four-point program," which focuses on: (1) building and maintaining motivation to abstain, (2) coping with urges, (3) managing thoughts, feelings, and behavior, and (4) balancing momentary and enduring satisfactions (Horvath, 2000). Relative to other mutual-help organizations, this philosophical statement is notable for its brevity, simplicity, and generality.

Each SMART Recovery group has a voluntary coordinator who has access to a mental health professional advisor between meetings. The voluntary coordinator may be in recovery from addiction, or may simply be a person who wishes to lead meetings as a form of community service. The professional advisor is also a volunteer, because, like all self-help organizations, SMART charges no fees. SMART Recovery provides meeting coordinators with a general meeting outline, but does not compel them to follow it (Horvath, 2000). The outline suggests that meetings begin with a welcome and opening followed by a brief personal update from each member on events, concerns, and problems experienced since the last meeting. A focus for the meeting's discussion is chosen based on the content of members' personal updates, and the bulk of the meeting is spent discussing the topic of choice and how it relates to SMART's four-point program. Members are encouraged to analyze behavioral and emotional states using methods derived from cognitive–behavioral therapy (e.g., identifying the activating event, how the member appraised it, behavioral choices, and consequences).

SMART members are expected to offer support and advice to each other in group meetings. SMART does not have sponsors per se, but one of the four statements in the organization's statement of purposes explicitly invites "individuals who have gained independence from addictive behavior to stay involved with us, to enhance their gains and to help others" (Horvath, 1997). Most SMART Recovery meetings are open to the public, but some are restricted to those trying to change addictive behavior (Horvath, 1997, 2000).

Membership

SMART Recovery self-help groups have not, at the time of writing, been the subject of a scientific study, so their membership characteristics are unknown. However, given that its root source was RR, one would suspect that the characteristics of SMART members are similar to those of RR members (i.e., primarily white, educated, socially stable people). In terms of size, the organization claims about 250 groups (Horvath, 2000), which, assuming eight members per group, would imply a membership of 2000 people. Almost all of these meetings are held in the USA, although the organization's website (www.smartrecovery.org) lists a small number of meetings in Canada and contact people in Scotland, England, Australia, and Sweden.

SOS/LifeRing Secular Recovery

Origins and history

James Christopher founded SOS after initially attempting to recover from alcoholism by attending AA. The organization was named "SOS" as an acronym both for "Secular Organization for Sobriety" and "Save Our Selves." Although he appreciated some aspects of AA, Christopher was uncomfortable with AA's emphasis on God, a Higher Power, and spiritual change (Christopher, 1992). These frustrations led Christopher to explore secular humanism as an alternative philosophical basis for recovery, and eventually to write an article recommending such an approach in the humanist magazine *Free Inquiry*. Positive responses to this article and to subsequent presentations of his proposal encouraged Christopher to start the first SOS self-help group in North Hollywood, California, in 1986. It subsequently spread within the USA and to a few other countries.

The largest chapter of SOS, which is centered in northern California, changed its name to "LifeRing Secular Recovery" in 1999 after a legal dispute with another party using a similar name (Unhooked online newsletter, 1999). LifeRing Secular Recovery remains integrated with SOS as a whole.

Philosophy and approach

SOS's values reflect its organizational connection to the Council for Secular Humanism. Its approach is rational and secular, and echoes existentialist themes concerning the value of authenticity and individual responsibility (Christopher, 1992). SOS views recovery from alcoholism as an individual achievement independent of any spiritual or religious forces (Christopher, 1992, 1997). SOS's brand of individualism is not solipsistic however (cf. RR), because the organization strongly emphasizes the importance of mutual support among members.

SOS views alcoholism as an illness that has genetic, biological, and psychological roots. SOS also believes that abstinence is the only adequate solution to substance dependence. However, it explicitly rejects AA's concept that alcoholism is a disease with moral and spiritual components. SOS attributes the achievement of sobriety to a member's responsible, existential decision to make sobriety a life priority (i.e., recovery is not a gift from a spiritual power).

SOS members provide mutual support and encouragement during group meetings, but without any reference to a unifying spiritual framework. Meetings are fairly unstructured, last for about 75 minutes, and have an average of eight attendees (Connors & Dermen, 1996). SOS members usually attend no more than one SOS meeting per week, probably because few groups are available in most areas. Although SOS's texts espouse openness to all viewpoints (Christopher, 1992), members report that negative comments about religion and AA are not uncommon in group meetings (Connors & Dermen, 1996).

Membership

Claims of SOS membership have been as high as 20 000 members (Connors & Dermen, 1996) and 1200 groups (White & Madara, 1998), but the reality is likely to be less impressive. In reporting a survey of SOS members, Gerard Connors and Kurt Dermen (1996) noted that SOS's list of active and potential meeting conveners included only 350 people. As 10% of the surveys mailed out were returned as undeliverable, 350 active groups with a total of 3000 members would probably be a generous estimate of SOS's actual size. The organization is based almost entirely in the USA, with Canada and England being the only other countries to have more than a few groups.

Connors and Dermen's (1996) survey of SOS had a sample size of 158 out of 4000 mailed out to meeting conveners, which means either that SOS is much smaller than claimed, or that a minority of members completed the survey, or both. Its authors therefore cautioned that their results were preliminary. Most (73%) respondents were male and employed full-time (53%). Like other secular self-help organizations in the USA, SOS attracts a membership that is almost entirely Caucasian (99%), well-educated (35% baccalaureate degree, 31% post-graduate degree), and non-religious (70% no religious affiliation, 68% self-described atheist or agnostic). Members reported a history of severe alcohol problems, with the majority reporting multiple physical dependence symptoms.

A significant minority also had a history of drug abuse, with marijuana/hashish (38%), sedatives/tranquilizers (24%), and amphetamines/stimulants (21%) being the most widely used. Members of SOS, like members of other "AA alternatives," often concurrently attend AA or NA. Co-attending respondents reported disliking the spiritual elements of AA, but considered contact with AA members – i.e., the fellowship – helpful in their recovery (Connors & Dermen, 1996).

Women for Sobriety

Origins and history

Women for Sobriety's history begins with Jean Kirkpatrick – an outstanding sociology graduate student at the University of Pennsylvania and a successful AA affiliate (Kirkpatrick, 1977; N.B. to address a common misconception, this is not the Jeane Kirkpatrick who became US Representative to the United Nations). Upon winning a prestigious fellowship to complete her dissertation, Kirkpatrick became wracked with self-doubt about whether she really deserved the award and whether it would be taken away from her. She relapsed, and abused alcohol for the next 13 years. She returned to AA, but did not find it helpful for ameliorating her low self-esteem, self-doubts, and the stigma of being a woman alcoholic.

Kirkpatrick had continued her education, earning her Ph.D. and reading widely. Inspired in part by philosophical works of writers such as Ralph Waldo Emerson, she decided to create a new self-help program for women with a philosophy that differed from AA's. She began her new mutual-help organization in 1973 under the rubric "New Life," but eventually changed its name to "Women for Sobriety" (WFS). Kirkpatrick subsequently wrote a book about her recovery and her organization, which received wide media attention. WFS's growth and public profile were enhanced by a cultural zeitgeist: its approach resonated with many themes of the then-ascendant US feminist movement. Kirkpatrick died in 2000, but WFS headquarters (located in Quakertown, Pennsylvania) continues as a non-profit organization that is overseen by a board of directors composed of recovering women.

Philosophy and approach

Kirkpatrick designed her organization in direct contrast to what she believed were male-biased aspects of AA (Humphreys & Kaskutas, 1995). She considered AA's emphasis on minimizing grandiosity and instilling humility appropriate for arrogant, self-involved men, but damaging to women alcoholics who more commonly suffered from low self-worth and lack of confidence. Women for Sobriety is primarily concerned with building up rather than minimizing the self (Humphreys & Kaskutas, 1995), as illustrated by its 13 affirmations, e.g., "I have a drinking problem that once had me," " Problems bother me only to the degree I permit them to," and "I am a competent woman and have much to give life" (Kirkpatrick, 2000).

Other intentional differences with AA are as follows. First, in order to prevent dependency, WFS does not use sponsors or encourage lifetime membership. Second, members are encouraged to take personal credit for abstinence as a way of building their self-confidence. Third, although daily meditation is encouraged, the organization's program makes no reference to a Higher Power or God (Kirkpatrick, 2000). Fourth, WFS has no tradition of anonymity and each member has the option of going public about her recovery (Kaskutas, 1996a). Fifth, intellectual analysis is viewed as a vehicle for change, as reflected in the slogan, "We are what we think." This contrasts with AA's dictum, "Utilize rather than analyze." All that said, WFS does share some ideas and approaches with AA. It views abstinence as the only acceptable drinking goal, asserts that spiritual growth is part of the recovery process, and, of course, considers peer mutual help to be a valuable resource.

WFS (2001) offers guidelines for the conduct of its meetings (at www.womenforsobriety.org/). The moderator begins by reading the 13 affirmations, sometimes supplementing them with other program literature. Each member then introduces herself in a fashion that again inverts AA's traditions. Rather than intoning, "I am Jean and I'm an alcoholic," members begin by saying, "I am Jean and I am a competent woman," and then briefly describe a positive event or success from the preceding week. The moderator then begins discussion of a topic and members share their experiences and ideas about it. Meetings end with members joining hands and saying, "We are capable and competent, caring and compassionate, always willing to help another, bonded together in overcoming our addictions."

Individual WFS self-help groups are peer-led but the organization's headquarters retains some centralized control. A woman who wishes to moderate a group must obtain certification from headquarters, which requires having a year of sobriety, studying program literature, and passing a test about WFS's philosophy (Horvath, 1997). Centralized control is also evident in the provision of information about where group meetings occur. Other mutual-help organizations provide easy access to their meeting locations by posting them on the

World Wide Web, whereas WFS's website requires visitors to contact headquarters personally to request access to such information. WFS's procedures thus raise significantly the behavioral cost of starting new groups and finding those that exist. Why the only alcohol-related self-help organization founded by a sociologist adopted cumbersome procedures and growth-impeding organizational structures remains a mystery.

Membership

Recent estimates of the size of WFS center around 150–300 groups and 1000–2000 members. Almost all of these groups are in the USA, with a few chapters existing in Canada, England, Australia, and New Zealand. Interestingly, in the latter two countries, WFS receives some government funding (Horvath, 1997).

Kaskutas (1992a) mailed surveys to WFS's North American membership and attained an excellent response rate (73%). Like other AA alternatives in the USA, the organization attracts a membership that is Caucasian (98%), middle class, and well educated, a large proportion of whom (about a third) continue to attend AA (Kaskutas, 1992b). However, unlike SOS and RR, WFS has a low proportion of atheists (4.6%), perhaps because the program explicitly supports spiritual practices. The severity of members' drinking problems is reflected in 49% of them describing the turning point that led them to seek help as blackouts, liver cirrhosis or other sickness, withdrawal symptoms, or loss of control over drinking (Kaskutas, 1996b).

Comparisons and contrasts

Seven universal and nine optional features of self-help organizations were presented in Chapter 1. All of the above organizations, by definition, possess the universal features (e.g., members share a problem or status, valuation of experiential knowledge, etc.). They also have two of the optional features in common: (1) a developed philosophy and program of change, and (2) groups nested within a larger organization. Self-help groups lacking these characteristics are rarely the subject of extensive research projects and hence were not selected for discussion here.

Two other optional features show only modest variation across the 19 organizations. A residential structure with 24-hour support is characteristic only of Oxford Houses, and some chapters of AA in Mexico City. An Internet presence of at least a minimal level (e.g., a website for the organization or a particular group or member) was found by the author for all of the above organizations, but the amount of Internet resources utilized differed in predictable ways. Self-help groups and organizations made more use of the Internet if they were based in geographic areas of greater wealth and greater computer access (e.g., Danshukai groups in Japan, and all groups throughout the USA, but most particularly in California). The absolute amount of an organization's Internet activity is hard to quantify, but obviously increases with number of members. The proportion of an organization's activity that occurs on the Internet, in contrast, seems to increase largely as a function of scarcity of face-to-face groups, with MM being the most extreme example. No scale or system exists for objectively assessing amount of "Internet presence," so the above observations are only the author's subjective impressions based on unstandardized online data collection.

The 19 organizations show more variation across the other five optional dimensions, as displayed in Table 4. The spiritual heritage of organizations varies depending upon what national religious traditions influenced the founders, and the period during which the organization was created. Organizations founded in the USA are obviously the most likely to use some version of the Christian-influenced 12 steps, but US organizations created in recent decades have tended to have less spiritual emphasis (e.g., MM, RR). This may reflect the waning influence of Christianity in developed western nations since the time that organizations like AA and Blue Cross came to prominence (Wilson, 1999), and the consequent greater acceptance within the general population of non-spiritual approaches to resolving substance-abuse problems.

Organizations tend to have either both, or neither, of two characteristics: (1) acceptance of external funding, and (2) engagement in outside advocacy. A tradition of anonymity to the outside world at once rules out both of these activities. In contrast, once an organization is obtaining funding from government, advocacy may follow naturally in order to maintain it.

The outliers on the professional role dimension are the two founded under totalitarian governments: Abstainers Clubs and CTAs. The democratization of eastern Europe has obviously already weakened the dogma that members of mutual-help organizations should be subordinate to controlling professionals. Cultural values may persist long after political systems change, but in the coming decades it seems likely that the eastern European mutual-help clubs will evolve a stronger norm of peer leadership parallel to that of their counterparts in other developed societies.

Organizations founded in the USA tend to allow participation only by the primary holder of the status the group addresses, which may reflect the American cultural emphasis on individual autonomy from social and cultural bonds (Bellah *et al.* 1985). The relative influence of temperance movements in

Table 4. *Comparison of addiction-related mutual-help organizations on five key dimensions*

	Spiritual heritage	External funding	Advocacy	Professional role	Relations attend?
Alcoholics Anonymous	Christian	None	No	Min	No**
Abstainers Clubs	None	Gov't	Yes	Strong	Yes
Al-Anon	Christian	None	No	Min	No
All Nippon Sobriety Assn	Other	Gov't	Yes	Mod	Yes
Blue Cross	Christian	NGO	Yes	Min	Yes
Clubs of Treated Alcoholics	None	Gov't	No	Strong	Yes
Double Trouble in Recovery	Christian	Gov't	No	Min	No
Free Life	None	None?	Yes	Min	Yes
JACS	Other	None?	No?	Min	No?
The Links	None	Gov't	Yes	Min	Yes
Moderation Management	None	NGO	No	Mod	No
Narcotics Anonymous	Christian	None	No	Min	No
Nicotine Anonymous	Christian	None	No	Min	No
Oxford Houses	Christian	Gov't	Yes	Min	No
Pui Hong Association	Other	Gov't?	Yes	Mod	No?
Rational Recovery	None	NGO?	Yes	Mod	No
SMART Recovery	None	NGO	No	Mod	No
SOS	None	None	No	Min	No
Women for Sobriety	Other	Gov't*	No	Mod	No

* Only in Australia and New Zealand, **In all but a few locales, including among some Native-American tribes and perhaps in some parts of Poland and rural Mexico.
? Indicates that the reported data are the author's best guess.
NGO = non-governmental organization; Gov't = government agency; Min = minimal; Mod = moderate.

different countries may also help to account for why some organizations developed a norm of non-substance-using supporters attending self-help groups while others do not.

Two other general comments are worth making. First, all of the organizations were influenced by AA, with the exception of Blue Cross and the Pui Hong Self-Help Association. This includes organizations that adopted AA's approach almost completely (e.g., Al-Anon, NA, Nicotine Anonymous), those that were inspired by it and took pieces of its approach into a larger philosophy (e.g., The Links, JACS, Danshukai), and those that designed their approach in intentional contrast to it (e.g., RR, WFS). In these positive and negative ways, AA clearly has had an astonishingly broad and powerful influence on the world's addiction-related self-help organizations. Second, even though they were not selected for description on this basis, the organizations primarily focus on alcohol problems. Individuals who have problems with other drugs may attend alcohol-oriented organizations; such individuals are the explicit target of only DTR (all substances), JACS (all substances), NA (illicit drugs), Nicotine Anonymous (tobacco products), Oxford Houses (all substances), and the Pui Hong Self-Help Association (opiates). This likely reflects the higher prevalence of alcohol problems than drug problems, the worldwide influence of AA, and the greater social stigma and criminal penalties attached to drug use around the world. This latter factor creates challenges for establishing a stable organization that individuals are willing to attend.

In summary, this chapter has demonstrated that, of all self-help group movements, those addressing substance abuse are probably the most robust and widely disseminated. The worldwide popularity of addiction-related self-help groups is undeniable, but this does not in itself prove that they are effective. The ensuing chapters turn to this vital question.

3

Does self-help group participation lead to positive addiction-related, psychiatric, and medical outcomes?

Conceptual background

Frederick Glaser and Alan Ogborne (1982) expressed a common sentiment when they said that what they "would most like to know" is whether addiction-related self-help groups "really work?" (cf. Leach, 1973). They focused upon AA, but the question has relevance to all self-help organizations. This chapter addresses the most common approach to answering this important question, namely asking whether self-help groups produce the same sorts of benefits one hopes for from professional addiction treatment programs, i.e., reduced substance use and lower associated psychiatric, social, and medical problems.

The case for evaluating whether addiction self-help groups "really work"

The need and warrant to evaluate publically funded and licensed healthcare organizations is self-evident. However, one might ask why scientists should attempt to evaluate the outcomes of participation in a voluntary social movement (Mäkelä, 1993). Self-help organizations do not compel attendance, do not seek any licensure or accreditation, and in most cases do not receive any public monies, so one might take the perspective that the "effectiveness" of self-help groups is no more pressing a question than the effectiveness of stamp-collecting clubs. If citizens choose to attend voluntary associations and find them beneficial and enjoyable, who are scientists to interfere or even to comment?

A social responsibility to evaluate putative helping interventions exists even when no public money or licensure is involved. Many self-help organizations make public claims of being able to help addicted people. Society cannot assume that such claims are correct without evaluating them carefully, even when the best of intentions are present (Glaser & Ogborne, 1982). Evaluation research

94

thus has a role in protecting vulnerable citizens from potentially ineffective self-help organizations.

Evaluation research also has a role in protecting effective self-help organizations from professional guilds. Some professionals will never accept the idea that non-professional interventions can work, will never provide the resources to study them, and will not accept the results of any studies that fail to show the relative superiority of professional services. (Chapter 5 discusses the source and nature of these biases.) Society at large cannot, therefore, leave judgements about self-help groups' effectiveness to those professionals who put their guild interests ahead of the public interest. Evaluation research serves society's interest in finding out what resources help addicted citizens, even when such information is upsetting to powerful vested interests.

A laissez-faire attitude about whether self-help groups are effective is therefore contrary to the public interest. Evaluators have a responsibility to conduct impartial outcome studies of mutual-help groups and, to let addicted individuals and society at large know which organizations are effective and which are not.

Evaluating self-help groups as analogous to professional healthcare interventions

Many addiction researchers believe that self-help groups can be evaluated in the same way as professional treatment programs. That is, researchers should examine the characteristics of individuals entering and leaving these organizations to determine whether group participation has reduced alcohol and drug use, substance-related problems, and psychopathology. Analogizing self-help groups to professional addiction treatments thus leads to particular choices about independent and dependent variables in outcome research, as well as to particular methods and conceptualizations.

Other scholars take exception to such an analogy, however (Rappaport, 1993). E. Kurtz (1992), for example, writes that, "Evaluating AA under the heading of "treatment" is like studying the formation patterns of bears flying south for the winter . . . both bears and Canadian geese change their usual activities with the onset of winter. Both AA and alcoholism treatment can benefit people whose lives are disrupted by the drinking of alcohol. But to leap from either observation of shared likeness to a larger equation that implies identity is as false in one case as in the other" (p. 397). In essence, Kurtz argues that if researchers simply transfer treatment evaluation concepts and approaches wholesale to the evaluation of self-help organizations, they will misunderstand the phenomenon, because "reality constrained into the wrong category is reality distorted" (p. 397).

Self-help groups are clearly not the same as treatments, but they do share certain goals and activities with them. The "treatment-evaluation perspective" on self-help groups is thus simultaneously useful and incomplete. Researchers studying friendship might reasonably examine whether having a friend makes depression less likely, but no-one would argue that the rich benefits of friendship are limited to reducing psychopathology. Likewise, while asking "treatment-style" questions (e.g., do those who attend AA consume less alcohol?) is valid and important, other important questions about AA (e.g., how do long-term AA members experience spiritual change?) will be ignored if this were researchers' sole guidepost. Accordingly, this book considers the treatment-evaluation perspective on self-help groups neither as useless nor as perfect, but as one possible perspective on a complex phenomenon. This chapter reviews work guided by the treatment-evaluation perspective, whereas Chapter 4 considers treatment-outcome research conducted from the perspective that self-help groups are community-based voluntary associations. Finally, Chapter 5 adopts a third perspective by discussing whether self-help group participation has an impact on healthcare costs. None of these perspectives is complete, but together they will offer as nuanced a picture of the effects of addiction-related self-help group participation as can be mustered from scientific inquiry to date.

Randomized clinical trials as a regulating ideal in treatment research

Some evaluators think that discussions of treatment-style evaluations of self-help groups should begin (and perhaps even end) with tightly controlled randomized clinical trials. Randomized controlled trials typically standardize the delivery of the intervention, select a homogeneous patient sample, and deny participants choice of treatment. Few randomized trials have been conducted with addiction self-help groups, and clinical trials are never likely to become the dominant evaluation technique in this field, for reasons that will be explained. Should a discussion of research on self-help groups' effectiveness thus begin and end with apologies about the hopelessly inferior, non-randomized evaluations that predominate? Two points argue against this pessimistic conclusion – one related to randomized trials in general and one specific to their application to self-help group outcome research.

Randomized trials are not necessarily the best guide to useful knowledge

Randomized trials are a powerful instrument for knowledge construction because they have high internal validity (i.e., they are excellent for making a causal inference about a treatment effect). But this internal validity often comes at a high cost in generalizability and utility (Tucker, 1999; Wells, 1999). Most notably, because of their extensive exclusion criteria, across medical disorders, randomized trials enroll a very small and unrepresentative subset of all patients (Humphreys, Loomis, & Joshi, 2002). In alcohol treatment outcome research, for example, common exclusion criteria rule out most patients from participating in research trials, and disproportionately exclude African-Americans, low-income individuals, and individuals with comorbid psychiatric and medical problems (Humphreys & Weisner, 2000).

Further, the common conviction that randomized trials always generate more accurate estimates of treatment effects is, as an empirical matter, simply incorrect. The *New England Journal of Medicine* – perhaps the most respected source of controlled clinical trials in the world – recently published literature reviews comparing the observed outcomes of medical treatments that had been studied both by randomized trials and by other evaluation approaches. Across methodologies, outcome results were almost always similar (Benson & Hartz, 2000; Concato, Shah, & Horwitz, 2000).

The implicit conceptual model underlying randomly assigned patients to treatments also has limitations. The idea that treatments are applied by outside forces before change begins and then are not affected by any subsequent changes in the patient is poorly matched to chronic, dynamic disorders like addiction, in which patient factors (e.g., motivation, progress, or regress) and treatment factors are in constant interplay (Moos, 1997a, b). Such processes are much easier to understand when patients have the option of choosing which treatments they want, how they want them, when they want them, and so forth, all of which is impossible in the context of the typical randomized trial.

Randomized trials have additional shortcomings specific to self-help group evaluation

Solid randomized clinical trials have been conducted in the addiction self-help area (e.g., Kingree & Thompson, 2000; Sisson & Mallams, 1981) and more are needed, but such studies will never in themselves fully map the substantive terrain (Humphreys & Rappaport, 1994). Randomized trials depend on professional control of who receives intervention and how they receive it, whereas, by definition, self-help groups specifically reject professional control of these decisions. Participation in self-help groups simply cannot be denied to "controls" by researchers (as access to a new medication or surgical procedure can be), and indeed, as will be described in this chapter, in every controlled trial some patients in "no intervention" and "non-self-help group" conditions have gone to community self-help groups anyway. Clinical researchers also cannot force self-help groups to standardize what they do or how often, or to exclude people based on pre-established criteria. This creates a paradox for randomized trials of self-help groups, in that the more the researcher controls the group for research purposes, the less what is being evaluated is truly a self-help group as opposed to a professionally controlled paraprofessional helping program (Humphreys & Rappaport, 1994). The best opportunities for randomized trials in the self-help group evaluation arena thus tend to be those in which the researcher can control the intervention but the self-help group remains in control of itself, as was the case in studies like Project MATCH (Matching Alcoholism Treatment to Client Heterogeneity; Project MATCH Research Group, 1997, 1998), which randomly assigned individuals to professionally delivered interventions that were designed to facilitate group participation (see also McCrady, Epstein, & Hirsch, 1996).

Correlational studies and quasi-experiments are no panacea either

The foregoing critique of randomized trials should not be taken as an uncritical endorsement of more naturalistic evaluation designs, which have shortcomings mirroring the strengths of randomized trials, i.e., greater external validity but poorer internal validity. Most particularly, countless studies have documented cross-sectional associations between higher involvement in an addiction-related self-help group and fewer substance-abuse problems. These studies provide results that are consistent with the hypothesis that self-help groups are effective, but obviously do not expose it to a rigorous falsification test. Such cross-sectional correlations may result from all individuals for whom the group was ineffective having already dropped out, or from good-prognosis individuals who would have recovered anyway attending the self-help group unnecessarily.

A stronger class of naturalistic evaluations improves upon cross-sectional single-group studies by using comparison groups and repeated measures (Emrick *et al.*, 1993). These enhancements are valuable but do not necessarily address self-selection bias as effectively as does random assignment. Such outcome studies typically use some form of covariance adjustment to "statistically control for" differences between samples, for example pre-existent differences in alcohol consumption between AA participants and non-participants. This approach can be informative, but should not be equated with situations where the samples really were equal at baseline owing to random assignment or good luck. Covariance control variables almost always under-correct for bias because, like all measurements, they contain error (Kahneman, 1965). Further, studies that use covariance control have to interpret a counterfactual, i.e., what would the outcomes have been like if these groups were the same . . . but in reality they were different! (see Cronbach, 1982; Meehl, 1970; Miller & Chapman, 2001).

Naturalistic longitudinal outcome research (some of which uses covariance control) includes quasi-experiments with matched comparison groups (e.g., Humphreys & Moos, 2001), instrumental variables analysis (e.g., Fortney *et al.*, 1998; Humphreys, Phibbs, & Moos, 1996), multi-wave structural equation modeling approaches (Kelly, Myers, & Brown, 2000, 2002; Pisani *et al.*, 1993), population-based studies (e.g., Smart & Mann, 1993), and inventive methods for checking on third variable explanations using standard regression techniques (e.g., Fiorentine, 1999). All of these approaches are superior to cross-sectional, correlational survey studies. Yet, like every other evaluation design, each of them provides an imperfect picture of a complex phenomenon.

The above methodological discussion supports conclusions about self-help group outcome studies which are similar to those reached by investigators working in other areas of addiction research (Dennis *et al.*, 2000). Randomized trials are one of many useful methods of evaluating outcomes, and methodological diversity is a strength, not a weakness, of evaluation science (Humphreys, 2002). Studies that have examined self-help groups' effectiveness using a variety of research designs will now be reviewed in that spirit.

Outcome studies of specific addiction-related mutual-help organizations

Of those mutual-help organizations described in Chapter 2, the author was unable to identify English-language studies of effectiveness – as interventions for substance abuse and its psychological and medical comorbidities – in six: Abstainers Clubs, Blue Cross, Free Life, The Links, SMART Recovery, and Jewish Alcoholics, Chemically Dependent Persons, and Significant Others. Therefore no empirically supported conclusions will be drawn at this point about the effectiveness of these organizations per se. The studies reviewed below nonetheless have some relevance to understanding them because all mutual-help organizations have some potentially curative factors in common. Evaluation research on the other 13 organizations, some of which is quite limited, is reviewed below. Organizations are discussed in alphabetical order, with the exception of AA (which is discussed separately on p. 109), because it has been studied by far the most extensively and can therefore have its research findings discussed in more detail. Except as noted in the text, all the studies described below were conducted in the USA, and thus the potential cultural-boundedness of what follows should be kept in mind.

Al-Anon Family Groups

In a study of 227 alcoholic husbands whose wives participated in different types of treatment, abstinence rates were 86% when the wife attended Al-Anon and 46% when she did not (Wright & Scott, 1978). The wife's participation in other forms of treatment showed more modest or no positive relationship to abstinence, suggesting that the observed benefits of Al-Anon were not attributable to self-selection.

Positive outcomes were also identified in a comparison of 116 wives of alcoholics who were Al-Anon members with 46 who were not (Bailey, 1965). Almost all (88%) of the Al-Anon members' husbands were in AA, compared with 48% of non-Al-Anon members. Within husband AA members ($n = 172$), rates of sobriety were 66% among those with Al-Anon spouses versus 43% among those without. Al-Anon thus supported both AA affiliation per se and the likelihood that AA affiliation would be successful.

Several mechanisms might explain Al-Anon's effect on members' mental health. Al-Anon members are much more likely than non-members to see alcoholism as a disease rather than a character weakness, which may relieve resentment and anxiety. Changes in coping behavior have also been identified as a curative mechanism in Al-Anon. Over time, members cease attempting the near-impossible – and therefore maddening – task of controlling their spouses' behavior (Gorman & Rooney, 1979; L. F. Kurtz, 1994).

Al-Anon participation seems to benefit members' mental health and to support sobriety in an alcoholic spouse, but this does not necessarily imply that it leads the alcoholic loved one to seek treatment. This question was addressed in a randomized trial of 130 significant others of alcoholics (Miller, Meyers, & Tonigan, 1999). Importantly, whereas previous studies examined samples composed almost entirely of non-Hispanic Caucasian, female wives of alcoholics, this investigation included a significant proportion of Latino- and Native-American participants, some males ($n = 12$), and some individuals with relationships to alcoholics other than that of spouse. Participants randomized to community reinforcement training had significantly higher rates of treatment engagement by the alcoholic than did individuals randomized to Al-Anon facilitation counseling or to a Johnson Institute intervention in which family members confronted the drinker. Depression, state anger, family conflict, and relationship unhappiness decreased significantly in all three conditions by 6-month follow-up. These results largely replicated those of an earlier, smaller randomized trial (Barber & Gilbertson, 1996).

In summary, one is struck by the close match between what Al-Anon claims to offer and what research shows about how members change. Al-Anon promises to help the member but not to force the alcoholic loved one to change. Evaluation research indicates that these promises are realistic, i.e., members improve psychologically but alcoholic others are no more likely to enter a treatment setting or stop drinking. Yet if alcoholic loved ones decide to attend AA, Al-Anon membership is an ally in their sobriety, which is again just as Al-Anon would predict.

Al-Anon groups for Adult Children of Alcoholics (ACA) have also been evaluated. The strongest study was conducted with a primarily African-American sample of substance-abuse patients in a 120-day residential treatment program (Kingree & Thompson, 2000). Participants ($n = 114$) were randomly assigned to regularly attend during treatment either ACA self-help group meetings or substance-abuse education classes. Past 30 days' abstinence rates post treatment were more than twice as high in the self-help group condition. Because patients in both conditions attended AA/NA/CA meetings, these superior outcomes appeared uniquely attributable to Adult Children of Alcoholics.

Results were equally impressive for psychiatric outcomes. Patients in both conditions showed significant and comparable decreases in depressive symptoms at 30-day follow-up, but by 6-month follow-up, only patients in the ACA self-help group maintained these gains. Levels of depression returned to their baseline level in the non-self-help group condition. Self-help group involvement may have consolidated early treatment gains by providing "extensive" support that was available after treatment ended (Humphreys & Tucker, 2002).

Alateen has also been the subject of an evaluation research project (Hughes, 1977). The study lacked a longitudinal design, but did employ two appropriate, demographically matched comparison groups. Among teenage children of alcoholic parents, Alateen members had significantly less problems with self-esteem, emotional upset, school performance, and juvenile delinquency than did non-members. Further, Alateen members had psychological and school functioning that was comparable to that of adolescents whose parents were not alcoholic. These initial findings generate optimism about Alateen's effectiveness, but they have not yet – to the author's knowledge – been built upon in subsequent research.

All Nippon Sobriety Association and the Sobriety
Friends Society (Danshukai)

Danshukai keeps unusually careful records of members and is open to professional inquiry, which helps to explain why a large amount of outcome data are available for the organization. Organizational records of continuous abstinence among a growing membership across Japan are fairly consistent over time, with a 1980 report (Suwaki, 1980) noting that 64% of the then 25 000 members had been abstinent for a year or more, and a later report noting a 63% abstinence rate among 48 000 members (Suwaki, 1988). This latter report also indicated that 28% of members had been abstinent for over 3 years, and 14% for over 5 years. A study of 366 members conducted by an outside researcher supported the credibility of these organizational records by identifying similar (in fact, slightly better) outcomes. Members had a median length of 4 years of continuous abstinence, and 25% had more than 10 years. Further, almost all members were currently in a period of abstinence, even if they had sustained it for less than a year (Sugita *et al.*, 1985).

Other evaluations have included comparison groups. A study of 482 alcoholics compared Danshukai members with alcoholic outpatients who did not go on to attend self-help groups (Shido *et al.*, 1986). Danshukai members had much longer sobriety periods (53 months vs. 31 months) despite similar age of onset, age of peak drinking, and severity of drinking. Self-help group attendance was also a robust predictor of good long-term drinking outcomes in a study of 329 former alcohol inpatients, even after considering a range of other prognostic variables (Noda *et al.*, 1988, see also Maruyama, Higuchi, & Hayashida, 1994). The difference in 10-year survival rates among males was striking: 83.3% for those affiliating with Danshukai versus only 52.6% for non-attenders.

An evaluation of the effect of structured family visits on hospitalized alcoholic patients provided further evidence of the effectiveness of Danshukai as aftercare (Ino & Hayasida, 2000). Married patients receiving the family visits were more likely to attend Danshukai meetings and professional outpatient aftercare sessions, and those who did so had significantly higher abstinence rates (48.1% vs. 36.7%). These effects did not hold in unmarried patients, perhaps because Danshukai meetings are organized to support couples attending together. This study did not distinguish self-help groups and outpatient counseling sessions in its data analysis, which is unfortunate because other studies of discharged inpatients in Japan (e.g., Suwaki, 1979) suggest that the benefits of Danshukai attendance may be augmented by concurrent outpatient treatment. The results of the study are nonetheless encouraging because self-help group involvement was clearly caused in part by forces external to the patient (i.e., a family visit organized by treatment staff), and therefore the superior outcomes cannot be put down to self-selection.

Clubs of Treated Alcoholics

English-language studies of CTAs are neither numerous nor recent. The most impressive study followed up several thousand patients treated in Zagreb in 1969 and found a 91% club-affiliation rate among abstainers (Sikic, Walker, & Peterson, 1973). Yugoslavian club members ($n = 134$) reported sharp drops in alcohol consumption and sick leave days, although this finding is based upon members' retrospective reports of their pre-membership problems (Matijevic & Paunovic, 1973). In a more recent outcome study, about one-third of Yugoslav affiliates reported at least 5 years of affiliation and continuous abstinence (Bennett, 1985).

A prospective longitudinal evaluation of CTAs with an appropriate comparison group has yet to be conducted, at least in a language accessible to the author. Further, these Balkan outcome studies may not generalize to Italy, where clubs have a different character. There obviously remains much more to learn about the impact of clubs on alcoholics and their families.

Double Trouble in Recovery

Only one longitudinal outcome study of DTR has been conducted (Laudet *et al.*, 2000b). The baseline sample was a cohort of 307 participants in 25 groups, of whom 278 were located at 1-year follow-up. This 90.5% follow-up rate increases confidence in the results and is in itself a singular achievement given that the majority of participants had psychotic spectrum disorders in addition to substance dependence. Most study participants were male (72%), African-American (58%), currently on medication (92%), involved in outpatient treatment (93%), and also attending other 12-step groups such as AA and NA (75%).

Abstinence rates increased from 58% at baseline to 72% at follow-up and correlated significantly with the number of DTR meetings attended. Psychiatric symptoms, in contrast, did not improve over the course of the study. Selection effects likely contributed to these results; individuals still attending DTR at follow-up had more severe mental health symptoms, but less severe substance-abuse problems, at baseline relative to non-attenders. Yet the observed outcomes do not appear *solely* attributable to selection bias because the number of outpatient treatment sessions attended, which presumably shares some self-selection influences with number of self-help group meetings attended, was uncorrelated with reductions in substance use and psychiatric symptoms (Laudet *et al.*, 2000b).

This study suggests, but does not prove, that DTR conveys some benefits to an extremely troubled and disadvantaged population. But, for the same reason that this result is exciting (i.e., the vulnerability of the population concerned), it demands replication before being accepted as definitive.

Moderation Management

MM has been unusually open to collaborative research projects. The organization allowed a research team to answer its national information and referral telephone line, provide the usual services, and then administer consenting callers a structured assessment of alcohol problems. The same measures were administered at MM self-help groups to new and established members. This design created a unique opportunity to evaluate whether attrition processes create the illusion that addiction-related mutual-help groups are effective when researchers examine a cross-sectional sample of current participants. If only "easy cases" attend or stay involved after initial contact, cross-sectional analysis would show a spurious correlation between self-help group affiliation and better outcomes.

Telephone callers to MM ($n = 444$) consumed significantly fewer drinks on typical drinking days and drank less frequently than did either new group members ($n = 47$) or established members ($n = 118$). Selection into MM groups is therefore adverse, i.e., the "easy cases" are *less likely* to affiliate than are those with a worse prognosis (Stewart *et al.*, 2002).

Experienced members did not differ from new members on amount of alcohol consumed but did have fewer alcohol-related problems. MM stands alone as a harm-reduction self-help organization that reduces adverse consequences of drinking rather than drinking per se (Stewart *et al.*, 2002). This study's results are consistent with two conclusions. First, MM may help non-dependent problem drinkers reduce alcohol-related harm. Second, selective attrition may be causing cross-sectional studies to understate, rather than overstate, the benefits of substance-abuse-related self-help groups.

Narcotics Anonymous

Evaluations of NA as a sole intervention are difficult to conduct because many members simultaneously attend Cocaine Anonymous (CA). Some NA members also attend AA, despite not having an alcohol problem, because of AA's wide availability and reputation for having a large corps of experienced potential sponsors. So, while the studies in this section are described as NA studies, the outcomes observed may also reflect the impact of sister 12-step organizations.

NA outcome research is of recent vintage, with the first sophisticated studies being conducted in London in the early 1990s by George Christo and colleagues (Christo & Franey, 1995; Christo & Sutton, 1994). In their first study of NA members ($n = 200$, 50% male), increased self-esteem and reduced anxiety were associated with length of membership and duration of abstinence, in a roughly linear fashion. The NA sample had higher average anxiety levels than samples of university students and employed adults. However, members who had been in NA for 3 years or more had anxiety levels that were similar to the non-addicted comparison groups, which, though not definitive, is consistent with the hypothesis that long-term NA participation reduces anxiety as well as drug use. The study is also notable for being one of the few that studied NA in the community rather than drawing its sample from a treatment program (see also Toumbourou *et al.*, 2002). This research group's next project replicated the association of NA involvement with decreased drug use 6 months after professional treatment.

A longitudinal study of 253 urban African-American drug patients conducted in the USA also provided evidence of NA's effectiveness. Those individuals who attended NA and other 12-step groups after treatment discharge showed a 50% greater decrease in drug use and related problems at 1-year follow-up than those patients who did not attend NA. Self-help group members also experienced significantly greater reductions in medical and alcohol problems (Humphreys, Mavis, & Stöffelmayr, 1994). This study found that these apparent benefits of NA were equally present for males and for females, a finding which has since been replicated in other projects (e.g., Hillhouse & Fiorentine, 2001). This study relied on self-report data, but studies that have assessed drug use with urinalysis (e.g., McKay *et al.*, 1994) have also found that post-treatment NA involvement reduces drug use.

Post-treatment 12-step self-help group involvement has been a strong predictor of better outcomes for drug patients in a number of other large, prospective, multi-program evaluation studies in the USA, including the Drug Abuse Treatment Outcome Study (Etheridge *et al.*, 1999), the NIDA Collaborative Cocaine Treatment Study (Weiss *et al.*, 1996, 2000), the VA multisite outcome study (Humphreys *et al.*, 1999b), the VA community residential facilities study (Moos *et al.*, 2001), and the Los Angeles Target Cities Evaluation Project

(Fiorentine, 1999; Fiorentine & Hillhouse, 2000). The consistency of NA predicting better outcomes emerges despite these studies employing diverse samples, measurement strategies, procedures, follow-up periods, and strategies of adjusting for possible self-selection factors. Minding the caution that none of these evaluations were randomized, collectively they increase confidence in NA as a complement to substance-abuse treatment programs, and the value of clinicians making strong efforts to connect drug-dependent patients with NA and related self-help groups (e.g., CA).

The only study that evaluated whether drug-related self-help groups affect infectious disease risk was conducted with injection drug users in Portland, Oregon. Participants ($n = 317$) received, at baseline, an HIV-related preventive education program and encouragement to attend drug treatment (Sibthorpe, Fleming, & Gould, 1994). At 6-month follow-up, enrollment in professional drug treatment had no effect on needle-sharing and injection frequency, but involvement in NA did. Self-help group members had decreases in risk behavior that were twice as large as those in non-attenders. Although only a single study with no control group, this project's results are exciting given that intravenous drug use behaviors are now a primary route of AIDS transmission in the developed world. To the extent that NA involvement reduces such risk behavior, the organization may be making a major impact on public health beyond reducing drug use per se.

A final important outcome study was not focused on NA, but evaluated a sufficiently similar organization to merit adumbration here. Opiate-dependent patients in the USA and Hong Kong ($n = 168$) were randomly assigned, at treatment discharge, to usual aftercare services or to "Recovery Training and Self-Help." This intervention comprised professionally led cognitive–behavioral relapse prevention counseling and peer-led, non-12-step, self-help group involvement. Abstinence rates were 50% higher in the experimental condition at 6-month follow-up in both countries (McAuliffe, 1990). This randomized trial supports the value of mutual-help activities among drug-dependent individuals, and so, like the NA-specific research just discussed, it increases confidence that NA's method can be effective.

Nicotine Anonymous

Research established the value of self-help groups in reducing tobacco use prior to the founding of Nicotine Anonymous. For example, an evaluation team randomly assigned half of a sample of 43 companies to have a smoking cessation program supplemented by self-help groups that were led by employees who were attempting to stop tobacco use (Jason *et al.*, 1987). Initial rates of quitting smoking were significantly higher for the 21 companies that had self-help groups available (average of 41% vs. 21% of participants). Self-help group participants also smoked significantly fewer cigarettes per day, with lower tar, nicotine, and carbon monoxide content. Although conducted before the advent of Nicotine Anonymous, this clinical trial provided indirect evidence that the organization could be helpful.

The only longitudinal outcome data specific to Nicotine Anonymous come from a larger clinical trial that examined methods of eliminating smoking among recovering alcoholics recruited from AA meetings (Martin *et al.*, 1997). Participants ($n = 205$, 55% male) were randomly assigned either to a 20-day group psycho-educational treatment supplemented by Nicotine Anonymous meetings, or to one of two behavioral treatment conditions (one with nicotine gum, one without). The behavioral treatments were modified to include 12-step content and were administered by ex-smoking members of AA. Initial quit rates favored the behavioral treatment without nicotine gum, but by 12-month follow-up, all groups had a similar quit rate of about 27%.

Had the study been designed to study self-help groups per se, the experimental conditions would no doubt have been more distinct instead of all including a 12-step self-help component. Nicotine Anonymous' effectiveness might be inferred from it producing a quit rate approximate to that obtained by other successful treatment programs in the field (Martin *et al.*, 1997). However, the outcome equivalence across conditions may mean that joining Nicotine Anonymous is not more helpful to an AA member than finding a supportive ex-smoking AA sponsor. More definitive conclusions await the conduct of outcome studies that are specifically intended to evaluate Nicotine Anonymous.

Oxford Houses

Leonard Jason *et al.* (1997b) studied rates of continued residence among 132 new Oxford House residents. The sample's representativeness was assured by the enrollment of 95% of the entering population in the US state where the study was conducted. Continued residence may safely be equated with abstinence and economic self-sufficiency because of the close monitoring that occurs in Oxford Houses. Eviction is an excellent proxy for substance use and/or antisocial behavior for the same reason. At 6-month follow-up, 36% of participants were still in residence, 32% had departed on good terms, and 32% had been evicted. These results surpass typical addiction treatment outcomes of low-income populations with long histories of antisocial behavior.

In addition, whereas 92% of the continuing residents reported engaging in criminal behavior at baseline (e.g., property crime), none did so at follow-up – a considerable benefit to society (Jason *et al.*, 2001). Survival analysis showed that length of residence in Oxford Houses is not predicted by race or ethnicity, implying that the apparent benefits of the program are accessible to a variety of individuals (Bishop *et al.*, 1998). This research team is currently conducting a randomized trial of Oxford Houses that should provide further information on the outcomes of participation, which, based on the above work, appear very positive.

Pui Hong Self-Help Association

Ch'ien (1980) compared a random sample of 100 new association members with 100 graduates from professional treatment services who chose not to join. The majority (57%) of association affiliates remained narcotic-free at 2-year follow-up compared with only 9% of non-affiliates. Self-selection is a threat to internal validity in this study, but Ch'ien (1980) argued persuasively that selection bias could not be a complete explanation given the absolute size of the abstinence rate among affiliates (any treatment program would envy the majority of its clients being completely abstinent for 2 years), coupled with the fact that, prior to the formation of the association, Hong Kong's professional treatment network could find little evidence of success. A different sample of former patients who joined the Pui Hong Self-Help Association had a re-admission rate of only about a third over 12 months post-treatment (Ch'ien, 1980). This is low by the addiction treatment field's standards and therefore suggests that the association is reducing relapses.

Rational Recovery

The only outcome data available on RR comes from a single cross-sectional study that compared 250 members who had been in the organization for 3 or more months with 110 newcomers (Galanter, Egelko, & Edwards, 1993). Experienced members had higher rates of abstinence (73% vs. 38% for newcomers) and lower levels of neurotic distress. Engaged members reported far more drinking and psychological problems prior to their involvement in RR. These findings are all consistent with the hypothesis that RR is effective, but the cross-sectional, single-group study design leaves them as suggestive rather than definitive evidence.

Secular Organization for Sobriety

Most of the 158 SOS members surveyed by Connors and Dermen (1996) were currently abstinent (70.1%) or mostly abstinent (16.2%), despite generally long and severe drinking histories. The survey was cross-sectional, and many respondents were concurrently attending other self-help groups and/or psychotherapy, rendering causal conclusions and the effects of SOS participation tenuous. To the author's knowledge, SOS has never been evaluated in a longitudinal study with appropriate comparison groups.

Women for Sobriety

WFS's effectiveness can be assessed based on only a single cross-sectional survey, albeit one that had a high response rate and coverage (73% of the North American membership). Key results of relevance were that the average member had been sober for 3.5 years and that WFS involvement was associated with higher self-esteem, less negative thinking, and more emotional calm (Kaskutas, 1996a, b). Whether such positive outcomes are attributable to WFS affiliation or to almost all members being socially stable, well educated, and economically advantaged remains an open question.

Outcome studies of AA

AA and other self-help organizations are not equatable with professional treatment, as explained in Chapter 1. Studies that label themselves as AA outcome studies – but are actually studies only of the effectiveness of 12-step-influenced professional treatment programs (e.g., Alford, 1980) – will therefore not be addressed here. Studies examining the unique effect of AA participation as a supplement to professional treatment are germane and will be discussed, but are still not identical with community-based evaluations of AA for several reasons. First, samples recruited in treatment usually include many individuals who have already unsuccessfully affiliated with AA in the past (Humphreys, Kaskutas, & Weisner, 1998a; Mäkelä, 1993). This unrepresentative subsample's subsequent experiences of AA as aftercare likely differ from those of first-time affiliates. Second, AA studies that begin in a treatment setting can only determine whether AA augments the efforts of professionals. Left unexamined is the critical question of whether AA in some cases makes professional treatment unnecessary (i.e., when an individual goes to AA first). Some professionals find this an uncomfortable question, but because of the healthcare policy implications it deserves as much attention as the question of how treated alcoholics are affected by AA involvement.

Any conclusions about AA's effectiveness must consider the work of the indefatigable meta-analytic research team led by Chad Emrick and Scott Tonigan (Emrick *et al.*, 1993; Tonigan, Toscova, & Miller, 1996). After reviewing about 200 studies (most of them US-based), this team developed estimates of the size of AA's effect on drinking and related outcomes. Their overall conclusion was that AA affiliation was positively correlated with better outcomes on measures of drinking and drinking-related problems. More modest associations were identified between AA involvement and better psychological health, social functioning, employment situation, and legal situation. The research team estimated effect sizes for AA where possible. Using Jacob Cohen's (1992) well-known terminology, they ranged from "small" to "medium." Given the largely correlational research base, these apparent benefits of AA participation may be an artifact of self-selection. A few research projects have found that prior motivation to reduce alcohol consumption predicts AA affiliation, a selection bias that might exaggerate AA's effectiveness in some studies (Isenhart, 1997; Morgenstern *et al.*, 1997). Yet more studies identify an opposite selection bias that understates rather than overstates AA's benefits. Across studies conducted in inpatient and outpatient treatment samples (Emrick *et al.*, 1993), in correctional facilities (Seixas, Washburn, & Eisen, 1988), and in communities as different as Mexico City (Rosovsky, Casanova, & Pérez, 1991) and London (Edwards *et al.*, 1966), AA attracts problem drinkers who have more serious alcohol problems and therefore a worse prognosis. Hence, even though individual correlational studies of AA may have significant selection bias in one direction or the other, all such studies combined (i.e., those meta-analyzed by Emrick *et al.*) should have no consistent selection bias.

Most of the studies considered in the meta-analysis were cross-sectional. Cross-sectional studies often overstate the effect of interventions, and were this true for AA the meta-analytic team's main conclusions would be too optimistic. This concern does seem warranted because the longitudinal research that has been conducted, for example the studies of George Vaillant (1995), has generally found even stronger relationships between AA involvement and better outcomes than has cross-sectional research. Because individuals can participate in AA indefinitely, longer-term outcome studies are particularly likely to identify AA as the most influential factor in long-term recovery (Cross *et al.*, 1990; Humphreys, Moos, & Cohen, 1997). From the vantage point of an individual's whole life course, professional treatment interventions come and go rather quickly, whereas AA affiliation can literally become a lifelong influence (Vaillant, 1995; Vaillant & Milofsky, 1982).

All meta-analytic conclusions are captives of whatever research has been done in the past, which raises a final caveat. The body of AA research reviewed by Emrick *et al.* (1993) combined studies that examined AA in inpatient, outpatient, and untreated samples. Even if these types of research were separated for analysis, inpatients have still been greatly over-represented in AA research. Upon further analysis, the research team concluded that AA's effects were more in evidence in outpatient than inpatient samples (Tonigan, Toscova, & Miller, 1996), which would imply that over-reliance on inpatient recruited samples has led the field to underestimate AA's effectiveness.

This meta-analytic research program also drew some instructive methodological conclusions. Most AA studies have lacked sufficient statistical power to detect effects, primarily because they have employed small samples (Tonigan, Toscova, & Miller, 1996). Tonigan *et al.* estimated a Type II error rate of 0.33 to 0.71 across different types of outcomes. This implies that, when a significant relationship between AA and outcome is present in reality, most research studies as currently designed will fail to detect it. A related problem is that, until recently, reliable, multi-dimensional (i.e., tapping more aspects of AA affiliation than meeting attendance) measures of AA involvement were not available, further reducing statistical power (Allen, 2000; see also Montgomery *et al.*, 1995). In addition to inducing some humility in all those who would draw strong conclusions about AA's effectiveness or ineffectiveness, these conclusions suggest obvious avenues for improving AA research in the future (Humphreys, 2002).

Experimental and quasi-experimental studies of AA as a sole intervention

Turning from the meta-analysis to specific outcome studies, only three randomized trials have included a condition in which AA in the community was the sole intervention. The author agrees with E. Kurtz (1993) that these studies are frequently cited as stating things that they do not actually say, or as having certain characteristics that they do not. Hence, each of them will be discussed in some detail

The Ditman et al. (1967) trial

Participants in this study were "chronic drunkenness offenders" facing criminal sentencing. A judge randomly assigned participants to either attend five

AA meetings ($n = 86$), go to an outpatient treatment program ($n = 82$), or receive no intervention ($n = 73$) over a 30-day period. Offenders in the three conditions did not differ on rate of re-arrest at 1-year follow-up, which was the sole outcome measure. The researchers never assessed alcohol consumption, alcohol-related problems, or psychological functioning, which is a serious shortcoming because such clinical outcomes are uncorrelated in substance-abusing samples with measures of "institutional recapture" (e.g., recidivism to treatment or jail; Humphreys & Weingardt, 2000; Lyons *et al.*, 1997). Neither did this study monitor or describe whether individuals in the control condition voluntarily received any treatment or attended AA; only a small amount of such participation would have meant that some "no intervention" controls received more intervention than participants assigned to AA and treatment. Finally, all participants in all conditions were on probation and under legal order not to consume alcohol. Other studies from this research program demonstrate that such legal pressure alone significantly reduces drunkenness arrests (Ditman & Crawford, 1966), which implies a homogenization of experimental conditions and attendant difficulty in finding outcome differences.

The author has heard many treatment professionals confidently cite the Ditman study as evidence that "AA does not work," apparently unaware that were this study considered a source of reliable conclusions, professional treatment would be considered not to work either. Upon careful reading – which one hopes always precedes citation – the Ditman study does not support any conclusions about the effect of AA or treatment on alcohol consumption and related psychological and medical comorbidities.

The Brandsma, Maultby, & Welsh (1980) trial

This randomized clinical trial is less well known because it was never published in a peer-reviewed journal. Most of the participants were referred by the courts for alcohol-related offenses, with the remainder being referred by other agencies or by themselves. Five conditions were compared: insight therapy, rational behavioral therapy led by a professional, rational behavioral therapy led by a recovering paraprofessional, AA, and no treatment. The AA condition was actually a group created by the research project and led by two AA members. Unlike in a real AA meeting, attendance records were kept, so it was not anonymous, and if a participant missed a meeting, a research staff member contacted them and "reminded them of the condition of their probation" (p. 34).

Out of 532 potential subjects who were screened for participation, 260 were accepted into the study. Excluded individuals had more severe alcohol problems and less socioeconomic resources than those individuals who enrolled in the study. Of the 260 screened in, 197 actually initiated treatment. The researchers made the debatable decision to drop from the study any individual who attended less than 10 sessions, reducing the final outcome sample even further to 104 (i.e., 19.5% of those screened, 40% of those accepted into the study).

Individuals assigned to the AA-style group were less likely to attend 10 sessions and more likely to have a drinking binge than were individuals in all the other conditions. However, relative to untreated controls, at the end of treatment AA members had much lower drinks per day on drinking days (2.5 vs. 11.2) and mean ounces of ethanol per day (1.2 vs. 5.3). None of the groups differed in the year after treatment on any outcome, but this may have been due to the drop-outs and exclusion criteria reducing statistical power (i.e., at follow-up only 12–24 subjects remained in each of the five comparison groups). An additional complication (present in all AA trials) was that some participants in the control and treatment groups attended AA on their own, reducing the distinctiveness of the various experimental assignments.

This evaluation study is a little acerbating because, despite having the space of a whole book to describe it, the research team never reported the most basic analysis for a randomized trial – namely, intent-to-treat results! Determining whether the higher rate of attending less than 10 sessions in the AA condition (i.e., differential attrition) accounted for the sharp drops in drinking in that condition is therefore impossible. In a review of alcoholism treatment outcome studies, John Finney and Susanne Monahan (1996) rated this trial as too flawed to support any conclusions, which is perhaps a bit strong given that it did at least include random assignment and a longitudinal design. However, this study's flaws and idiosyncracies definitely render it less informative than the final randomized trial on AA as a stand-alone intervention.

The Walsh et al. (1991) trial

A more sophisticated research project studied factory workers who had come into contact with an employee assistance program owing to alcohol abuse (Walsh *et al.*, 1991). Although often described as a comparison of "AA vs. Treatment," this randomized clinical trial actually compared AA combined with treatment with AA alone. The two experimental conditions of primary interest here were compulsory inpatient treatment combined with concurrent and post-treatment AA ($n = 73$) versus direct referral to attend community-based AA groups only ($n = 83$). The researchers monitored compliance with assigned condition, substance use, and job performance over 24 months.

Subjects in both conditions experienced significant and comparable improvement on 12 employment-related performance measures. However, the inpatient treatment + AA condition produced better outcomes on several substance abuse-related measures. The AA-only condition resulted in absolute reductions in substance use and related problems over time, but was relatively less effective at preventing relapse than the inpatient treatment + AA condition. AA without treatment seemed particularly less effective at reducing substance abuse among participants who abused cocaine as well as alcohol.

As in the other randomized trials just discussed, Walsh *et al.*'s participants were aware of being carefully monitored, and faced negative consequences (e.g., job loss) for continued drinking. The above results may therefore not generalize to voluntary help-seekers. In addition, the study's comparison of AA alone to AA + inpatient treatment has reduced relevance to modern healthcare policy decisions in light of the subsequent sharp contraction of inpatient alcoholism treatment in developed nations (Bao, Sauerland, & Sturm, 2001). External validity is also limited by the fact that alcoholics who seek inpatient treatment differ significantly on baseline variables from those who use AA as a primary intervention (Timko *et al.*, 1993). Nevertheless, in its conduct and design characteristics, Walsh *et al.*'s. 1991 study stands head and shoulders above the other two randomized trials of community-based AA participation as a sole intervention. Just as important of course are its results, which show that, on average, individuals who begin attending AA make significant improvements on substance abuse and related outcomes, but also that, for many people with serious substance-abuse problems, AA is simply insufficient as a sole intervention. More perhaps than any other study, the Walsh *et al.* (1991) project refutes the idea that treatment systems are not necessary because mutual-help organizations can eliminate substance-abuse problems on their own.

The Humphreys and Moos (1996) quasi-experiment

The author and his colleague Rudolf Moos had the good fortune to find a sample of alcohol-abusing individuals initially seeking AA ($n = 135$) or outpatient treatment ($n = 66$) who were initially equivalent in almost every respect, despite not being randomly assigned to condition. Specifically, the two groups did not differ significantly at baseline on sex, marital status, employment status, race, days intoxicated, alcohol-dependence symptoms, depressive symptoms, prior treatment experience, or current help-seeking/motivation (all were seeking help). The only differences between the groups were slightly lower income, less education, and more adverse consequences of drinking in the AA sample, which, when considered with the non-significant differences on the other variables, suggests that any departures from overall equivalence gave only a modest prognostic advantage to the outpatient sample.

Both groups were substantially improved at 1- and 3-year follow-ups, decreasing ethanol consumption and alcohol-dependence symptoms by about 70%, and depressive symptoms by about 30%. Despite their somewhat worse prognosis at baseline, AA affiliates improved as much as those who sought outpatient treatment. The fortuitous similarity of groups at baseline supports the conclusion of comparable effectiveness for AA and outpatient treatment. This study did not include an untreated comparison group, but other studies of these same participants have found that both the outpatient and AA samples improved more than untreated alcohol abusers (Timko *et al.*, 1994).

Longitudinal studies of AA's effectiveness in combination with treatment

AA's effect has been evaluated more extensively in clinical populations than in community samples. In naturalistic studies of alcohol treatment samples in a variety of settings and societies, AA involvement correlates with better alcohol-related and psychological outcomes (Emrick *et al.*, 1993; Johnsen & Herringer, 1993; McLatchie & Lomp, 1988; Thurstin, Alfano, & Nerviano, 1987; Van de Velde *et al.*, 1998). No knowledgeable person disputes the existence of this association, but whether it results from effectiveness, self-selection, or both is a subject of debate. The subset of studies that have stronger research designs provides the best opportunities to throw light on this issue, and therefore receives primary attention here.

The New Orleans Homeless Substance Abusers Project provided powerful evidence of how 12-step treatment and self-help groups can benefit severely troubled individuals (Devine, Brody, & Wright, 1997; Wright & Devine, 1995). Participants ($n = 670$, 75% male) were randomly assigned to a control condition (detoxification only) or to a 12-step-oriented treatment program with supplemental self-help group involvement. Individuals in the 12-step-oriented condition experienced significantly greater gains by 6-month follow-up on days housed and days without substance use. Self-help group involvement at follow-up was almost eight times higher in the experimental condition than in the control condition. Attending AA/CA/NA meetings was thus largely determined by a random assignment rather than self-selection, which is of singular importance given its large observed benefits in terms of sobriety and days housed. These benefits fully accounted for the superior outcomes for participants randomized to a professional 12-step treatment. The main value of the treatment program was not its concurrent benefits but its ability to connect patients to self-help groups which, in turn, supported improvement over the long term (Devine, Brody, & Wright, 1997).

Project MATCH (Project MATCH Research Group, 1997, 1998) compared cognitive–behavioral therapy and motivational enhancement therapy with twelve-step facilitation (TSF) counseling in a randomized clinical trial of 1726 patients (inpatient arm 774, outpatient arm 952) diagnosed with alcohol abuse or dependence. TSF was provided by a professional counselor, but otherwise drew most of its design from AA and other 12-step organizations. For example, TSF counselors emphasized to patients that alcohol dependence was a disease that could be arrested but not cured through lifelong abstinence, and that attending AA meetings would facilitate recovery.

Discussion of Project MATCH's results will be limited here to the overall pattern of 1-year and 3-year outcome differences between TSF counseling and the other two treatments. All three treatments produced significant reductions in alcohol consumption, alcohol-related problems, and psychiatric symptoms over the course of the study. Each treatment yielded comparable changes in research participants, with two exceptions. First, relative to the other treatments, TSF counseling produced higher levels of AA meeting attendance and AA-related activities (e.g., working the 12 steps, Tonigan, Connors, & Miller, 2002). Second, at each follow-up, TSF counseling generated significantly higher rates of abstinence. This result was as expected given AA's opposition to viewing moderate drinking as an acceptable goal for alcohol-dependent individuals.

Project MATCH's (1997) central goal of course was to evaluate the hypothesis that patient characteristics could be used to match the patients to appropriate treatments and thereby augment outcomes. The much-underappreciated achievement of this landmark study is that it proved conclusively that the matching hypothesis is generally wrong (some in the field wanted to kill the messenger, which is simply unfair).

Many Project MATCH participants in the cognitive–behavioral therapy and motivational enhancement conditions attended AA meetings even though, unlike TSF patients, they were not specifically encouraged to do so. AA attendance and drinking intensity were *positively* correlated in the cognitive–behavioral outpatient arm at 6 months (Tonigan Connors, & Miller, 2002); both – other than that anomaly benefit from AA participation – did not differ by treatment condition in Project MATCH. Further, across all Project MATCH study sites and settings, the associations between greater AA involvement and better alcohol-related outcomes were of comparable strength (Tonigan, 2001).

Contemporaneous with Project MATCH, the US Department of Veterans Affairs (VA) evaluated 12-step and cognitive–behavioral treatment provided in inpatient programs with outpatient aftercare services. Male substance-abuse patients provided data at intake, discharge, and multiple follow-ups (Moos, *et al.*, 1999). Almost all participants were alcohol dependent, half were also drug dependent, and one-fifth had a comorbid Axis I psychiatric disorder. The five 12-step-oriented treatment programs emphasized clinical activities such as attending AA/NA group meetings, incorporating the 12 steps into daily life, reading AA/NA literature, and accepting one's addiction. Surveys of staff indicated that they believed addiction was a disease and that they spent most of their time on 12-step treatment activities. In contrast, the five cognitive–behavioral treatment programs provided patients with relapse-prevention groups, cognitive skills training, and cognitive–behavioral group therapy. They applied the cognitive–behavioral approach very purely, spending less than 5% of treatment time on 12-step-related activities.

A total of 2045 men were followed-up at 1 year. Outcome results were quite similar to those of Project MATCH. Cognitive–behavioral and 12-step oriented treatment both produced significant decreases in patients' drug and alcohol use, substance-abuse-related problems, psychiatric symptoms, and criminal behavior (see Moos *et al.*, 1999, for 1-year results; Ritsher, Moos, & Finney, 2002, for 2-year results). The different treatments were comparably effective, with the only exception again being that 12-step-oriented treatment had an advantage in promoting complete abstinence. At 1-year follow-up, for example, rates of abstinence from drugs and alcohol for the past 3 months were 45% for patients treated in 12-step-oriented programs versus 36% for patients treated in cognitive–behavioral programs.

Patients entering 12-step and cognitive–behavioral treatment programs did not differ in their prior level of self-help group involvement. Yet 1 year after treatment, 12-step treatment had produced significantly higher rates of ongoing AA/NA involvement (Humphreys, 1999), replicating the other studies just reviewed (see also Smith, 1986). The VA study found stronger evidence than Project MATCH that 12-step self-help group involvement may be more beneficial to patients who received 12-step versus cognitive–behavioral treatment. At 1-year follow-up, abstinence rates for 12-step-treatment patients increased from 19%, for patients less involved with self-help groups after discharge, to 75% for more involved patients. In contrast, after cognitive–behavioral treatment, abstinence rates increased from 25% for patients less involved in self-help groups to only 65% for highly involved patients (Humphreys *et al.*, 1999a).

Finally, a recent analysis of 2-year data from the VA study provided strong evidence that AA's positive outcomes were not attributable to self-selection on motivation to change, psychopathology, or alcohol problems. In a multi-wave structural equation modeling analysis, AA involvement 1 year after treatment predicted better alcohol-related outcomes at 2 years, but alcohol-related problems at 1 year did not predict AA involvement at 2 years (McKellar, Stewart, & Humphreys, 2003). In separate structural models, AA attenders and non-attenders had comparable prior motivation to change and psychopathology. In other words – AA's relationship to better outcomes was not due to "easy cases" staying in the organization. A skeptic could still argue that other self-selection factors were at work, but it is striking that the three most commonly invoked hypotheses of this sort had no empirical support.

Another important study examined heterosexual couples who were receiving alcohol-related behavioral couples therapy (McCrady, Epstein, & Hirsch, 1999). Couples were randomly assigned to receive couples therapy only ($n = 30$) or to have it supplemented with relapse prevention training ($n = 31$) or with a TSF-style intervention ($n = 29$). The TSF-style intervention appeared similar to that used in Project MATCH, except that it covered Al-Anon more thoroughly as a resource for the non-alcoholic partners in the study (all of whom were women).

The TSF-style intervention was highly successful at increasing attendance at 12-step self-help groups, but 6-month outcomes were roughly comparable across conditions (e.g., about 50% of patients were abstinent or engaged in non-problem drinking), and what differences there were favored the two purely behavioral conditions that did not include TSF. In other words, echoing other findings just reviewed – supplementing cognitive–behavioral marital therapy with 12-step self-help group involvement did not appear to enhance the effectiveness of the treatment.

The above studies were all conducted in specialty addiction-treatment programs. TSF interventions may have applicability beyond that context. In an intriguing study of patients hospitalized for medical treatment after an alcohol-involved accident, Richard Blondell *et al.* (2001) compared the effectiveness of (1) usual care with (2) a 5–15 minute physician-delivered brief intervention and (3) this intervention coupled with a 30 to 60-minute visit by an experienced AA member. Almost two-thirds (64%) of patients who received an AA "12-step call" were abstinent 6 months after hospital discharge, compared with 51% of brief-intervention patients and 36% of usual-care patients. Even more impressive, 49% of those patients receiving an AA visit initiated alcohol treatment and/or self-help group attendance, compared with less than 15% of the patients in the other two conditions. These findings merit replication and extension given the exciting possibility of peer-delivered TSF interventions being able to have an impact in general medical settings.

Summary of AA effectiveness studies

Considered as a body of work, the studies of AA as a sole intervention in the community and in combination with professional treatment are more extensive and better designed than those for any other addiction-related mutual-help organization. Thus, it is encouraging that this more extensive inquiry has strengthened rather than weakened the case for the effectiveness of mutual-help groups. The average effect of AA as a stand-alone intervention is no greater than that of other ambulatory interventions, but it is of meaningful size. AA may add more to 12-step treatment outcomes than to cognitive–behavioral treatment outcomes, but nonetheless, across interventions it usually helps patients maintain and build upon treatment gains. As noted, many studies of AA have serious methodological flaws, yet one is struck by how conclusions regarding AA's effectiveness are equally strong or stronger when design characteristics are better.

Three intriguing questions about AA's effectiveness

The remainder of this chapter addresses three questions that flesh out the general conclusion that AA is an effective intervention for reducing alcohol consumption and related psychiatric and social problems. First, through what processes does AA produce positive outcomes? Second, as several million people are affiliating with AA, could AA actually affect population-level indices of health? Third, even though AA is helpful *on average*, are some individuals harmed by AA involvement?

Mediators of AA's influence on drinking outcomes

Evaluators use the term "mediator" in a variety of ways. It will be employed here specifically to mean a link in a causal chain, i.e., if A leads to B and B leads to C, then the relationship of A to C is "mediated" by B (Finney, 1995). The common mediational question about AA is what B factors account for self-help group participation (A in the above example) leading to less alcohol consumption and related problems (C in the above example).

Jon Morgenstern and colleagues (1997) found that individuals who became involved in AA augmented their commitment to abstinence, self-efficacy, and negative appraisal of substance abuse as a source of harm. AA members also enhanced their use of active coping behaviors. These mediators led to subsequent decreases in substance use. Morgenstern's sample had been treated in private hospitals and included a high proportion of women (42 out of 100 subjects). Yet greater use of active coping responses also emerged as a mediator of change in 12-step groups in a sample of male patients treated in the public sector (Humphreys *et al.*, 1999b), suggesting the generalizability of this result.

Robert Fiorentine and Maureen Hillhouse (in press – a, b) provide findings similar to Morgenstern on the importance of commitment to abstinence and the appraisal of substances as harmful as mediators of recovery, but put these changes in the context of their "Addicted-Self Model of Recovery." This dynamic model holds that individuals who feel themselves unable to control substance use are more likely to participate in 12-step treatment programs and 12-step self-help organizations, which reinforce the self-perception that one is permanently addicted. The effectiveness of AA/NA is mediated, therefore, not only by increased self-efficacy concerning abstinence, but also by *decreased* self-efficacy to use substances moderately (Fiorentine & Hillhouse, in press – b).

A related line of research has focused on the positive influence of internalizing AA's philosophy of alcoholism, and indeed of human existence (E. Kurtz, 1982). In anthropology, the concept that healing involves changes in "assumptive world" (Frank, 1973) has a long history, and parallel work in psychology has emphasized that a "sense of coherence" improves health (Antonovsky, 1984). This process has been described in many different ways and from many different perspectives, but Paul Antze's (1979, 1987) concept of the "cognitive antidote" is probably the most widely invoked. Antze argues that when new members join AA, they encounter an organized world view represented in program literature, in the 12 steps and the 12 traditions, and in the stories told by members. This philosophy intends to counter the problematic world view with which the member joins the organization. For example, because AA's founders saw alcoholism as stemming from self-will run riot, AA's cognitive antidote emphasizes members' powerlessness and need for help from a Higher Power. These sorts of changes have been described from the perspective of psychoanalysis as an alteration in the relationship of the ego to the superego and id (Tiebout, 1954), from a cognitive perspective as a change in attributions and cybernetic epistemology (Bateson, 1971; Beckman, 1980; Brundage, 1985), and from a theological perspective as spiritual growth (E. Kurtz & Ketcham, 1992). The theoretical pieces in this area constitute some of the most intriguing and engaging writing about AA. Almost none of these authors provide extensive, systematic, empirical data supporting their conjectures, but subsequent research may show that world view transformation (however described) is a mediator of AA's effect on alcohol consumption.

The above mediators are largely intrapsychic in scope, reflecting perhaps the tendency of addiction research, especially that done by US psychologists, to focus more on intrapersonal variables than environmental ones (Humphreys & Rappaport, 1993). AA and other self-help groups are human organizations and thus some of their mediators are social rather than intrapsychic. The three most likely candidates for social-context-driven mediators in AA are abstinence-specific social support, opportunities for altruism, and access to recovering role models.

Generic social support has only a modest influence on the course of addictive disorders, but abstinent-contingent support (e.g., friends who are only supportive when one is not drinking) can be quite influential (Beattie & Longabaugh, 1997). The desire to meet others who share one's situation is a common motivation for attending self-help groups of all sorts (Richardson, 1983a, b), and AA members therefore appreciate finding other alcoholics who are committed to abstaining and to creating social events upon that assumption (e.g., "sober dances," recovery weekend retreats). Multiple studies have found that increases in such abstinence-specific support mediates the effect of 12-step group participation on future substance use (Kaskutas, Bond, & Humphreys, 2002; Humphreys, *et al.*, 1999b). Project MATCH also supported this hypothesis: TSF counseling was particularly helpful as an "inoculant" for those participants who had a drinking-supportive social network (Longabaugh *et al.*, 1998).

By design, the AA's social environment also provides opportunities for members to help others. The "helper-therapy" principle operates across self-help organizations (Maton, 1988; Riessman, 1965), and indeed the survival of all self-help organizations depends on members taking advantage of opportunities for altruism (Montaño Fraire, 2000). Altruism may mediate AA's effects on drinking. Individuals who engage in AA service work, for example sponsoring others and working the 12th step, have better drinking outcomes (Emrick *et al.*, 1993; Sheeren, 1987). Further, a 10-year follow-up study of 158 former alcoholic inpatient reported an astonishing 91% remission rate in the subset of individuals who had been AA sponsors (Cross *et al.*, 1990).

The social environment of AA also offers opportunities to meet experienced recovering members, which may aid the process of the recovery in two ways. First, sponsorship offers a helpful role model who can provide emotional support and practical advice (Ripley & Jackson, 1959). Second, whether they are sponsors or not, the presence of experienced members with whom one identifies can instill hope (Van der Avort & Van Harberden, 1983). No pun intended, the initial stages of recovery from alcoholism can be quite "dispiriting." When newcomers see experienced members prospering further down the difficult road they themselves hope to travel, it increases their faith that the future might be better than the present.

How specific are the mediators of AA's effectiveness?

The foregoing list of mediators may seem disappointingly pedestrian next to the stereotype that AA members invariably experience "bolt from the blue" spiritual transformations that cause them to stop drinking forever. Some AA members do indeed experience dramatic changes in their spiritual life (see Chapter 4), but AA clearly shares mediational processes with other self-help groups and with professional treatments. Changes in active coping behaviors, cognitive appraisal of the advantages and disadvantages of drinking, and self-efficacy may seem more the stuff of cognitive–behavioral psychotherapy than of a 12-step self-help organization. But even the most spiritually minded AA meetings and texts offer extensive practical advice, which any cognitive–behavioral theorist would endorse even though the jargon would be unfamiliar: monitor for relapse-promoting cognitive distortions ("no stinking thinking"), adopt behavioral changes that are congruent with more positive mood ("fake it until you make it"), and use stimulus-control methods to eliminate alcohol consumption ("avoid slippery people, places, and things"). Such parallels explain why proximal changes evident in cognitive–behavioral programs (e.g., in beliefs and coping responses) occur in 12-step treatment programs as well (Finney *et al.*, 1998). As for the other mediators, access to role models, altruism, and instillation of hope are all important mediators of positive outcomes in group psychotherapy (Yalom, 1975) and in other self-help groups (Lieberman, 1986; Salem *et al.*, 2000). Those who market AA as the "only way" or as a "way without parallel" are thus on weak empirical footing (Toch, 1965).

Many different AA mediators have been identified by research, which raises the question of whether all members need all of them to become abstinent. Multi-modal addiction interventions are sometimes conceptualized as having fully interactive mediators of change across patients, for example the hypothesis that every mediator increases every individual's chance of abstinence by 5%. An equally plausible concept, however, is that each mediator of change increases by a few percentage points the proportion of substance-dependent people who benefit (i.e., different members benefit from different mediators). The latter conceptualization is probably more true of AA, which offers many mediators of change to fill whatever need a given member happens to have – be it sober friends, a new perspective on life, advice on coping strategies, or the chance to help other alcoholics.

Finally, mediational research augments understanding of AA but cannot escape being a series of snapshot photographs taken of a flowing river. AA involvement at baseline may lead neatly to better self-efficacy at follow-up interview 1, and more days of abstinence at follow-up interview 2, but a more complex process would be in evidence were daily observation between the time points possible. The first AA meeting might improve self-efficacy a little, which reduces drinking a little, which increases self-efficacy as well as making more AA attendance more likely, and so on in a positive spiral. This is not a critique of AA mediational research such as that just reviewed, but a recognition that human beings, interventions, change processes, outcomes, and environments are always in more complex interplay than science can easily map.

AA's potential for population-level benefits

The received view within the public health field holds that individual-level interventions for current cases never reach enough afflicted individuals to affect population-level indicators. Individual medical treatments (e.g., coronary artery bypass graft) are too expensive, time-consuming, and inaccessible to significantly change population-level health (e.g., national rates of sudden cardiac death). Self-help organizations could be an exception to this general rule because they are free of charge, easy to establish, and simple to access. For example, at one time almost 2% of the adult population of Norway had participated in weight-loss self-help groups of demonstrated effectiveness, which may have been sufficient coverage to aggregate to improvements in population-level rates of cardiovascular diseases (Grimsmo, Helgesen, & Borchgrevink, 1981; Humphreys & Ribisl, 1999), although this possibility was never researched.

AA is the only addiction-related self-help organization prevalent enough to potentially produce population-level effects. Reginald Smart, Robert Mann, and colleagues' research program evaluated whether AA's growth in the USA and Canada accounts for drops in population-level liver cirrhosis rates, drunk-driving arrests, and other alcohol-related offences (Mann *et al.*, 1991; Smart & Mann, 1993, 1998; Smart, Mann, & Anglin, 1989). Their primary analytic method was to create change scores based on two time points (e.g., 1974 and 1983) for each independent and dependent measure and then use correlations or regression models to assess (presumed linear) associations, e.g., whether the change in the number of AA members in each of the 50 US states correlated with the change in drunk-driving arrests in those same states. Analysis typically included a covariate to try to control for the effect of changes in alcohol consumption. The specific results of their studies differ somewhat from paper to paper, because they examine different time periods, regions, and outcomes, but their usual finding is that increases in the growth in Alcoholics Anonymous correlate with decreases in liver cirrhosis rates and alcohol-related criminal offences even after accounting for decreases in alcohol consumption. The size of the association was estimated in a US data set as each 1% increase in AA membership causing a 0.06% decrease in cirrhosis mortality (Mann *et al.*, 1991). If this is in fact accurate, AA's extraordinary growth has resulted in a sizable contribution to public health and substantial reductions in human misery and economic costs.

However, Harold Holder (1997) has made some compelling arguments for why this conclusion may be premature. The apparent positive effects of AA's growth in the Mann and Smart studies do not all have a plausible causal mechanism. AA could be expected to reduce liver cirrhosis rates because it draws members from the highly alcohol dependent subpopulation whose heavy drinking accounts for almost all cases of liver cirrhosis. In contrast, AA's growth should have little effect on population rates of drunk-driving arrests and alcohol-related road-accident fatalities because these are primarily caused by non-alcohol-dependent individuals (Bruun *et al.*, 1975). Holder raises the added concern that comparing percentage change between one time point and another does not take account of autoregression and lagged effects (Holder, 1997). Because liver cirrhosis takes years to develop, a large expansion of AA from 1940 to 1949 might not show any benefits until the 1950s and 1960s, for example.

The time period studied by Smart and Mann was characterized by important cultural changes, notably a general drying trend of reduced consumption and attitudes that supported such changes (Holder, 1997). AA is therefore probably not the only variable accounting for its apparently powerful population-level effects in this research program (in other words, the analytic model is probably underspecified). All that said, if one is willing to surrender the search for a prime mover, one could easily conceive of how AA, declining consumption, changing attitudes, and other factors might together have caused declines in liver cirrhosis rates and alcohol-related offenses. With declining alcohol consumption, social comparisons between one's own drinking and those of others may have become more stark for alcohol abusers, making them more likely to seek out AA. Synergistically, if a culture develops a "dry Zeitgeist," relatives and friends of heavy drinkers may be more likely to push them to seek help from AA. These forces could increase AA involvement rates. Increases in AA's prominence may, in turn, strengthen the cultural anti-heavy-drinking Zeitgeist (including a greater tendency for non-dependent drinkers to be careful about drinking and driving), and also, of course, lower consumption by inducing abstinence in the small alcoholic subpopulation that accounts for a large part of population ethanol consumption (American Psychiatric Association, 1987). More sophisticated methodologies with more measurement points would be needed to test for these dynamic, reciprocal effects. Such analysis would likely reveal greater complexity within the processes involved and reduce the estimate of the population-level effect size for AA, but would probably still support Smart and Mann's basic conclusion that AA has at least some positive impact on population-level rates of liver cirrhosis, and perhaps also on alcohol-related crime. The impact may be modest and may be dependent on other cultural factors to appear (see Smart, Mann, & Anglin, 1989). Yet its existence is a reasonable conjecture in light of the other positive findings on AA discussed earlier and the enormous size of the organization.

Weaknesses and possible harms of AA

Behavior therapists postulate that AA harms some members through an "abstinence violation effect" (AVE) (Kanfer & Schefft, 1988; Marlatt, 1978; Ogborne & Bornet, 1982). Such theorists consider AA's maxim "One drink, one drunk" to be a self-fulfilling prophecy. The AVE hypothesis holds that when AA members have one drink, negative AA-inculcated cognitions are activated, for example the thought that one is a helpless, permanently diseased individual who cannot control drinking. These cognitions are hypothesized to facilitate a more severe relapse. This is an intriguing idea, but that may be all it is given that it has never been rigorously tested within the context of AA. The AVE hypothesis may in some ways have simply been another of the many parries and thrusts that occurred between AA advocates and behavior therapists during the controlled-drinking controversy of the 1970s. Supporting this conjecture, interest in the AVE hypothesis has faded noticeably in the scientific literature, as the heat from that fight has mercifully diminished.

Other concerns about AA have a stronger empirical foundation. Lifetime attendance is a hard teaching, and for some AA members it may have un-intended adverse consequences (Bean, 1975a). Research disconfirms the belief that everyone who drops out of AA eventually relapses. Of 780 patients who received 12-step-influenced treatment and were continuously abstinent for 1 year, two-thirds were not attending NA/AA at follow-up (Godlawski, Leukefeld, & Cloud, 1997). More generally, most formerly alcohol-dependent individuals are not AA affiliates, even in the USA, where the organization is most prevalent (Dawson, 1996; Hasin & Grant, 1995). AA dropout of course can be linked to relapse, but it can also be due to innocuous reasons (e.g., plain old boredom) or to positive ones, for example abstinence allowing greater participation in important work and family roles (Godlawski, Leukefeld, & Cloud, 1997). The relationship between how many AA meetings members attend and how well they are functioning is non-linear (Caldwell & Cutter, 1998; O'Leary *et al.*, 1980; Zywiak, Hoffman, & Floyd, 1999), which suggests that some members hit a plateau of AA benefit beyond which more involvement in itself will not further improve their lives. In cases where AA encourages unneeded involvement that competes with other important relationships and activities, it may be limiting members' lives. No systematic information exists on how often this occurs, or on what would have to be weighed against it, i.e., how many members stay in AA for longer than they deem necessary and benefit as a result.

AA's myth that "it works if you work it" also may have adverse consequences because it implies that anyone for whom AA is ineffective did not make a serious effort to "work the program." This idea would have appalled AA's co-founders, but in the author's observation some current AA members believe and express it nonetheless. Following the AA program is no guarantee of success. A US-based study of 927 individuals seeking alcohol treatment at a variety of agencies found that a significant minority had worked the AA program quite extensively (e.g., attended meetings, read literature, done service, been sponsored and sponsored others, etc.), but were nevertheless having severe drinking problems and were in need of treatment (Humphreys, Kaskutas, & Weisner, 1998a). For these patients, AA was clearly not sufficient intervention, even though they had made a good-faith effort to affiliate with it. If they had absorbed within AA meetings the sentiment that they had "failed AA" in some way, their recovery from alcohol problems may have been complicated by unreasonable self-blame and shame.

AA is the only addiction-related self-help organization that has a sufficiently developed research literature to discuss weaknesses and potential harms. One would suspect, however, that the above problems sometimes occur within other addiction-related self-help organizations as well. Investigating possible harms thus remains an important task for future research on self-help organizations, just as it does for professional treatment interventions.

Summary

The famous psychotherapist Carl Rogers used to say, "The facts are friendly." This same optimism might be paraphrased for present purposes as, "The facts we have so far are friendly." Surveying the literature as whole, empirical results are generally consistent with the conclusion that addiction-related self-help organizations have effects that are similar to those desired of professional treatment programs, such as reduced alcohol and drug use, diminished depression and anxiety, and improved social functioning.

These positive signs are not to be minimized, but should also be placed in context. The outcomes of many addiction-related self-help organizations, at least as far as the author could determine, have either never been evaluated or only have been evaluated using weak research designs. Other organizations, for example the All Nippon Sobriety Association and CTAs, have some data suggesting that alcohol-dependent members benefit from participation, but no data on the effects of participation on the non-alcoholic supporters who accompany their loved ones to meetings. Further, most outcome studies have been conducted in the USA, and may not generalize to other cultures, or indeed even to all parts of the USA, which is a large and diverse country in its own right.

The shortcomings of existent research evaluations point clearly toward improvements needed in the future, many of which are already under way. More studies must be longitudinal, include comparison groups, and have large samples. More studies must measure self-help participation as a broad construct and not count meetings as the only index of participation (Allen, 2000; Humphreys, Kaskutas, & Weisner, 1998b). Those who participate in, or simply have an interest in, addiction-related self-help organizations should take a role in helping evaluation researchers implement such improvements, which the author believes will increase rather than decrease confidence in the effects of self-help groups on "treatment-style" outcomes.

4

A different perspective on change in self-help organizations: spirituality, identity, life stories, friendship networks, and politicization

Moving beyond the treatment-outcome perspective

The previous chapter concluded that participation in addiction-related self-help groups can promote improvement on important clinical outcomes, for example reduced substance abuse, psychopathology, and medical comorbidities. From some perspectives, inquiry should stop here, because the likely value of self-help groups as a treatment for substance abuse has been established. However, the clinical treatment-evaluation perspective on self-help groups is a necessary but insufficient lens through which to understand the effects of self-help group involvement. Self-help organizations resemble professional treatments in some respects, but they also have unique aspects that can influence members in ways not typically associated with healthcare interventions, and indeed some members who have already resolved their substance-abuse problem seek out self-help groups specifically for these other benefits (Kaskutas, 1994, 1996a). This chapter evaluates the implications of this reality for outcomes that are not usually considered part of the clinical treatment-evaluation perspective.

A focus upon such outcomes follows naturally from the recognition that, in many ways, self-help organizations are more akin to communities than to treatments. Individuals participate in them for indefinite periods, structure social activities around them, actively work to keep them in existence, make friends within them, and so forth. In the process, members encounter a philosophy and set of values that some scholars termed the "mutual-help organization's "ideology"" (e.g., Antze, 1979; Cerclé, 1984; Kassel & Wagner, 1993; Suler, 1984). In this chapter the term "world view" will be employed instead because it conveys broader coverage than "ideology," which is often restricted in meaning to political matters (Humphreys, 1993b). Self-help organizations' world views offer perspectives on issues such as the nature of addiction, human relationships, the relationship of members to spiritual forces/God, and the nature of the self (Hayes, 2002; Humphreys, 1993b; Kennedy & Humphreys, 1994). Members who participate in self-help groups for extended periods thus not only encounter a program for addressing addiction, they also interact with a social network, philosophy, and set of behavioral norms that may affect their life far more broadly. The scope of evaluation must be broadened to do justice to such effects because they are rarely included in the treatment-evaluation paradigm: spiritual change, identity/life-story transformation, social network reconstruction, and politicization/empowerment.

Proposing that evaluators must broaden the "usual" treatment-evaluation perspective to fully understand the effects of self-help groups isn't to deny that the usual treatment-evaluation perspective could stand broadening in many treatment studies as well (Moos, Finney, & Cronkite, 1990). The four outcome domains discussed here are simply more important in self-help group evaluations than they are in even a broadened professional treatment-evaluation perspective, even though both self-help groups and treatments have behavioral norms, and organizing philosophies, and make efforts to address factors other than addiction. First, individuals rarely stay in contact with treatment programs for as long as they can with self-help groups, so it is harder for, say, identity transformation to occur in treatment programs. Second, the ethics of professionals prevent them from producing some of the outcomes to be discussed here. For example, self-help group members can befriend, date, or even marry each other; treatment professionals are typically bound not to enter into such relationships. Further, self-help group members may experience political empowerment by having control of the organization and using their influence to advocate for a political agenda, whereas professionals always control their own treatments, and patients are therefore kept in the role of service recipient.

Finally, and perhaps most importantly, the outcomes discussed here move well beyond clearly valenced health states into subjective questions of human values. Virtually no-one wants to have delirium tremens or major depression, and hence professionals are on safe moral and political ground when they strive to eliminate such problems in their patients' lives. But when professional change agents venture into patients' spiritual and political views, the objectivist stance possible with strictly medical outcomes deserts them (Humphreys, 2000b). Whether one should believe in God or not, or have a certain political perspective or not, or have a certain type of friends or not, are value-laded outcomes about which competent observers may disagree. Many healthcare professionals are appropriately wary about ranging into such territory, and, in parallel fashion, many citizens do not want publically funded experts inculcating certain political, social, and spiritual views under the rubric of health care. Democratic societies want healthcare professionals to return patients to health, but usually want subjective, existential questions about how citizens shall live resolved in voluntary sector organizations, such as families, political parties, communities, religious organizations, and, for present purposes, self-help groups.

None of what follows can establish that self-help groups are "effective" in the sense of bringing about changes that virtually all human beings would view as desirable. In examining how self-help groups may produce changes in spirituality, identity, friendships, and political views, this chapter is being descriptive rather than prescriptive. It remains for each observer to decide whether to be pleased, disappointed, or uninterested in how self-help groups change members beyond reducing their substance abuse and associated psychological and medical problems.

Scope and background

Researchers' academic disciplines strongly influence their choice of research method and focal questions. The majority of researchers discussed in the prior chapter were in psychiatry or psychology and preferred quantitative methods and clinically oriented measures. In contrast, the majority of authors of the research reviewed in this chapter are from fields such as sociology and anthropology. These investigators prefer qualitative data and ethnographic research methods, which brings a different set of strengths and weaknesses to the present chapter's research. The research in Chapter 3 was useful primarily for understanding normative change (e.g., average percentage decrease in alcohol consumption across participants). Research in this chapter primarily focuses on the subset of members that becomes involved with organizations for extended periods, including after substance abuse has remitted. A well-known scientific trade-off is therefore operative: research samples are smaller and less representative, but ideothetic and phenomenological changes are more richly described.

Almost all of the research summarized in this chapter was undertaken in 12-step self-help groups, and was conducted in the USA. Even more caution than usual is therefore warranted about the generalizability of the findings to all organizations and countries.

Finally, the focus here will be on our outcomes of interest, *in themselves*, even when they may mediate changes in clinical variables. Whereas, for example, the last chapter discussed how changes in friendship networks mediate the effect of self-help groups on substance use, this chapter examines the benefits of friendship-building in self-help groups per se. Adopting this perspective overcomes the limitations of the treatment-evaluation perspective in which such changes are only important to the extent that they eventually produce the "real outcomes" (i.e., those that seem important if self-help groups are equated with treatments).

Domain 1: spiritual change

Recovery from serious health problems is believed, across most cultures, to include a spiritual component (Galanter, 1997). Many self-help organizations emphasize the role of spirituality in recovery from substance-abuse problems, as mentioned in Chapter 2. Most members of these organizations consider spirituality to be a key site of world view transformation (Humphreys, 1993b). Several conceptual issues require clarification before empirical work on spiritual change can be discussed.

Definition of spiritual change

As a resident of California – ground zero for overuse of the term "spiritual" – the author is well aware that this term has acquired a great deal of surplus meaning. This vagary has crept into instrumentation, such that some spirituality assessment instruments include questions about exercise, sexual fulfillment, and belief in extrasensory perception (e.g., Christo & Franey, 1995; Whitfield, 1985). To have any meaning as a term, "spiritual change" cannot be equated with a good massage, a handful of crystals, an encouraging tarot card, or even feeling happy. Spiritual change will be more strictly defined here as transformations in an individual's relation to ultimate concerns, such as the meaning of life, suffering, and death, or as fundamental alterations in moral behavior based on changes in belief about the existence/non-existence of transcendent forces (e.g., a deity or deities, an immortal soul), and in some cases, experiences of a mystical or ecstatic nature. Under this definition, the finding that NA members believe that their spiritual Higher Power will help them with future stressors (Christo & Franey, 1995) would be considered relevant here, whereas the finding that Abstainers Club members are significantly more optimistic about the future than is the general population of Poland (Światkiewicz, 1992) would not. As a final delineation, spirituality is not isomorphic with the social phenomenon of religion, which can enhance, limit, or be unrelated to spiritual experience (Maslow, 1964; Miller, 1998).

*Is it possible and appropriate to study spiritual change
in self-help organizations?*

William Miller (1990) described spirituality as "the silent dimension" in addiction research, and for support of his argument one could point to some extensive academic studies of AA virtually omitting description of the spiritual aspects of the organization. Despite their central place in the lives of most human beings, spiritual concerns have rarely been given sustained and serious attention by addiction researchers. The social sciences have been at pains to differentiate themselves from religion and philosophy, in other words to be identified as "Sciences" with a capital "S" rather than as humanities. Other reasonable explanations for the lack of attention and occasional hostility of social scientists toward spiritual concerns have been put forward (e.g., Galanter, 1999; Miller, 1990; Morgan, 1999). The most important to discuss for present purposes is the nagging, subjective worry of some researchers that one cannot be a good scientist and take spirituality seriously at the same time.

William James, one of the more influential intellectuals of the twentieth century, provides an informative model of how scientific inquiry and interest in spirituality can co-exist. In *The Principles of Psychology* (1890/1981) and *The Varieties of Religious Experience* (1902/1985), James developed a pragmatic, descriptive, and respectful approach to religious and spiritual experience. Respect did not mean swallowing dogma, but simply taking the lived experience of human beings seriously as a source of data (E. Kurtz, 1999a). James studied relationships between observables (e.g., phenomenological changes in spiritual experience and changes in drinking behavior) without making any larger theological assumptions, a model that any good scientist could emulate. If one documents, for example, that individuals who come to believe in a God pray more often and also abstain from cocaine, one is firmly in the scientific tradition of natural history as long as one does not leap to conclusions about non-observables (e.g., that God exists and stops cocaine use when petitioned through prayer).

Many "tough-minded" psychologists and psychiatrists (e.g, Ellis & Schoenfeld, 1990) have difficulty in adopting such an open-minded and respectful attitude when studying spirituality, mystical experiences, and the like, because they have faith that no science can be built around phenomena that are subjective and impossible to see, hear, touch, or taste. As Mark Keller (1990) sagely observed, however, intellectual disciplines that lavish so much attention on "expectancies," "cognition," "alcoholic personality," and many other subjective phenomena that cannot be heard, touched, or tasted, don't really have the standing to throw stones in this case!

Spiritual change in AA and NA

AA involvement has often been likened to a "conversion" (e.g., Greil & Rudy, 1983; Petrunik, 1973), a term employed in divergent ways across and within scientific disciplines (Blasi, 1985). The common connotation of "conversion" as Zeus' thunderbolt is certainly inconsistent with the expectations of AA's founders (Maxwell, 1984) and with ethnographic research on a wide variety of 12-step organizations showing that most spiritual changes are gradual and non-dramatic (e.g., Denzin, 1987; Humphreys, 1993b; Kennedy, 1995; Kloos, 1999; Ronel, 1993; Rudy, 1986; Taylor, 1979).

Neither is spiritual change universal in AA. About one-fourth of a sample of AA members in Merseyside, England, considered the 12 steps to be "too religious" and 12% reported no changes at all in their beliefs and values (Jones, 1970). Only one out of five AA members living in Oxford Houses spontaneously reported changes in spirituality and belief in a Higher Power in open-ended interviews (Nealon-Woods *et al.*, 1995). Yet about two-thirds of a sample of highly involved AA members reported a greatly changed view of God in a different study, when prompted by specific questions about spirituality (Horstmann & Tonigan, 2000). Cultural factors also influence how AA/NA spirituality is experienced. Within the USA, African-American AA members more commonly report a spiritual awakening than Caucasians (Kaskutas *et al.*, 1999). In Sweden, a more secular society, less than a third of AA members express certainty that God exists (Mäkelä, 1993). Every estimate of the prevalence of spiritual change in AA/NA thus seems strongly influenced by how spirituality is defined and measured, what members are studied, and where the study is conducted.

AA/NA and the other 12-step organizations they have inspired (e.g., Overeaters Anonymous) place spiritual change at the heart of the recovery process. The 12 steps and other program literature, for example, devote more attention to spiritual matters than to substances themselves (Antze, 1987; Maton, 1989; Miller & Kurtz, 1994). AA/NA's spirituality emphasis on surrender differentiates it from some other self-help organizations. Highly involved AA members score higher on a measure of "surrender" than less involved AA members and RR members (Reinert *et al.*, 1995), and higher than SMART Recovery members on a range of spiritually related beliefs (Li, Strohm, & Feifer, 1998). Those AA members who experience spiritual surrender tend to describe it as an ego-deflating experience (Antze, 1987), that is, an admission that the member is not a God but has essential human limitations (e.g., can't control substance use; E. Kurtz, 1982). Spiritual change in AA/NA thus can have a paradoxical flavor, with some members describing it to researchers as *both* "ultimate degradation" and "miraculous and powerful" (Petrunik, 1973).

AA/NA members who experience spiritual change do not embrace any particular set of beliefs about God or a Higher Power, but tend to echo certain themes in the description of it (Antze, 1987). For example, God/Higher Power is often ascribed descriptors like "looking out for me," "a wise helper," or "a source of strength." Spiritual change is completely unrelated to external attributions for relapses (Christo & Franey, 1995), which again highlights that acceptance of a Higher Power in AA/NA need not imply an external locus of control for one's own behavior. Some AA/NA members base their concept of a Higher Power in a particular religion (e.g., "Jesus Christ is my Higher Power"), but do not typically use this language in group meetings. Forming a positive view of God/Higher Power may be a powerful healing experience for some committed AA/NA members, given that substance-dependent people are somewhat more likely than the general population to view God as punishing, judgemental, and angry and to feel alienated from mainline religions (Fowler, 1993; Gorsuch, 1993).

AA/NA spiritual transformation bears surprising similarity across cultures studied comparatively to date. In a series of studies of NA in Israel, Ronel (1997, 1998) documented that 12-step spirituality requires more creative reinterpretation for Jewish Israelis than it does for American Christians. Despite this difference in process, the outcomes are remarkably similar: Israeli NA members describe their conception of a Higher Power in ways that are hard to distinguish from the words of American AA members (Ronel & Humphreys, 1999).

In addition to directly affecting experience/views of the divine, AA and NA may influence intermediate variables often thought of as spiritual in nature. Only a smattering of studies and conceptual papers have addressed this topic. Denzin (1987), Hart (1999), and Ronel (1993) all cite examples of AA/NA members becoming less resentful and more forgiving, and O. Hobart Mowrer *et al.* (1975) argued that 12-step groups' emphasis on honesty and confession helps members to share shameful "pathogenic secrets" that separate them from the human community. A different study reported positive correlations between AA step-11-related practices (e.g., prayer and meditation) and purpose in life (Carroll, 1993). Finally, Gregory Bateson's (1971) widely cited formulation of AA as a context that helps alcoholics to replace a "symmetric" (e.g., competitive) relationship with the world with a "complementary" one is entirely consistent with the view that AA helps to minimize selfish traits that block a sense of harmony with the universal order (Brundage, 1985).

Possible negative effects of AA/NA spirituality   Some problem drinkers consider the spiritual aspects of AA to be a significant barrier to attending the organization (George & Tucker, 1996; Klaw & Humphreys, 2000). Systematic evidence is lacking on how serious a problem this poses in 12-step organizations. Dually diagnosed 12-step group attenders rated "Accepting a Higher Power" last on a list of 29 challenges of recovery in the only identified study of this issue, which is a reassuring finding (Laudet *et al.*, 2000a). Those twelve-step self-help group meetings observed by the author varied in their frequency and type of "God talk," so many individuals may deal with their discomfort by finding less spiritually oriented meetings rather than dropping out of the fellowship entirely.

Spiritual change in Al-Anon-affiliated ACA

One of the few studies of spiritual change in this organization found that a surprisingly small number of members mentioned spiritual concerns in interviews or in meetings (Cutter & Cutter, 1987). Participants in this study frequently referred to spirituality as something which they "tuned out" or as "the hardest part of the program" (Cutter & Cutter, 1987, p. 30). In contrast, in the author's own subsequent study of Al-Anon-affiliated ACA groups, 90% of members reported significant change in their spiritual outlook (Humphreys, 1993b). This pronounced difference in results may be explained in part by intensity of contact with the organization: the earlier study was based on one group observed for 12 consecutive weekly meetings, whereas the author's study was based on five groups observed for 120 meetings over a year and a half. The greater familiarity of the author to participants may have made them more comfortable in discussing spirituality. Further, the author's study was restricted to committed members of the organization, who may be the subset of participants most likely to experience spiritual change in Al-Anon-affiliated ACA groups (Cutter & Cutter, 1987). These observations again highlight how methodological characteristics influence results on the prevalence and depth of spiritual change in 12-step mutual-help groups.

Both studies found that many Al-Anon adult-children-focused group members considered spiritual change to be challenging even when they experienced it (Cutter & Cutter, 1987; Humphreys, 1993b). Most of Humphreys' (1993) sample entered Al-Anon with negative views about God, religion, and/or spirituality. This animadversion often stemmed from experiences of childhood victimization (e.g., incest). A typical comment was, "When I first came to adult children of alcoholics meetings, I was pretty much an atheist. My parents are church goers, so I always saw the hypocrisy in Christianity. You know – if you are so religious why do you treat me like this? I prayed as a child but then quit. I think I lost faith somewhere amidst the abuse." A related sentiment was, "I always knew there was a God, but was often annoyed at him for what he let happen." An additional indicator of spiritual alienation in the sample was that none of the 20 participants who completed life-story interviews were actively involved in a mainline church.

Spiritual change centered around contradictory impulses, namely the desire to surrender personal control to a Higher Power and the fear of doing so (Humphreys, 1993b). The former impulse tended to be driven by a wish not to feel responsible for all of life's problems and anxieties, and the desire to feel loved or cared for in a way one was not in childhood. The latter impulse stemmed more from fear that release of control would mean disaster and rejection by God, or from unwillingness to accept the humbling idea that the member could not control all of life's outcomes.

Humphreys (1993b) found no consistent pattern in the beliefs of members regarding their Higher Power. Some construed it in terms of a religion (e.g., Christianity, Bahá'i), some as a non-anthropomorphic, positive force (e.g. "A common flow of life", "nature"), and others in an idiosyncratic fashion.

Spiritual change in Women for Sobriety

Affirmation 8 reads: "the fundamental object of life is emotional and spiritual growth," which, along with some of Kirkpatrick's (1981) writings, implies that spiritual change is important in WFS. Between 40% and 60% of WFS members accede to close-ended statements along the lines of: "My sobriety comes from God" and "My spiritual program keeps me sober" (Kaskutas, 1992b). In contrast, when asked open-ended questions about the benefits of the organization, members rarely mention spiritual change, and when they do, often do so in the negative, e.g., express satisfaction that WFS requires no belief in, or reliance upon, God or a Higher Power (Kaskutas, 1994).

These conflicting findings must be understood in the light of many WFS members co-attending AA. These members endorse spiritual beliefs about sobriety at much higher levels than those who attend only WFS (Kaskutas, 1992b). Many members thus seem to "get their spirituality" from AA but rely on WFS for emotional support, an all-female environment, and an alternative perspective on their problems (Kaskutas, 1994).

Is there then a type of spiritual change unique to WFS, for example for those members who have never been to AA? The organization's founder made reference to the writings of Ralph Waldo Emerson and the Unity Movement, including those concerning the value of appreciating one's place in the natural world, and of bringing the mind into harmony with the good in life (Kirkpatrick, 1981). This sounds like some strains of Taoism and Buddhism, except that those belief systems consider minimization of the self as central to accepting one's (small) place in the flow of life, whereas WFS celebrates the importance of the individual, self-will, and self-mastery. Some members engage in spiritual practices, for example meditating and reflecting on their place in nature (Humphreys & Kaskutas, 1995), but the spiritual changes unique to WFS generally seem of a modest nature.

Understanding spiritual change in substance-abuse-related self-help organizations

The above findings are intriguing, and raise two provocative questions. First, how does spiritual change differ across those organizations that have been studied? Second, does this spiritual change imply that self-help organizations are cults or religions?

Contrasts in spiritual change across AA/NA, Al-Anon, and Women for Sobriety

Humphreys and Kaskutas (1995) concluded that world view transformation in the above organizations exists on a continuum, with poles representing counter-Enlightenment and Enlightenment-style spirituality. At one end, AA and NA mirror classic Christian warnings that self-concern and pride are barriers to a relationship with God. In these organizations, the journey to spiritual growth involves inculcation of humility and acceptance that, despite one's inherent flaws, one is nonetheless cared for by a spiritual Higher Power. At the other end of this continuum, WFS has a more modern, psychologized conception of spirituality in which low self-esteem and lack of self-appreciation are seen as barriers to spiritual growth. Hence, building up self-mastery and self-regard are the gateways to spirituality. Al-Anon-affiliated ACA groups are a middle ground between these extremes, in which building a connection to a Higher Power involves both self-minimization (e.g., accepting limits on one's control) and self-enhancement (e.g., accepting that one is worthy of spiritual love).

These different interpretations of spiritual change stem from how the founders of these organizations viewed members' problems (Humphreys & Kaskutas, 1995). AA's founders saw alcoholism as stemming from "self-will run riot," and believed that alcoholics could have no relationship to God until they admitted that they themselves were not masters of the universe. WFS's founder viewed women alcoholics as stigmatized and ashamed; to her, AA's approach was akin to trying to extinguish a fire with gasoline. WFS instead focused on building up the self as the way to connect to larger spiritual concerns. Al-Anon-affiliated ACA viewed its members as being self-abnegating in some ways, but selfish in others, and adopted a middle course. In summary, each of these self-help organizations' world views prescribes a different "cognitive antidote" to combat the problems they believed their members faced (cf. Antze, 1979).

Are spiritually based self-help organizations cults?

Self-help group involvement changes some members' spiritual outlook. This raises the question of whether such organizations should be understood as cults or religions, a much debated issue in the field (Alexander & Rollins, 1984; Bean, 1975b; Brandes, 2002; Bufe, 1991; Cain, 1967; Galanter, 1990; Jones, 1970; Madsen, 1974; Room, 1993; Rudy & Greil, 1988; Wright, 1997). This debate has important academic and policy implications. In the academic world, such analogizing may open new perspectives on self-help organizations and link them to other knowledge bases (e.g., on the sociology of religion). The policy world engages the question for a different reason. If spiritually oriented self-help groups are cults or religions, the US practice of legally mandating some individuals to attend them may violate the separation of state and religion, a perspective that has been upheld in some US court cases in recent years (Conlon, 1997).

The author will use the term "cult" in this discussion as it is commonly understood (e.g., organizations like the Jonestown/Guyana Group, The Aum Shinrikyo cult, etc.), recognizing that, in some academic disciplines, it has more specific meanings (e.g., in "crisis cult" theory; Madsen, 1974). Both cults and self-help organizations involve meeting in groups, changes in personal behavior and outlook, promises of improving members' lives, and a set of rituals. Yet were these characteristics sufficient to qualify an organization as a cult, many civic organizations (not to mention graduate training programs) would be cults. The pronounced differences between cults and self-help organizations are much more significant (Riessman & Carroll, 1995): self-help organizations do not have coercive recruitment and retention practices, do not take control of members' financial assets, and do not have a single, charismatic leader with power to dictate personal aspects of member's lives (e.g., with whom they may have social and sexual relationships). With one exception, no addiction-related self-help organization has ever used internal coercion and threats to promote retention, robbed members of their worldly possessions, or assumed global control over members' lives.

The exception alluded to was the Synanon communities in the USA in the mid 1970s. US Synanon was originally a creditable therapeutic community operated by former drug-dependent individuals, but eventually degenerated into a cult which used many coercive measures on its members (e.g., control of diet, forced sterilization, breakdown and reassignment of intimate couples), adopted a paranoid posture toward the world at large (e.g., stockpiling weapons, threatening critics of the organization), and elevated founder Charles Dederich to demi-god status (Janzen, 2001). Scholars view this disturbing cult as an aberration within the history of addiction-related self-help organizations (White, 1998), as do members of self-help organizations themselves. German Synanon, for example, specifically differentiated itself from US Synanon because it recognized that Dederich's cult had completely strayed outside the bounds of movement norms (Fredersdorf, 2000).

Are spiritually based self-help organizations religions?

The meaning of the word "religion" has changed drastically through history, and remains elusive today (Wulff, 1991). Wilfred C. Smith's (1963) definition of religion is among the most widely cited and respected and will be relied upon here: religion comprises a set of cumulative traditions (e.g., rituals, writings, stories, physical structures) and a set of beliefs about some transcendent reality in which participants have faith.

Self-help organizations certainly meet Smith's (1963) former criterion, but do not require specific beliefs about, or any faith in, any transcendent reality. This distinction can best be illuminated by contrasting 12-step self-help organizations to Christian religions. According to the distinguished theologian Raymond Brown (1997), Christianity is defined by particular beliefs, e.g., that Jesus of Nazareth was the Son of God, that he was crucified for human sins, and that he was resurrected on the third day. Individuals who read The New Testament, attend Christian church services, follow the Golden Rule, are charitable and moral, but reject all of the above beliefs are not Christians in the theological sense (Brown, 1997). Brown (1997) thus agrees with Smith (1963) that religion requires specific beliefs about a transcendent reality.

In contrast, within 12-step self-help groups, all beliefs yield to practical behavioral considerations about achieving and maintaining abstinence. If conflicts arise between those behaviors and a member's beliefs, the belief must yield. This reflects AA's American origin (Ronel, 1997), in that pragmatism has tended to trump conceptual philosophy in American culture. AA/NA do not mandate that any member should believe in the 12 steps, that alcoholism is a disease, that a Higher Power has any transcendent aspect, etc., as long as the desired practical result is obtained, i.e., the individual stops drinking and attends meetings (Bales, 1944; Maxwell, 1984). To wit, Mäkelä *et al.* (1996) have shown that the interpretation of AA's "Higher Power" varies enormously across and within cultures (see also Bloomfield, 1991). This aspect of AA – which upsets many religious individuals who wish the organization to communicate some specific dogma (e.g., Bridgman & McQueen, 1987) – was consciously put in place by the founders (E. Kurtz & Ketcham, 1992). They understood that any demands for belief would drive away at least some members, which would defeat the singleness of purpose of the organization (i.e., instilling sobriety in alcoholics). Indeed, the founders' concern about this issue was so great that they specifically stated in the second printing of "The Big Book" that spiritual experience was various and no particular type was necessary for recovery (Maxwell, 1984). To put it more simply, AA's founders knew that they were creating a mutual-help organization rather than a religion.

To illustrate this contrast with a concrete example, if a churchgoer asks a member of the clergy, "I follow the 10 Commandments, care for the sick, am honest with those I love, but I think Jesus was not the son of God but just a nice person like any other nice person – am I a Christian?", the clergy member will answer "No" (Brown, 1997). If an AA meeting attender asks her sponsor, "I go to meetings and I am trying to stop drinking, but in my mind my Higher Power is just my AA friends, there is no supernatural deity out there taking care of me, and the 12 steps are a bunch of superstitious blather – am I an AA member?", the sponsor will answer "Yes."

One scholar (Trevino, 1992) made the intriguing argument that AA does meet the criteria of religion as described by the sociologist Emile Durkheim. For example, it treats collective conscience as a redeeming force that can overcome individual egotism, has sacred rituals and symbols, offers behavioral proscriptions and prescriptions, and values altruism. But religion as commonly experienced is not the same as religion as conceptualized by French sociologists (E. Kurtz, 1999b). Under Durkheim's definition, which excludes faith in specific transcendent realities, "religion" becomes so broad as a term that it is difficult to say what is *not* a religion (i.e., Physicians for Social Responsibility would be a religion, for example).

Thus, despite their references to spirituality, Higher Power, and God, spiritually oriented self-help organizations are not religions or cults (the fact that governments have, at times, suppressed them as such notwithstanding; see "Soviets seek US help in combating alcoholism," Holden, 1989). The changes just described are thus best considered as of a spiritual rather than religious nature.

Domain 2: identity and life-story transformation

The self is a key site of world view transformation for committed members of self-help organizations (Humphreys, 1993b). Self-help group participants are exposed to new perspectives on their identities (Cerclé, 1984; Rudy, 1986), some of which they may absorb into their conception of who they are. Members may come to think of themselves as "a co-dependent," "an oppressed woman," "a committed member of The Links," "in recovery," or as a "victim of alcoholism," to name only a few possibilities. They may also come to see themselves as possessing certain character traits, for example grandiosity, humility, manipulativeness, selflessness, and the like. A small but rich group of studies has documented such changes in identity among self-help group members.

Greater incorporation into personal identity of the status the organization addresses is a commonly identified outcome of addiction-related self-help group participation. What are the consequences of embracing a status that includes a problem, for example "recovering drug addict" or "adult child of an alcoholic"? Kip Kingree and colleagues conducted an interesting sequence of studies of this question (Kingree & Ruback, 1994; Kingree & Thompson, 2000). In an initial series of three correlational studies, degree of participation in 12-step self-help groups was positively associated with more strongly embracing into personal identity the status of being the child of the alcoholic. For example, highly involved members of Al-Anon-affiliated ACA groups usually agreed with statements like, "I have been handicapped as a result of my parent's alcoholism," and "People who are not children of an alcoholic do not really understand me." These findings *seem* to imply that self-help group participation leads to greater inculcation of the identity of adult child of an alcoholic, which in turn causes greater self-stigmatization. Yet in the initial series of studies, involvement in 12-step groups for adult children of alcoholics was either unrelated or positively related to self-esteem, and negatively related to depression.

A subsequent randomized study helped to clarify these seemingly contradictory results (Kingree & Thompson, 2000). Adult children of alcoholics who were randomized to attend self-help groups during alcoholism treatment reported greater embracement of adult child status and greater belief that this status conferred *positive* benefits, such as being more emotionally sensitive and better at coping with stress. These positive perceptions predicted reduced depression over time. The initial correlational findings were probably the result of those individuals who feel more status-stigmatized being more likely to attend groups rather than the group causing them to stigmatize themselves (Trice & Roman, 1970). Once involved, they are persuaded to view some previously problematic aspects of their identity as positive, which benefits them.

In evaluating whether incorporation of an addiction into identity during self-help group participation is positive or negative, the basis of comparison provided by how societies at large view addicted people must be borne in mind. All societies stigmatize addictive behavior to some degree and use it to assign individuals to disreputable social categories (e.g., "shiftless drunks," "dope fiends," etc.). Many people with substance-abuse problems therefore incorporate addiction into their identity and experience resultant shame and despair whether they ever attend a self-help group or not (Bean, 1975a). Although many self-help organizations encourage members to see addiction as essential to identity, they present a more positive picture of what this means – for example, that, as a recovering alcoholic, the member can help others to recover, is better at handling his defects (Sadler, 1977), or has become more mature. Similar identity-change processes occur within self-help organizations for people with serious psychiatric disorders (Kloos, 1999).

Self-help group members may also come to view organizational membership as central to their self-conception. The process of becoming committed to a self-help group includes incorporation of organizational and shared goals and values into personal identity (Donovan, 1984). This involves some willingness to give up individualistic interests, and to devote time to helping the group operate (Trice & Roman, 1970). The positive effects of such transformations are obvious: they make group affiliation more affirming and help to sustain membership, which in turn helps to sustain recovery. The downside, however, may be when organizational and individual needs are in conflict. In AA's world view, for example, there is no legitimate "exit strategy" (Trice & Roman, 1970) because the organization maintains that lifetime AA involvement is necessary to keep alcoholism in remission. Ramona Asher (1992) makes the same criticism about Al-Anon, arguing that when a member leaves there is "a knowing assumption that she'll be back because eventually she will need to be" (p. 193). Long-term members who identify strongly with the organization but who also desire to reduce meeting attendance may experience psychological distress over the decision. The frequency and severity of such conflicts between substance abusers' identity as organizational members and other pro-social identities they may wish to live out has not been studied systematically, and thus remains a subject of speculation.

Identity changes within self-help organizations have also been examined under the rubric of "life-story reconstruction." "Life story" is a term from narrative studies which conveys a more active and temporally based sense of human identity as something evolving over time and being actively constructed throughout, for example one's sense of where one came from, why life unfolded as it did, where the future will lead, and what it all means (Rappaport, 1993; Schank, 1990). This concept has unique value for analyzing addiction-related self-help groups because so much of group dialogue is in the form of stories, and members typically work actively to create a new life narrative that brings meaning to their addiction and their recovery from it (Humphreys, 2000a; Rasmussen & Capaldi, 1990). Researchers vary (usually by discipline) on whether they prefer to understand changing self-conceptions through the lens and argot of life-story reconstruction, identity change, or self-transformation, but the ground they cover collectively is similar enough for their work to be discussed together.

Carole Cain (1991) presented an intriguing analysis of the life stories of AA members who had different lengths of membership. Members' life stories became progressively more like the prototypical AA stories presented in AA texts as their length of AA membership increased. Highly experienced members' stories had the same general structure as the stories of Bill Wilson, Dr. Robert Smith, and other early AA members, and were more likely to exemplify key AA beliefs such as the destructive effects of "self-will run riot" and the uncontrollable nature of alcoholism. AA members' life stories, though grounded in real experiences and having unique aspects (see Aaltonen & Mäkelä, 1994), "grow with the telling" in a fashion that makes the member's life story more congruent with AA's world view and shared community narrative (Cain, 1991). Humphreys (2000a) documented similar processes in AA, and added the caution that to say that AA members change their life stories over time is not to demean them. Given the limits of human memory and perception, constructing a perfectly accurate life story is impossible (Ross, 1989) – and perhaps also undesirable!

AA members aid the process of life-story construction by providing differential reinforcement of AA-consonant stories in group meetings (Cain, 1991). AA members pay more attention when such stories were told, build upon them in their own stories, ignore discordant aspects, and so forth (Humphreys, 2000a). Parallel group communication processes have been observed in self-help groups for chronically mentally ill people (Jurik, 1987).

Constructing a new life story helps to solidify AA member's identity as alcoholics and as AA members (Cain, 1991; Humphreys, 2000a). As AA members incorporate their drinking years into a longer account of their life story – particularly when they can make their defects the subject of self-puncturing humor – their mastery over these experiences increases, and the break between the actively alcoholic and recovering phases of life is solidified (Denzin, 1987). Story telling has the further organizational benefit of helping to hook newcomers (Humphreys, 2000a; Maxwell, 1984). Indeed, AA's founders were so aware of this possibility that they insisted upon multiple speakers in meetings to give the organization multiple chances of finding a story that is sufficiently similar to a newcomer's that it would attract their interest (Alcoholics Anonymous, 1976; Maxwell, 1984).

The life-story reconstruction opportunities of self-help organizations can be perceived as life-story *destruction* demands by some individuals, and can drive them away. Many members of MM, for example, rejected AA because they felt that its narrative about their problems was inappropriate to their life experiences (Klaw & Humphreys, 2000). MM's philosophy was more congenial to these individuals because it allowed them to construct their life story around self-control, personal power, and rationality rather than the typical AA story themes of humility, surrender, and spirituality (Klaw & Humphreys, 2000).

Life-story reconstruction has been studied only within a few addiction self-help groups, but evidence from other fields suggests that it is a general phenomenon within social settings. For example, cross-person similarity in life stories has also been found in studies of self-help organizations for psychiatric problems and in church communities (Rappaport, 1993). Some of this similarity can be attributed to self-selection, but for committed members, interchange between community narratives and personal life stories is a dynamic process with true causal power.

Domain 3: friendship-network composition

Improved social skills, greater support for abstinence, and enhanced psychosocial functioning are important clinical-style outcomes of self-help group participation that were reviewed in Chapter 3. Friendship-network composition is a different outcome that may be orthogonal to social functioning and substance-abuse outcomes. It refers to who one views as a friend, spends time with, has fun with, cares about, trusts, and so forth. Addiction-related self-help group members appreciate friendship as an independent potential benefit of involvement. For example, alcoholic women who rely on AA to prevent relapse may continue to attend WFS meetings specifically because of their friendships with women alcoholics (Kaskutas, 1994).

Conclusions in this area must be tentative, because only a handful of studies are available and all have been conducted on US-based samples of 12-step group participants. Also, all findings must be interpreted with awareness that the process of ceasing substance abuse often involves the loss of friends (Ribisl, 1997), particularly those with whom drug and alcohol abuse was a valued, shared activity. Because social-network contraction and reorganization are likely to occur in the process of recovery of substance abuse, causal effects of mutual help group participation on friendships are harder to pinpoint.

Studies to date all suggest that 12-step self-help group members incorporate other group members into their friendship networks. For example, in a longitudinal study of African-American patients ($n = 253$, 64% male), those who affiliated with 12-step self-help groups after treatment had an identical number of friends at intake and 1-year follow-up, compared with an average 18% reduction for non-members over the same period (Humphreys, Mavis, & Stöffelmayr, 1994). In a similar study of over 2000 male substance-abuse patients, significant self-help group involvement increased number of close friends over a 1-year treatment and recovery process, and these findings were invariant across different racial/ethnic groups (Humphreys & Noke, 1997). Likewise, virtually all AA members in the UK make friends within AA, and the likelihood of making "a lot" of such friends increases with years of involvement (Robinson, 1979).

In Humphreys and Noke's (1997) study, the composition of friendship networks was profoundly affected by post-treatment self-help group involvement. Of patients who had close friends at 1-year follow-up, about half had almost no 12-step friends in their friendship networks (mean = 3% of friends), whereas the other half had networks almost entirely composed of 12-step members (mean = 91% of friends). Thus, the sample split into two separate worlds of friendship. Whether this insularity will persist over time is unknown. In the author's observation, many successful 12-step group affiliates begin to branch out socially and psychologically beyond the organization once sobriety is firmly established. However, the frequency and patterning of this process has not been carefully studied.

A few researchers have tried to characterize friendships between 12-step group members. Based on qualitative interviews with 20 gay male AA members, Robert Kus (1991) described 12-step friendships as more respectful, supportive, and trusting than friendships prior to membership. Similar conclusions were reached in a qualitative, ethnographic study of 20 (50% male) committed members of Al-Anon-affiliated ACA groups (Humphreys, 1993b). Quantitative research indicates that friendship networks composed of 12-step group members have more frequent contact and are perceived by participants as more supportive, trusting, and lacking in criticism than friendship networks that do not include 12-step group members (Humphreys & Noke, 1997; see also, Humphreys, Finney, & Moos, 1994; Toumbourou *et al.*, 2002).

Thus far the research paints a rosy picture, but there may be some thorns as well. Sponsors often advise 12-step group members to avoid places and people associated with substance abuse, so it is neither surprising nor necessarily lamentable that group involvement often reduces contact with substance-abusing friends (Kus, 1991; Trice, 1955). However, what about non-substance-abusing, supportive social network members? To the author's knowledge, no researcher has systematically evaluated the potentially adverse effects of social immersion in 12-step groups upon the member's spouse, family, and friends. The famous anecdote of Lois Wilson's shoe, described in Chapter 2, echoes similar statements that the author has occasionally heard family members make over the years, e.g., "He used to be with his drinking buddies all the time, now he's with his AA buddies all the time, either way I never see him so what's the difference?". The shared language and experience that facilitates friendship within self-help groups may make those not "in the know" feel left out and resentful, at least during the period when an individual has just joined a self-help group and is most intensely involved in it. Understanding the experiences of such individuals remains an important task for future research, and may help underscore the fact that, unlike improved social skills or better psychosocial functioning, change in friendship-network composition is an outcome whose worth may be appraised differently by competent observers.

Domain 4: politicization and empowerment

Self-help groups' influence on political activism has been well documented outside the addiction field (Chesler & Chesney, 1988; Humphreys, 1997c). The experience of coming together in support groups to talk about being abused in the psychiatric treatment system was an important part of the politicization process of many mental health consumer activists (Zinman, Harp, & Budd, 1987). Similarly, many successful political advocacy organizations evolved from an earlier stage as a mutual-help organization (e.g., Association for Retarded Citizens; Riessman & Carroll, 1995).

Little research has been conducted on whether participation in addiction-related self-help organizations affects political activity. Organizations such as Free Life and The Links engage in political activism, so they probably increase their members' political activity. One would further assume that reducing or ceasing alcohol consumption per se should indirectly support political activity by giving group members more time, energy, and resources to focus in this area.

Because of their tradition of taking no position on outside political issues, 12-step organizations represent a different situation than that of politically active mutual-help organizations. Essays pillorying 12-step organizations from a variety of political perspectives appear regularly in scientific and popular literature (see, e.g., Kaminer, 1992; Morrell, 1996; Rapping, 1997; Rieff, 1991). The specific complaints of these commentaries vary, but all of them fault 12-step organizations for allegedly leading millions of members away from whatever the commentator considers to be appropriate and correct political views, be it conservatism, progressivism, Christian evangelism, feminism, rugged individualism, or Marxism. In most cases, the argument rests on two assumptions about 12-step organizations: (1) they present a perspective on human problems that may clash with particular political perspectives, and (2) they prevent members from engaging in political activity.

The first assumption has merit. The perspective of 12-step mutual-help organizations on human suffering and how it may be addressed differs from that advanced in Christian conservative political parties, Marxist cells, progressive activist organizations, etc. Illuminating such differences, as for example Janice Haaken (1993) does in a coruscating feminist analysis of Al-Anon family groups, is an important goal for scholars of self-help organizations. But condemning 12-step organizations for such differences per se, as do commentators such as Wendy Kaminer (1992), borders on narcissistic reasoning because it assumes that one's own political views embody Absolute Truth and that therefore any individual or organization that does not endorse them is to be deplored or pitied. Readers who doubt the infallibility of their own political views are unlikely to find such critiques persuasive.

The second assumption is based on a misunderstanding of the 12 traditions. The tradition of avoiding political stances refers only to the 12-step organization itself and not to individual members who wish to speak and act for themselves (Alcoholics Anonymous, 1952/1953). Affiliation with 12-step mutual-help groups does not therefore inherently conflict with political activity, as demonstrated in the lives of individuals such as National Council on Alcoholism founder Marty Mann and US Senator Harold Hughes (L. F. Kurtz, 1997b; Room; 1997). Many 12-step group members are not politically active, but there is no evidence that their rate of political activity differs from the general population. On balance then, the most reasonable conclusion one can make about 12-step mutual-help group involvement and political activity is that they are orthogonal phenomena.

Summary

Collectively, the conclusions of this chapter must plant their feet on a small beachhead, because only a handful of studies have been conducted in each domain and many organizations remain entirely unexamined. Research to date is nonetheless intriguing, for it suggests that self-help group participation may have effects that are more commonly associated with voluntary associations and communities than with healthcare interventions. The challenge for self-help scholars is not to allow the many advantages of the treatment-evaluation perspective to blinker them to these other types of effects, which are worthy of continued study and reflection.

5

How should government agencies, healthcare organizations, and clinicians interact with self-help organizations?

External support of self-help organizations: benefits and risks

This chapter discusses different types of interactions between self-help organizations and government agencies, healthcare organizations, and individual clinicians. A sizable literature addresses how some techniques, ideas, and language from self-help groups can be combined with professional treatment interventions, for example writings on "recovery sensitive counseling" (Morgan, 1995), "social model" recovery programs (Borkman, Kaskutas, & Barrows, 1996), and therapeutic communities (De Leon, 1999). The present chapter complements such works by focusing instead on how supportive outsiders should interact with self-help organizations in cases where each party is autonomous and maintains its own sphere of operation.

Individual citizens of democratic societies do not need any complex rationale for attending self-help groups any more than they need one to go bowling. They wish to engage in a voluntary activity, and so they do so. In contrast, outside entities from the other sectors of society, for example public health departments, hospitals, and government agencies, are usually chary of intervening in the voluntary sector. In all free societies, citizens expect some compelling rationale before accepting extensive outside intervention into civil society (e.g., their marriages, families, religious organizations, and voluntary activities). What could justify anything other than a laissez faire policy toward self-help organizations? Two rationales come easily to mind: (1) direct health benefits and (2) healthcare cost reductions.

Direct health benefits

Chapter 3 concluded that self-help group participation can reduce substance use, psychopathology, and attendant social suffering and disorder. The scientific evidence reviewed in Chapter 3 has an obvious public policy implication: as self-help organizations can improve public health, governments and professionals should support them as one method of reaching this worthy, shared goal.

Healthcare cost reductions

Healthcare systems are under significant fiscal strain in virtually every society mentioned in this book. Treatment providers are being asked to offer more and more services despite having fewer and fewer resources. Societies that hope to ease demand on healthcare systems while simultaneously protecting their citizens' well-being may realize both these goals by promoting self-help group participation.

Determining whether self-help group participation decreases healthcare utilization requires high quality data. Kessler and colleagues' (1997, 1999) cross-sectional surveys of self-help group and healthcare participation were major contributions to knowledge, but offered the questionable conclusion that because self-help group participation and treatment utilization are positively correlated, self-help groups do not reduce demand for health care (Kessler, Mickelson, & Zhao 1997, p. 33). This conclusion cannot logically be drawn from cross-sectional associations, any more than one could conclude that there is no competition for customers among fastfood restaurant chains because people who eat at McDonald's also often eat at Burger King (Humphreys, 1998). The discussion here is therefore restricted to what Kessler *et al.* (1999) acknowledge is a more useful source of data, namely prospective studies with comparison groups and repeated measures of healthcare utilization and self-help group involvement. Such research provides ample evidence that self-help group participation lowers utilization of professional health care.

For example, Galanter (1984; Galanter, Castaneda, & Salamon, 1987) randomly assigned 235 alcohol-dependent patients to one of two treatment units in the same hospital. The units were identical except that the experimental unit had 50% less staffing and implemented self-help group principles. Despite the significantly lower costs of the experimental unit, it produced patient outcomes that were equal or superior to the more professionalized treatment unit.

Similar results were obtained in prospective studies by Humphreys and Moos (1996, 2001). In the first evaluation project, problem-drinking individuals who initially sought out AA ($n = 135$) had 45% lower alcohol-related healthcare costs than comparable individuals who initially sought out an outpatient treatment provider ($n = 66$). Yet clinical outcomes were equally positive in both groups. These results were replicated in a quasi-experimental study of 1774 drug and alcohol inpatients. Patients treated in programs that worked vigorously to facilitate involvement in 12-step self-help groups had 39% lower healthcare costs (about US$5000 per person) in the year following discharge than patients treated in programs not making such efforts. This difference was present even though patients in the two types of programs did not differ at treatment intake on prior healthcare utilization, psychiatric problems, substance-abuse problems, or demographic characteristics (Humphreys & Moos, 2001). Reduction in healthcare utilization again produced no ill-health cost consequences. Outcomes were, in fact, somewhat better for patients whose self-help group involvement had been facilitated. Importantly, while the first of these studies was conducted on a sample that was primarily Caucasian, 50% female, and had minimal concurrent drug problems, the sample of the replication study was primarily composed of racial and ethnic minorities, was all male, and included patients dependent on drugs, alcohol, or both. Confidence in these results is also increased by Walsh *et al.* (1991) identifying a healthcare cost offset of AA participation in their randomized trial (described in Chapter 3).

The above findings are not surprising when one considers that a large amount of healthcare utilization is orthogonal to physical health status. Many healthcare visits are attributable not to diagnosable medical disorders but to worry, loneliness, boredom, discouragement, and other problems that one does not need a doctorate in medicine to address (Surgeon General's Workshop on Self-Help and Public Health, 1990). When individuals join self-help groups, they begin to rely more on fellow group members for such needs (Kleist, 1990), experience less anxiety about their health problem (Nicholaichuk & Wollert, 1989), and become better educated about what health care can and cannot offer (Trojan, 1989). All of these benefits reduce unnecessary medical care utilization. This decreases healthcare costs and reserves health care – which is often a scarce commodity for addicted people – for individuals who actually need it.

Healthcare cost reductions are also a clearly established outcome in naturalistic, quasi-experimental, and experimental studies of self-help organizations for psychiatric disorders (Davidson *et al.*, 1997; Fairweather & Fergus, 1993; Gordon *et al.*, 1979; Kyrouz & Humphreys, 1996). Given that it is in evidence irrespective of the disorder studied and the evaluation design employed, the healthcare cost offset effect may be considered sufficiently robust to guide public policy decisions.

Acknowledging healthcare cost offsets need not imply an acceptance of public policy economic reductionism, i.e., that money is the measure of all that is good. The value of self-help groups, or any other voluntary organization that enriches social life, and health, cannot be reduced to what the state and other payers save in healthcare costs. Healthcare offsets are important only because they can justify public investment in initiatives that may help more self-help organizations offer citizens the benefits of participation, many of which have no economic implication but enrich life nonetheless.

Challenges to collaboration

The self-help group literature includes many calls for self-help organization/ professional-governmental collaboration that do not consider the barriers and risks to such arrangements (Katz, 1981). Organizations that follow the 12 traditions (e.g., AA) have been most concerned about those potential problems identified below, but they are potentially relevant to mutual-help organizations of all types.

Risks to self-help organizations

Self-help groups' grassroots nature, informality, and communal spirit are part of what makes them appealing to members. Borkman (2001) argues that these essential qualities were often minimized in the UK when the government began directly funding mutual-help organizations. Self-help organizations sometimes had to become more formalized and bureaucratized, engage in data monitoring, and be subject to some outside oversight in order to obtain government funding (Borkman, 2001).

Funding for the quasi-professionalization of self-help group functions can also remove opportunities for voluntary service work (e.g. staffing telephone referral lines), which some organizations (e.g., AA and NA) view as an essential part of their recovery program. Self-help organizations also risk losing flexibility when they need to be responsive to governmental authorities rather than only to their own members (Robinson & Henry, 1977; Room, 1997). Contact with the more powerful organizational cultures of governments and healthcare organizations might lead self-help organizations over time to adopt the culture of the traditional service agencies to which they were originally intended to be an alternative (Gartner & Riessman, 1976).

A risk also exists that the state, healthcare organizations, or individual professionals will exploit self-help organizations (Meissen *et al.*, 2000). Healthcare organizations and government agencies may try to use self-help groups as an inexpensive dumping ground for anyone who is difficult, undesirable, or uninsured (Branckaerts & Deneke, 1983; Riessman, 1987). For example, the author is aware of treatment agencies and correctional facilities that have brought a literal busload of individuals to community-based, 12-step self-help groups for "substance abuse treatment." Needless to say, when a few dozen coerced individuals with no understanding of, or interest in, AA are dumped into a group with 10 voluntary members, the character of the meeting is often ruined to the detriment of both coerced and voluntary attendees (Borkman, 1999; Speiglman, 1994).

Risks to society

Those who would design public policies concerning self-help organizations should be cognizant that some political leaders wax romantic about the virtues of individual and community effort as a way to deny public responsibilities (Robinson & Henry, 1977). In this vein, Katz (1986) charges that Thatcherite government officials in the UK spoke positively about "self-help, voluntary initiatives" for the sole purpose of discrediting publically provided services. A related concern more specific to the USA is that privately owned and managed healthcare companies will reduce healthcare benefits on the grounds that the enrolled populations can address their health problems in self-help groups.

Too much collaboration between government, professionals, and self-help groups can harm civil society in ways less tangible than service reductions. Independent voluntary associations are essential to healthy democracy (Putnam, 1993). Self-help organizations instantiate legitimate, public suspicions of an overreaching state and the prescriptions of alleged experts (Katz, 1986). These tendencies vary in strength across societies, but they always have an important democratic function when state and citizen interests are not isomorphic.

Some observers (Trojan, Halves, & Wetendorf 1986) considered health-related self-help groups as one of the few forms of strong consumer participation in the healthcare system in West Germany, and that such a counterweight was needed as a "prosecutor" of the healthcare system. Room (1997) makes the similar point that governments often pursue controls on alcohol only because of strong pressure applied by independent voluntary sector organizations. Such a perspective can be oversold – most self-help organizations in the UK are pro status quo for example (Robinson & Henry, 1977) – but it should not be overlooked. If self-help groups become dependent on outside funding, or too intermingled with the official government, they may become co-opted and lose their advocacy potential (Richardson, 1983b). An analysis of the Dutch situation offered the related concern that outside entities may support only those self-help organizations that do not challenge current institutions and policies (Harberden & Raymakers, 1986). Such a situation would weaken self-help organizations' ability to serve as a support for those citizens who feel wronged by, or otherwise wish to turn their backs on, state-provided services (Trojan, Halves, & Wetendorf 1986). One could add that, were the state and self-help sectors unified, individuals who felt mistreated by, or wished to turn their backs on, self-help groups would have no option either. Because voluntary sector, private sector, and public sector organizations serve as checks upon each other in democratic societies, policies in this area should never be formulated from the perspective that self-help organizations exist only to benefit the state and its health and welfare apparatus (Bakker & Karel, 1983).

Summary: moving carefully forward

The above detailing of risks should not dissuade efforts to create self-help supportive policies, but should make them more informed. The potential benefits to public health and reductions in healthcare demand are sufficiently large to justify efforts by governments, healthcare organizations, and individual clinicians to support self-help organizations. The rest of this chapter provides examples of policies that may maximize the benefits of collaboration while minimizing the risks.

Strategies for governmental support of addiction-related self-help organizations

The following international review of self-help supportive policies is intended to illuminate a range of alternatives rather than offer a universal prescription. Surveying the great diversity of self-help organizations in the Netherlands, Jan Branckaerts and Christiane Deneke (1983) emphasize the importance of policy being flexible and sensitive to local needs. Commentators in the UK likewise assert that global rules of interaction are problematic because mutual-help organizations and the organizations that interact with them vary dramatically in size, stability, mission, and degree of interest in outside systems (Grant & Wenger, 1983; Richardson, 1983a, b).

The observation that all policy efforts occur in a cultural and temporal context is apposite here for two reasons. First, whereas previous chapters were weighted toward US research, most useful policy and policy writing comes from Belgium, Canada, Germany (pre- and post-unification), the Netherlands, and the UK, with only a few additions from other societies discussed in this book. Second, much of the most detailed writing took place in the 1980s (e.g., the edited books of Hatch & Kickbush, 1983, and Humble & Unell, 1989), when self-help groups became a focus of major interest for a number of important bodies, including the WHO, the European Community Council of Ministers, the Canadian Department of National Health and Welfare, the UK National Health Service, and the US Office of the Surgeon General. One is dealing, of course, with a considerably changed world today.

Legitimating rhetoric

As in many areas of social policy, reality has not always matched rhetoric in the self-help area. President Carter's Commission on Mental Health, Surgeon Generals Koop's Workshop on Self-Help and Public Health (1990), and the important document, "*Healthy People 2000*" (US Department of Health and Human Services, 1990), all called for greater support of self-help organizations in the USA, but none of them provided it directly or seem to have stimulated other entities to do so. Government leaders in the Netherlands have also made many supportive pronouncements about self-help organizations without offering any real policy to match (Bakker & Karel, 1983; Harberden & Raymakers; 1986). Citizens should, of course, hold political leaders responsible for following words with action, but rhetoric can have value in itself. When high-profile individuals and organizations speak publically in support of self-help organizations (e.g., World Health Organization, 1995), they legitimate them simply by taking them seriously rather than viewing them as unprofessional, unimportant, or "cute." Further, positive words in the absence of action are preferable to an openly dismissive attitude toward addiction-related self-help organizations, which, for example, used to predominate in the UK (Long, 1985). Such condescension undermines self-help organizations' relationships with professionals and help-seekers.

   Differences between positive rhetoric and useful policy about self-help organizations sometimes reflect a dismissive attitude by policy makers, but in many cases they are a product of well-intended leaders not knowing precisely what to do (Unell, 1989). As many well-informed committees and workgroups have discovered, making public policy is easier when one controls the object of the policy (e.g., a government agency) than when one does not (e.g., a self-help group). Self-help supportive policy is new terrain for many governments, and an extensive record of accumulated wisdom is not available. Indeed, most governments do not yet have information about what policies may be *worse* than doing nothing. Positive rhetoric cannot be an excuse for indefinitely avoiding policy decisions, but it does at least create a positive atmosphere in which the required creative thinking about self-help supportive policies can occur.

Direct financial support of self-help organizations

A number of governments have directly funded mutual-help organizations operated by "consumer/survivors" of psychiatric services. National and some provincial governments in Canada, for example, have for years funded consumer-operated organizations that seek to serve as an empowering, alternative, helping resource to people with serious psychological problems (Nelson, 1994; Trainor *et al.*, 1997). Direct funding of addiction-related mutual-help organizations has been less common.

The difference in funding for substance abuse versus psychiatric self-help organizations is a direct consequence of the 12 traditions, which forbid the acceptance of direct outside financial support. The 12 traditions not only influence AA and its sister societies, but also indirectly affect non-12-step tradition organizations. The All Nippon Sobriety Association endures significant criticism from 12-tradition-influenced self-help organizations in Japan about its acceptance of grants (Oka, 1994b), and the relationship of Abstainers Clubs and AA in Poland has been strained by the Clubs' direct government funding (Woronowicz, 1992). Such funds no doubt facilitate many self-help group activities, e.g., securing meeting space and advertising, but the author's belief is that the risks of government/self-help-organization collaboration outlined earlier are greatest when money is involved.

A private foundation has given millions of guilders to Dutch self-help organizations over the years (Bakker & Karel, 1983). Foundation funding may present less danger of co-opting self-help organizations relative to governmental monies, although this question has not been systematically studied.

A policy of directly funding addiction-related self-help organizations confronts numerous barriers. Many organizations will not accept outside financial support. Others may damage their relationships with other self-help organizations or be co-opted by accepting government funding. Providing resources to self-help organizations other than cash per se (i.e., "in kind" resources) and investing in self-help supportive infrastructure therefore seem to be more attractive policy options.

In-kind resource provision

Some self-help organizations may resent, as paternalistic, the implication that "they can't be trusted with money" or the relatively lower flexibility of in-kind resources. On the positive side, most in-kind resources can be provided with a minimum of paperwork and monitoring, which is very attractive to many mutual-help organizations. Further, in-kind resources are already matched to current organizational activities (e.g., meeting space provided for group meetings) and therefore present less risk of distracting members from their core mission than might, for example, a grant focused upon offering some service the organization has not historically provided.

Opening institutions to self-help groups

Self-help groups are inexpensive to convene, but do of course require physical space, chairs, lights, heat, and the like. Most large institutions have empty rooms available during the hours self-help groups typically meet. Some also have spare offices that can be made available to self-help group leaders. Such institutions include hospitals, clinics, criminal justice facilities, religious organizations, community centers, libraries, and educational facilities. Japan is a model of such "space sharing," in which most alcoholism treatment units have a close relationship with Danshukai and/or AA, as do almost all local government public health centers, social welfare offices, and mental health centers (Suwaki, 1988).

Institutional openness should go beyond passive willingness to offer meeting space if so importuned. Institutions can pro-actively invite self-help groups to demonstrate their potential value to residents. Many addiction self-help organizations are willing to hold group meetings in hospitals, treatment programs, and correctional facilities that current institution residents may attend or observe. Yet a surprisingly high number of administrators do not avail themselves of this low-cost opportunity to assist their wards.

Other in-kind resources

Common in-kind resources needed by groups are telephone answering service, photocopying, hosting of their website, publication of meeting announcements, and printing of materials. Well-resourced self-help group support organizations (described below) can offer such services, but such organizations are not available in some societies and regions. Government and private organizations should consider making such in-kind resources directly available to self-help groups in these cases, as has been done, for example, by a printing press in Amsterdam (Bakker & Karel, 1983).

Investments in self-help support organizations

Non-profit organizations dedicated to supporting self-help groups have different names across societies. They vary in specialty as well, with some serving all self-help groups and others focusing on specific types (e.g., mental-health-related groups). Some are free-standing, whereas others are integrated into large agencies that support voluntary services of all forms. Self-help support organizations are distinct from self-help organizations, but their voluntary and paid staffs usually include some self-help group members. Self-help support agency workers understand the strengths, weaknesses, and unique character of self-help groups, which of course facilitates the agency's task of supporting groups without co-opting or harming them.

Most support for self-help groups in the UK is coordinated through agencies with oversight over many voluntary helping programs (Hastie, 2000). The Nottingham Self-Help Support Center, founded by Judy Wilson, is probably the most important UK organization focused exclusively on support for self-help organizations. The center maintains a database on self-help groups, provides technical assistance to groups and to professionals who work with them, supports the development of new groups, promotes self-help concepts, and facilitates networking between self-help groups and professional healthcare agencies (Hastie, 2000). Self-help clearinghouses in the USA and Germany engage in similar activities (Hermalin, 1986; Matzat, 2002). The American Self-Help Clearinghouse is particularly well known for its Herculean directory of several thousand self-help organizations, which is available on the World Wide Web as well as in print form (Madara, 1986; in press).

Self-help support organizations become more effective over time as they become familiar to professionals, self-help organizations, and the general public. For example, the number of telephone callers to the American Self-Help Clearinghouse has increased significantly over its existence (Madara, in press), and the self-help group movement in the Flanders region of Belgium was strengthened when a university began to become known as a center of self-help-related information (Branckaerts, 1983). The benefits of organizational persistence make it all the more unfortunate that self-help support organizations are often forced to live hand-to-mouth and year-to-year (Hastie, 2000). Lack of consistent financial support in some countries stems from the "category problem," i.e., funding streams are linked to individual illnesses (Bakker & Karel, 1983; Branckaerts & Deneke, 1983). Self-help support organizations span a range of health concerns, and, while therefore of potential interest to all, sometimes they are seen as not the responsibility of any one funding agency in particular (Branckaerts & Richardson, 1989). Governments could surmount the category problem by creating funding earmarks for self-help support organizations within general public health budgets. In addition to increasing the visibility of such organizations, consistent support would allow self-help clearinghouses to build the trusting relationships and unique skills required to work effectively with self-help groups.

The presence or absence of a national plan also strongly influences the effectiveness of self-help support organizations. Federalism is on the wane in the USA, so support for self-help clearinghouses is provided mainly at the state and local level. This produces a patchwork of services that varies from place to place, depending on funding. Borkman (1997) estimated that only 9 of the 50 US states have complete clearinghouse coverage; most of the 66 existent clearinghouses in the USA are local and cover only a few counties or a metropolitan area. Spain endures a similar situation. Catalonia has a well-funded, high-quality self-help clearinghouse that provides extensive support to groups, but Andalucia does not. In contrast, because Germany has made a national commitment to supporting self-help groups, self-help support organizations are stronger and more consistently available throughout the country (Matzat, 1989, 2002).

Media and information campaigns

Announcements about self-help groups tend to be one or two printed lines about meeting and location times in free or commercial newspapers. Such announcements are useful in that any public outreach efforts that attract new members increase the likelihood that a self-help group will survive over time (Wituk *et al.*, 2002). However, more visible uses of media and public information campaigns are also possible, as the selected examples below demonstrate.

A regularly broadcast television show in Poland features Abstainers Club members who tell the story of their alcohol problem and testify to the benefits of club participation (Branckaerts, 1983; Mäkelä *et al.*, 1996). Similar programs about other self-help organizations have been broadcast in Belgium, which has also been the site of large fairs/exhibitions for self-help organizations to present their approaches, views, and activities (Branckaerts, 1983).

Leonard Jason directed the only program of research that evaluated the effects of media campaigns on self-help group participation (Jason, 1985; Jason, La Pointe, & Billingham, 1986). Jason hosted a widely broadcast Chicago radio program about self-help organizations. Each week, a different self-help organization held a live group meeting on the air and then responded to telephone calls from listeners. A multiple baseline design study documented significant increases in contacts with each self-help organization in the weeks following its turn on the broadcast. Overeaters Anonymous, for example, received over 200 telephone calls as a result of the broadcast (Jason, La Pointe, & Billingham, 1986). Jason added an interesting footnote to his report of this project. The radio station's sales manager attempted to cancel the program because its self-help spirit undercut the idea that one should solve personal and health problems by purchasing commercial products and professional services (i.e., businesses who buy advertising on radio). Public financial support for self-help-promoting broadcast media may be necessary to overcome such challenges when they arise.

Outside fiscal support is also necessary at times because individual self-help organizations usually do not have the resources to conduct extensive media campaigns. Individual groups may also lack the infrastructure to handle a large response to a media promotion effort. One approach the author is currently evaluating, with the aid of a private foundation, is to create a coalition of self-help group leaders and provide them with resources to design shared media announcements and a shared contact point (i.e., a telephone number where information on groups may be provided). Experience to date has been positive for those self-help groups involved (Humphreys *et al.*, 2002).

Training and education for professional helpers

The US Surgeon General's Workshop on Self-Help and Public Health (1990) asked its 200 expert participants (about 50% self-help group leaders, 50% research, clinical, and policy professionals) to rate the most important policy options for supporting self-help groups. The highest rated was: "Incorporate information and experiential knowledge about self-help in the training and practice of professionals." As governmental and healthcare organizations are already involved in the funding and oversight of professional training, they have a natural route to achieve this worthy goal.

The process of professional training programs is as important as the content. In an illuminating study of graduate students in clinical psychology and social work, students had more positive attitudes toward, and wished to collaborate with, self-help groups if they perceived that their faculty mentors had such attitudes (Meissen, Mason, & Gleason, 1991). Whoever offers training about self-help groups should therefore believe in what they are doing. One approach that would accomplish this goal, and also ensure that some self-help supportive resources actually go to groups themselves, is to have self-help group members serve as trainers of professionals.

Policies for disseminating information related to self-help groups, for example directories of local groups, should recognize that many "professional helpers" are not doctors or psychologists. Many people seek advice about emotional problems from bartenders, hairdressers, and other informal helpers who should be covered by dissemination efforts. Self-help-related information should also be provided to religious leaders, who are highly trusted by disadvantaged groups in many societies (e.g., low-income individuals, recent immigrants) and are typically interested in learning about local self-help groups (Jason *et al.*, 1988).

Research support

Science has an important role in illuminating the nature, benefits, and shortcomings of self-help organizations and policies toward them. Evaluators taking on this important task should consider the particular nature of self-help organizations when selecting research methods and questions, rather than assuming that whatever is used to study treatment services would automatically be appropriate (Humphreys & Rappaport, 1994; Surgeon General's Workshop on Self-Help and Public Health, 1990). As the previous chapters show, quantitative methods may be informative in some instances, whereas in others qualitative approaches will be superior, depending on the question being asked. Collaboration between the evaluation researcher and the self-help organization may also be appropriate (cf. Kaufmann, 1994; Lavoie, Farquharson, & Kennedy, 1994; Rappaport *et al.*, 1985; Simmons, 1992; Wong & Chan, 1994). Collaborating addiction-related self-help groups can be excellent recruiting sites for hard-to-reach populations (Toumbourou, Hamilton, & Smith, 1994), may be willing to open their operations to outside inspection (see, e.g., Rudy, 1986), can encourage members to participate in the study (Kaskutas, 1992a), and can develop research questions that an outsider may not realize are important.

A wide range of scientific questions can be asked about self-help groups, as the projects reviewed in this book demonstrate. The three areas below are particular priorities for the purpose of informing policy development.

Needs assessments of self-help organizations

Policies toward self-help organizations should not be designed solely from the perspective of outsiders. Needs assessments are one method of including the voice of group members in the policy formation process. Two model studies in this area were conducted by a research team at the Self-Help Network of Kansas, led by Greg Meissen. The first was an interview study of 90 randomly selected mutual-help group leaders whose organizations addressed a variety of concerns, including addiction (Meissen, Gleason, & Embree, 1991). Participants reported on what they needed from self-help clearinghouses. Improving public awareness of groups was by far the most commonly mentioned need (61% of respondents), followed by more referrals to the group (31%), help with fund-raising activities (20%), need for in-kind resources such as speakers or meeting places (19%), and training for groups (16%).

This research team took a different perspective in a second study that asked what 23 mental-health-related groups needed from the larger statewide self-help organization in which they were nested (Gaston & Meissen, 2000). Primary needs reported were continued political advocacy by, and greater contact with, the statewide organization. Groups also wanted help in recruiting new members and encouraging current members to take on more group maintenance responsibilities. Consistent with Karl Weick's (1976) concept of "loosely coupled systems," the local groups valued the identification with the state organization and wanted advice and assistance, but also wanted significant autonomy in matters affecting their group.

More needs assessments of self-help groups would be informative, particularly in the addiction area. Results to date show that self-help groups prefer support that comes with minimal interference in their group process. In other words, potential self-help supporters should approach groups as collaborators and not as underlings.

Stakeholder-based evaluations of self-help groups and self-help supportive policies

Much of this book has been devoted to evaluations of the effects of self-help group participation, so there is no need to belabor the point that such studies will continue to be important to self-help organizations, both to demonstrate their positive effects and to draw attention to their ineffective practices. Future evaluations should also assess the impact of policies designed to support self-help organizations.

As the many studies in this book show, the effects of self-help groups can be evaluated in terms of how groups influence substance-use behavior, subjective phenomena, healthcare utilization, external professionals, etc. These varied impacts may not be valued by interested parties in the same way. One developing field that might guide such work is stakeholder-based evaluation (Bryk, 1983) in which the different interests in different outcomes (potentially including contradictory ones) are explicitly recognized and addressed. This perspective is particularly valuable for studying self-help groups, whose perspective on desirable outcomes may differ more from researchers' perspectives than would that of their fellow professionals in a treatment study (Lieberman & Bond, 1979).

National data-gathering efforts

Many societies undertake national surveys that assess utilization of formal and informal health care for different disorders. Such efforts often ignore mutual-help organizations as a source of help (Powell, 1994). When questions about self-help groups are added to inventories about help-seeking options, they are almost always less numerous, less well designed, and less sensitive than those devoted to professional services, even in societies like the USA where self-help group participation dwarfs professional service utilization (Powell, 1994). This professional-centric bias understates the importance of self-help organizations and provides poor information for policy planning. National surveys of addiction-related self-help groups and their members could aid policy development in all of the societies discussed in this book. Researchers conducting such surveys would be wise to make use of advisory panels composed of self-help group members who can describe what self-help organizations exist, where they are located, and how useful information can be elicited from them.

Self-help groups as participants in relevant policy arenas

The WHO recommended that self-help organizations be represented on governmental advisory and policy boards that address their concerns (Branckaerts & Deneke, 1983). This is sage counsel provided that representatives of self-help organizations on such boards are genuinely in touch with the actual needs and perspectives of their constituent self-help groups (Harberden & Raymakers, 1986).

The most significant recent development on this front occurred in Germany in 2000. The "red–green" coalition of Social Democrats and Green Party implemented new legislation concerning self-help initiatives in health, which, in addition to providing a large budget for such activities (over 70 million DM/year), mandated that self-help group members be involved in decision-making surrounding the funds and their use (Matzat, 2002). The author believes that no parallel level of funding or formal influence exists for mutual-help organizations in any other society, so the next years in Germany will be an important policy experiment to observe.

Strategies for individual clinicians and treatment agencies

Individual clinicians and treatment agencies may engage in some of the strategies suggested above for governments. Possibilities and issues unique to them receive separate attention below.

The need for a collaborative mindset

This section can best be introduced with an example of failed collaboration. Francine Lavoie (1983) relates the story of a mutual-help group of widows in Quebec. Local health professionals felt confident that they understood the organization, despite never having had any contact with it. They tended to dismiss it as a leisure club or to abuse it with inappropriate referrals. The few professionals who offered any help to the group wanted only to serve as expert lecturers to the presumably benighted participants. Other professionals publically criticized the self-help group for its "lack of interest in the real needs of widows." Lavoie asks rhetorically how a group of widows could be so ignorant of the needs of widows.

The effectiveness of widow peer-helping programs has been clearly established in multiple randomized clinical trials (Marmar *et al.*, 1988; Silverman, 1970; Tudiver *et al.*, 1992; Vachon *et al.*, 1980), using both no treatment control conditions and comparison with much more costly professional psychiatric treatments. The attitudes and behaviors Lavoie describes are therefore not driven by rationality or data, but by professional culture and attitudes toward non-professionals.

Some professionals believe that all self-help groups need their intervention, and that such professional intervention will, without doubt, improve the otherwise hopelessly inferior group (Salzer, Rappaport, & Segre, 1999; Van der Avort & Van Harberden, 1985). As Thomas Powell (1987, 1990) made clear in two important books on self-help/professional collaboration, techniques for collaboration are worth discussing only in the context of a collaborative mindset. All the techniques in the world will not produce collaboration in the absence of fundamental respect (Humphreys, 1999).

The challenge for each health professional is to accept that, even though mutual-help organizations may, by their very existence, embody a critique of professional services, they are still worthy of a collaborative relationship (Gartner & Riessman, 1976). Recalling that professionals and self-help organizations share the noble goal of improving the lives of afflicted individuals can facilitate such a collaborative spirit.

Professionals' attitudes toward self-help groups

Alexandre Laudet's thorough literature review established that positive global attitudes about addiction-related self-help groups among professionals often co-exist with other beliefs, behaviors, attitudes, and knowledge gaps that limit collaboration in specific cases. A study of (West) German treatment professionals supported this conclusion. Surface-level questions to professionals elicited extremely positive responses about self-help groups and lay-care initiatives generally, but in intensive interviews, the same professionals expressed fears about their patients becoming too independent and about their own funding being jeopardized by the success of voluntary initiatives (Deneke, 1983). Many professionals also fear losing status if self-help groups are successful (Matzat, 2002; McKnight, 1995), and, that self-help groups may undermine their authority with patients, for example by suggesting that members question their doctor's advice (Chesler & Chesney, 1995; Robinson & Henry, 1977). Just as self-help groups sometimes fear being controlled by professionals, professionals sometimes fear losing control to self-help groups, which can inhibit collaboration (Balgopal, Ephross, & Vassil, 1986; L. F. Kurtz, 1985).

Surveys of health professionals in Australia (e.g., Woff *et al.*, 1996), Germany (e.g., Deneke, 1983), and the USA (e.g., Hermalin *et al.*, 1979) show that agreement with "apple pie items" (e.g., "Self-help groups can be helpful") does not necessarily betoken any real cooperation. Only a very small proportion (e.g., 1–2%) of clinical staff express blanket negative attitudes about self-help organizations, yet at the same time only a minority have any significant interaction with them (e.g., speaking to a group, inviting them to meet at the clinic, asking them for specific information that could improve the specificity of referrals). Such barriers are in some cases attributable to lack of knowledge rather than lack of interest, and therefore may be ameliorated by educational programs (Deneke, 1983; Hermalin *et al.*, 1979). One optimistic sign for the substance-abuse field is that health professionals know more about addiction-related self-help organizations than about any other type of self-help organization (Deneke, 1983).

Turning more specifically to attitudes about AA, most professionals have positive views of AA (Ogborne, 1996), even though the field includes some vocal critics who see AA as ineffective, too dominant, over-rated, and under-evaluated (see, e.g., Bufe, 1991; Clark, 1987; Tournier, 1979). Linda Kurtz (1984) noted, for example, that some professionals view AA as too "ideological" (she went on to add, "as though professionals did not also adhere to ideologies"). Professional discipline does not exert an overwhelming impact on attitudes toward AA, but physicians tend to hold somewhat more positive views than other professions (see, e.g., Du Pont, 1999), particularly psychologists. For example, US emergency-room physicians consider AA to be more effective for alcoholism than mental health professionals, and also agree highly on the effectiveness of AA (Chang, Astrachan, & Bryant, 1994, reported the significance of this finding at $P = 0.000000005$!). Australian postgraduate medical trainees rate

AA as better-supported empirically than a wide variety of professional interventions, including medication, inpatient treatment, psychotherapies, and brief interventions (Roche, et al., 1995). Physicians may be more comfortable with AA than other professionals because it overlaps less with their clinical activities and therefore engenders little sense of competition. The same principle may help to account for psychologists having, generally, somewhat lower regard for 12-step self-help groups (Humphreys *et al.*, 1996).

Attitudes of self-help groups toward professionals

An anti-professional camp within the psychiatric self-help movement strives to seize control of treatment away from what it considers to be a repressive, uncaring, ineffective set of professional institutions (Trainor *et al.*, 1997). Such sentiments are not normative within mental health self-help groups or within the self-help group movement as a whole. In original research conducted in Canada and in an international literature review, Miriam Stewart (1990; Stewart *et al.*, 1994) documented that most self-help group members hold positive views of health professionals. Group members appreciate that health professionals provide a useful service for their problem, and may advocate to see such professional services maintained (see, e.g., Chesler & Chesney, 1995). Self-help group affiliates also value professionals as a useful source of information and referrals (Knight *et al.*, 1980). Although some members entered mutual-help groups out of disappointment with professionals, an even larger proportion did so to supplement the health care they continued to receive. Such positive attitudes are common within 12-step substance-abuse-related self-help organizations. Most AA members consider the adoption of 12-step techniques by professional agencies as flattery rather than a threat (L. F. Kurtz, 1984).

These generally positive attitudes co-exist in self-help groups with concerns that some health professionals would rather be "on top than on tap." Stewart's research showed that this fear has a rational basis. Less than 10% of self-help group members report that "leader/director" was an appropriate role for professionals in their groups, compared with over half of professionals. Indeed, professionals endorsed this power role as more appropriate than any other, including consultant, liaison, helper, referrer, and legitimator (Stewart *et al.*, 1994).

Avenues for collaboration

Fear and unfamiliarity are worth overcoming because individual professionals and self-help groups can derive rich rewards from collaboration. The remainder of this chapter discusses some avenues for cooperation, focusing heavily on a common, mutually valued, and low-cost opportunity: referral of current patients to self-help organizations.

Making effective referrals

Clinicians often wish to help their substance-abusing patients reap the benefits of self-help group participation. Professional addiction treatment services are often too expensive and scarce to provide the long-term, extensive support that many patients need. As a low cost, self-sustaining resource, self-help organizations can fill this void in the continuum of care (Humphreys & Tucker, 2002). Self-help groups can also provide resources that treatments usually do not. Psychotherapy groups in treatment usually do not include stable, drug-free role models, whereas addiction-related self-help groups usually do (Spitz, 1987). Self-help group involvement can also offer a community and a way of living that is hard to create within a treatment setting (Robinson & Henry, 1977). Making a different point, Margaret Bean (1975a) notes that many professionals find substance-dependent patients exasperating and do not want them as referrals. Self-help groups give clinicians the option of referring addicted patients to someone who will actually be glad to see them!

Professionals should not limit themselves to thinking of self-help group referral only as "aftercare." Facilitating affiliation and monitoring any problems with it are easier if treatment is still occurring. Self-help group involvement can also be encouraged *before* treatment, for example when patients are on a waiting list. The arrival of the "stepped care" concept in addiction treatment supports the use of the least invasive intervention first (Sobell & Sobell, 1999). A brief self-help group facilitation intervention for waiting-list patients would be a good investment of resources, because by the time treatment slots become available, some patients may be doing sufficiently well in a self-help group for the treatment provider to grant an open slot to a more severe case. When self-help groups serve as "the first line of defense," addiction treatment resources can be allocated more rationally (Humphreys, 1998).

Empirically supported referral strategies

Most research on effective facilitation of self-help group involvement has been conducted with 12-step groups. The only exception the author could identify is a Japanese study that brought alcoholic patients' family members to the inpatient ward to non-confrontationally express concern and support. The intervention increased family members' and patients' attendance at Danshukai meetings (Ino & Hayasida, 2000).

A "personal touch" also enhances referrals to 12-step self-help groups, as demonstrated in a randomized clinical trial conducted in an alcohol outpatient clinic (Sisson & Mallams, 1981). Control patients ($n = 10$) were assigned to a "standard referral" in which the clinician gave them a list of meeting locations and suggested attendance. None of these patients attended a self-help group meeting. In contrast, the self-help group attendance rate was 100% in the "enhanced referral" condition, in which the clinician made an in-session phone call to a 12-step group member who talked with the patient and agreed to accompany her/him to a meeting (Sisson & Mallams, 1981). Personal contact with a current group member also augments the power of referrals to self-help groups for serious psychiatric disorders (Powell *et al.*, 2000).

An evaluation of an unsuccessful referral intervention provided useful information to professionals on how *not* to arrange personal contact with current self-help group members (Caison, 1997). Current AA/NA members were asked by a professional to telephone recently discharged substance-abuse inpatients several times a week, and to rate these inpatients "self-efficacy for self-help group attendance" using various psychological Likert scales. Inpatients in this experimental condition were no more likely to attend AA/NA meetings than controls who had no callers assigned to them. This intervention failed because it asked experienced AA/NA members to apply foreign psychological concepts, language, and methods. This was neither comfortable nor appropriate for the AA/NA members, as evidenced by 72% of them not completing all the requested telephone calls. This study shows that trying to convert 12-step group members into junior psychologists/social workers is not effective. Healthcare providers should allow self-help organization members to use their own methods and language to link patients to groups.

Finally, referral to 12-step groups is more likely to generate affiliation after treatment if 12-step ideas are presented during treatment (see Humphreys, 1999, for a review). Practical advice and exercises for accomplishing this are included in Project MATCH's "*Twelve Step Facilitation Handbook*," which is available free of charge from the US National Institute on Alcohol Abuse and Alcoholism (Nowinski, Baker, & Carroll, 1995).

Consultation and an experimental attitude over a priori matching

The negative findings of Project MATCH notwithstanding (Project MATCH Research Group, 1997, 1998), many clinicians are still entranced with the idea that addiction treatments will one day be selected and outcome optimized by using a priori decision rules. A wiser and more empirically sound approach is to construe the self-help group referral process as a consultation, in which patient preferences, needs, and experiences enter in more significantly than they would under strict a priori matching rules. Clinical judgement of course plays a role – for example, a clinician would not encourage severely dependent patients to attend MM – but to the extent possible the clinician's task is to present patients with a menu of reasonable alternatives rather than a single recommendation.

Referring clinicians should ideally be aware of what self-help organizations are available locally and how groups vary within available organizations. A clinician who knows which local AA meetings are specialty-focused (e.g., for women, gay people, etc.), which are first-step meetings, and which have distinct social-process traditions (e.g., extensive "God talk," strong sponsorship) can provide a better referral than a clinician who does not know. Referring treatment providers should present self-help group attendance options to the patient along with a recommendation reflecting their best clinical judgement. After the patient and clinician have agreed to a course of action (e.g., to try one SMART Recovery and one AA meeting in the next week), the clinician can supplement encouragement to attend with practical problem-solving on how to do so, including connecting the patient to an experienced member if appropriate.

Knowing for certain, a priori, which self-help option will work best is not necessary for making a recommendation. Self-help group meetings are not surgery: attending a meeting that doesn't fit one's needs and desires is never fatal or expensive. Clinicians and patients can safely adopt an experimental attitude rather than obsess in advance of experience over which organization or group is the perfect "match." In the author's clinical experience, this approach diffuses defensiveness and resistance on the part of patients, who rarely object to a modest proposal like, "Why don't you visit one or two self-help groups before next week and we can talk then about how you think it went." The process of experimentation and consultation should be continued until the patient finds a comfortable niche, or determines that self-help groups are simply not a useful aid to recovery.

Common worries about referral

The weak centralized control within self-help organizations by design allows local chapters to adapt to the needs of different cultures and special populations. Self-help groups have broad appeal as a result, attracting, for example, members of diverse racial and ethnic backgrounds (Alcoholics Anonymous, 2002; Caldwell, 1983; Davis, 1994; Harper, 1976; Hillhouse & Fiorentine,

2001; Hoffman, 1994; Hudson, 1985; Humphreys, Mavis, & Stöffelmayr, 1994; Humphreys & Woods, 1993; Jilek-Aall, 1981; Kaskutas *et al.*, 1999; Mäkelä *et al.*, 1996; Simoni & Perez, 1995; Tonigan, Connors, & Miller, 1998), and gays and lesbians (Bloomfield, 1990, 1991; Hall, 1996; Kus, 1991; Saulnier, 1994). Nevertheless, many clinicians have important concerns about referring patients from a few populations either to 12-step self-help groups in particular or to self-help groups in general.

Dual-diagnosis patients

Discussion of whether addicted patients with serious psychiatric comorbidities should be referred to self-help groups centers on two concerns. Fears that 12-step self-help groups may discourage medication compliance are addressed in a separate section below. This section discusses problems in group affiliation that may stem from psychiatric disorder per se. US and Australian survey data indicate that clinicians worry about whether self-help group members will reject or exclude individuals who display severe psychiatric symptoms (Humphreys, 1997b; Woff *et al.*, 1996). Such social exclusion could have negative consequences for patients but also for their relationship with the clinician who made the referral.

The only data on this issue come from studies of AA, and thankfully, do not support inordinate fears of referral. AA members may, in fact, be more tolerant of psychiatric patients than the general population. Almost all of a sample of 125 AA contact persons had personally had positive experiences when interacting with mentally ill individuals, and believed that dually diagnosed people could be valuable AA members (Meissen *et al.*, 1999). A study of dually diagnosed inpatients also had encouraging results: most were comfortable with AA's approach and meetings, a high proportion (37%) had attended regularly, and schizophrenic spectrum disorder patients were as likely to affiliate as were those with less severe forms of psychopathology (Pristach & Smith, 1999). This latter finding is particularly remarkable because most people are uncomfortable around individuals who have marked positive symptoms (e.g., hallucinations, delusions; see Powell *et al.*, 1996). AA members may be more tolerant than the general population because alcoholics themselves often experience florid psychiatric symptoms during heavy consumption of or withdrawal from alcohol.

Project MATCH (Project MATCH Research Group, 1997, 1998) hypothesized that alcohol patients with high comorbid psychopathology would have poorer outcomes with twelve-step facilitation (TSF) counseling than with other treatments. This hypothesis was not supported; such patients benefitted from TSF and from their subsequent self-help group affiliation.

The above results support a clinical policy of referring dually diagnosed patients to self-help groups and then monitoring progress and potential problems with affiliation. The menu of self-help referral options for addicted patients who have comorbid psychiatric disorders should include organizations for dually diagnosed people (Vogel *et al.*, 1998; Zaslav, 1993), dual-recovery-focused meetings of AA/NA (L. F. Kurtz *et al.*, 1995), and psychiatric self-help organizations (e.g., Recovery Inc., Depressive and Manic-Depressive Association, GROW). Referrals should be supportive and educative but not coercive (Powell *et al.*, 1996). Dually diagnosed patients are as justifiably put off by aggressive pushing of self-help concepts as are other addicted patients (Noordsy *et al.*, 1994).

Patients on medications and 12-step programs

12-step literature (e.g., Alcoholics Anonymous, 1984) explicitly supports outside medical treatment and enjoins members from "playing doctor." Indeed, AA co-founder Bill Wilson once asked methadone pioneer Vincent Dole to develop a similar medication for alcoholics (Payte, 1997). Some individual members of 12-step organizations nevertheless equate "clean and sober" with the absence of medications as well as drugs and alcohol. Buxton, Smith, & Seymour (1987) describe several cases of one 12-step group member encouraging another to stop taking psychiatric medication, with adverse consequences. Similarly, the new 12-step fellowship "Methadone Anonymous" would not have formed had its members felt completely comfortable combining methadone maintenance with NA attendance (Gilman, Galanter, & Dermatis, 2001). Clinicians whose patients are taking methadone, anti-depressants, or other psychotropic medications thus sometimes have reservations about referrals to 12-step self-help organizations.

These are legitimate concerns, but must be understood in context. First, there is no evidence that 12-step group members are any more skeptical of psychotropic medication than is the general public. Many people are critical of patients who take medications, including those non-12-step treatment professionals who make the inane charge about methadone maintenance that, "You can't treat drug addiction with drugs." Second, as anyone who has provided health care is aware, there are times when individuals benefit significantly by taking themselves off medication without medical permission. After all, in the USA alone, about 100 000 patients a year die as a result of taking prescribed medication *as directed* (Lazarou, Pomeranz, & Corey, 1998). One should therefore not fall into the error of assuming that patients' lives invariably improve in direct proportion to the number of medications they take.

Two studies provide systematic data on these issues. In a study of AA contact persons, 93% agreed that dually diagnosed members should continue taking their psychiatric medication, reflecting perhaps AA's efforts to publicize its policy in this area (Meissen *et al.*, 1999). Robert Rychtarik *et al.* (2000) found that only 29% of a sample of 277 AA members had ever been encouraged by another member to stop taking a medication of any form, and on average, this had occurred 7 years previously. Only 12% of this sample would recommend that a fellow member should stop taking a hypothetical new anti-relapse medication (Rychtarik, *et al.*, 2000).

At least in AA in the USA, 12-step self-help group members are unlikely to be condemned for taking medications. One would hope that other 12-step organizations, for example NA and DTR, follow AA's model of clarifying to members the acceptability of prescribed medication. Clinicians working with medicated clients should refer such patients to 12-step organizations when appropriate, but should monitor medication effectiveness, compliance, and any experienced stigmatization over time.

Patients who are averse to 12-step spirituality

The previous chapter reviewed evidence indicating that 12-step organizations are not religions, and that the perceived importance and interpretation of 12-step spirituality vary widely across members. However, 12-step groups do discuss spirituality and God, and sometimes have a Christian overtone. These aspects of AA/NA are off-putting to some patients and therefore should be a concern for clinicians (Fletcher, 2001; McCrady & Irvine, 1989; Tonigan, Miller, & Schermer, in press). Patients who are averse to 12-step spirituality comprise two groups: Atheists and affiliates of religions other than Christianity.

Atheism is one of the very few patient characteristics that US clinicians consider to be a strong contraindication of referral to AA/NA (Humphreys, 1997b). Yet in a study of over 3000 patients, theists and non-theists were equally likely to follow through on a referral to a 12-step group and to benefit from participation on substance-use outcomes (Winzelberg & Humphreys, 1999). Clinicians must therefore be wary of a self-fulfilling prophecy, i.e., not referring atheists and therefore never seeing them benefit from participation.

Atheistic patients may be referred to secular mutual-help organizations such as SMART Recovery and SOS as well as to 12-step organizations. Referrals to non-12-step organizations have important diagnostic value because they help to determine whether a patient's objection to "God talk" in AA/NA is genuine or is actually just an objection to taking any steps toward changing addictive behavior. More than once the author has had the experience of hearing allegedly motivated addicted patients lament, "I'd like to go to AA, but I hate the spiritual part," and then see them react with horror to learn that non-spiritual alternatives are available for them to attend!

Religious patients who follow a faith other than the Christianity that influenced the 12 steps may be uncomfortable with AA/NA spirituality. Many Jewish substance abusers in Israel (Ronel, 1993, 1997) and in the USA (Master, 1989) participate comfortably in 12-step groups and derive benefit from them, even though this at times involves re-interpreting aspects of 12-step spirituality to fit their own religious views. There seems, therefore, to be no general bar to Jewish participation in 12-step self-help groups, but if it arises with a specific patient, the clinician has several options. The patient could be referred to a non-12-step self-help group, to one of the many 12-step group meetings that are free of "Big Book thumpers," or to JACS (see Chapter 2).

Twelve-step spirituality may have less appeal outside of Judeo-Christian cultures (L. F. Kurtz, 1990). On the positive side, Native American adaptations of AA have been described (Duran, 1994; Jilek-Aall, 1981), and the proportion of Native Americans identified in AA's annual surveys (e.g., 2% in 1998; Alcoholics Anonymous, 1999) is higher than that in the US general population. In contrast, 12-step mutual-help organizations have had very limited success in establishing a presence in the Islamic world (Mäkelä, 1991), and, to the author's knowledge, no article on Islamic minority participation in 12-step groups in other countries has appeared.

Adolescents

Adolescent subjects are grossly under-represented in most areas of addiction research, including research on self-help groups. In one of the few available discussions, Gifford (1991) made the strong argument that AA is almost never appropriate for adolescents now that NA is more available, and that adolescents should never be referred to both. However, he provided no systematic data to support his prescription.

Substance-abusing adolescents seem to benefit from affiliation at 12-step self-help groups (Brown, Mott, & Myers, 1990; Kelly, Myers, & Brown, 2000, 2002), but research in this area is in an early stage. Science appears completely silent to date on whether adolescents can benefit from the non-12-step self-help organizations discussed in this book. Building knowledge in this area remains a critical task for researchers and clinicians. Clinicians treating adolescents in the mean time will have to use their best judgement about self-help group referrals and closely monitor the results.

Helping to start self-help groups

Individual professionals have been involved in the founding of many self-help organizations, as described in Chapter 2. They can also help to spread groups of existing self-help organizations, as have community agencies in Takatsuki City, Japan, for a number of years (Noda *et al.*, 1988). Methods of being the "midwife" to new self-help groups are variable, and can be as simple as bringing together a few interested individuals (e.g., current or former patients). In some organizations, such as MM, professionals can facilitate a group until indigenous leadership develops.

A workshop sponsored by the Canadian government included among its recommendations that professionals should have a "phased withdrawal" plan whenever working with self-help groups (Lavoie, Farquharson, & Kennedy, 1994). The desired end goal should always be a self-sustaining peer-operated group. Most professionals who help to start self-help groups appreciate this point, but others do not, which has led to instances of self-help group members eventually having to confront their initial leader for not letting the group become independent over time.

Technical assistance, lectures, research help, and media referral person

Although it needs no elaborate discussion, self-help groups are often interested in technical assistance from professionals, for example information about treatment options, disease course and management, research findings, and so forth. Some self-help groups also appreciate having a supportive professional to whom to refer journalists for added information when a news story is being produced about the group or the disorder it addresses. Self-help organizations also sometimes request assistance from professionals when conducting research projects. All of the above interactions can bring resources to both parties, for example the professional can invite the group to present its work to the treatment agency, can refer journalists to it, can approach it as a research collaborator, and so forth.

Attending self-help groups as a professional

Helping professionals are welcome in all self-help groups if they themselves wish to seek help for an addiction, and are welcome in most as a non-addicted visitor under some circumstances. Both of these situations are discussed below.

The addicted professional as a group member

Many addicted professionals attend either generic self-help groups or specialty groups devoted to their professions. Specialty organizations include Caduceus Clubs for physicians, Anesthetists in Recovery, Nurses in Recovery, and even an organization for recovering lawyers (in anticipation of the usual waggish query, members are recovering from addiction and not from being lawyers). Whether addicted professionals benefit more from specialty or generic self-help organizations (e.g., AA) has never been evaluated.

It is natural to wonder how being a self-help group member influences the quality and type of addiction treatment services a professional provides. Direct comparisons of the efficacy of recovering versus non-recovering counselors are rare. In the only identified randomized trial, alcohol-abusing patients ($n = 273$) assigned to a recovering counselor were more likely to reduce their drinking over time than were patients assigned to a non-recovering counselor (Argeriou & Manohar, 1978). This outcome difference was probably the result of patients staying in treatment somewhat longer if they were assigned to a recovering counselor rather than a non-recovering counselor. Patients whose counselor is in recovery may feel less shame about their addiction and therefore be more likely to continue attending treatment sessions.

Contrary to some professional lore, personal recovery status is a less powerful determinant of beliefs about addiction than professional discipline and education. When level of education is taken into account, recovering staff are no more likely to endorse a 12-step style disease model than non-recovering staff, at least in the USA (Humphreys, Noke, & Moos, 1996).

Dual relationships are the most significant potential problem raised by treatment staff being self-help organization members, for example when a patient attends an NA meeting in the community and sees his treatment counselor in attendance. Such situations can be awkward on both sides. Confidentiality problems may also arise when counselors on a treatment team know important facts about clients only because they were disclosed in an off-site self-help group meeting and feel unsure whether to account for them in team treatment planning. Alternatively, after a hard day a counselor may wish to go to his/her own mutual-help group meeting to complain about another staff member whom a former patient attending the group would recognize from even a general description. The various ethical codes of professional societies usually provide helpful guidance in such situations, and added consultation should be sought from agency supervisors.

Mental health professionals who have been members of self-help groups are more likely to collaborate productively with them (Meissen, Mason, & Gleason, 1991). Similarly, agencies with larger proportions of staff who are personally "in recovery" are more effective at linking patients to 12-step self-help groups during and after treatment (Humphreys, Mavis, & Stöffelmayr, 1992). The potential dual relationship challenges described above thus do not prevent "crossover staff" from making a unique contribution to patient care.

The non-addicted professional as a visitor

Many self-help organizations allow interested professionals to visit some or all of their group meetings. Professionals can come to any meeting of Danshukai, for example, and to "open meetings" of AA and NA. In the author's opinion, all professionals in the addiction field should avail themselves of this opportunity, for two reasons. First, such visits serve as continuing education into the nature of mutual-help organizations in general and of local meetings in particular, which facilitates informed referral of patients to groups. Second, treating addicted patients is often discouraging because only the relapsed patients come back. Going to a self-help group and seeing formerly addicted individuals thriving can be a great morale boost for addiction-treatment professionals.

Epilogue: summing up, moving forward

Some answers for the Martian

This volume opened with a hypothetical visitor from Mars who, knowing nothing of human ways, was struck by the disparity between the widespread use of addiction-related mutual-help organizations and the comparatively low level of interest shown in them by scientists, clinicians, and policy makers. The Martian asked whether anything was known about what self-help organizations are and where they come from, what effects they have, and how professionals might interact with them. This book had to scour a wide range of disciplines and countries to assemble a respectable amount of scientific findings relevant to these questions, but provides what the author hopes are informative answers to each of them. The preliminary nature of some of these answers underscores how much remains to be learned about addiction-related mutual-help organizations and their interactions with clinicians, treatment agencies, healthcare systems and governments. This epilogue briefly touches on some of the main conclusions of the book as well as important unanswered questions that require attention in the future.

What are addiction-related self-help organizations and where do they come from?

Mutual-help organizations for addiction must be understood in the context of a much larger self-help group movement in the modern world, as explored in Chapter 1. Both addiction- and non-addiction-related mutual-help organizations are voluntary associations operated by peers who share a problematic status, rely upon experiential knowledge, value reciprocal helping, do not charge fees, and include personal change among their organizational goals. The social trends that nourish addiction-related mutual-help organizations also support mutual-help organizations focused on other concerns: improved public health and wealth, weakening of familial ties, limitations of professional assistance, the rise of health consumerism, and the benefits of participating in groups. The bright dividing line between the allegedly distinct topics of "addiction" and "other disorders" established by policy makers, clinicians, and academics seems particularly inappropriate when applied to mutual-help organizations. Much of the knowledge acquired about self-help groups for addiction clearly applies to groups for other health and social concerns, and vice versa.

In contrast, the work reviewed in this volume supports a clear distinction that is often *not* made, namely between self-help organizations and other ways of helping addicted individuals. Self-help organizations share some techniques and values with professional treatment agencies, support groups, patient education programs, voluntary care initiatives, and even self-help books, yet are nonetheless clearly a unique phenomenon and should be researched, conceptualized, and valued as such. The common conceptual blurring of professional treatment and self-help organizations is particularly worrisome, not only for its factual inaccuracy, but because it might place each entity in the position of being expected to offer something it cannot (e.g., treatment agencies may be expected to exist without funding; self-help organizations may be asked to become formally licensed, accredited, and monitored).

The work reviewed in Chapter 2 revealed that, despite its pre-eminent scope and influence, AA is only one of many addiction-related mutual-help organizations in the developed world. Certain cultural forces in developed societies are conducive to all addiction-related mutual-help organizations, yet each organization has a history and character of its own. Each of the societies discussed in this book offered a set of cultural, religious, and political traditions in which addiction-related mutual-help organizations evolved, and these forces were strong enough to create significant differences even within the "same" international organizations (e.g., AA, Blue Cross, The Links). Scientific data on mutual-help organizations support neither exceptionalism (i.e., that what is learned in one culture applies nowhere else) nor universalism (i.e., that what is learned in one culture applies everywhere else). Valid generalization is possible, but must be done in the context of each society's traditions of language, government, religion, civil society, and substance abuse, to name only a few prominent factors. Although less commonly appreciated, the same care is needed when generalizing within the increasingly diverse societies that compose the developed world.

What effects do self-help organizations have?

Evaluation of the effects of self-help group participation always occurs within some conceptual context and from the perspective of some stakeholder, as detailed in Chapters 3–5. The treatment researcher may wish to know whether self-help groups reduce substance abuse, the qualitative sociologist may wonder about how groups change spirituality and friendship, the hospital director may care primarily about how group participation affects healthcare costs, and group members themselves may want all or none of these things. Much inquiry remains to be done within all of these perspectives, but a few conclusions are possible given current knowledge.

First, participation in addiction-related mutual-help organizations seems, on average, to reduce substance use and associated problems with psychological, physical, and social functioning. However, the effect of many organizations on these outcomes has never been evaluated rigorously or even at all. More "treatment-style" evaluations of self-help organizations are needed, particularly more that employ prospective and longitudinal designs, include comparison groups, use multi-dimensional measures of group involvement, and examine large, diverse samples. These evaluations should comprise randomized clinical trials but should not be limited to them. Methodological pluralism will strengthen rather than weaken researchers' ability to evaluate the effects of self-help group participation.

Second, participation in addiction-related self-help organizations causes a subset of members to experience significant changes in their spiritual life, world view, identity, life-story, friendship networks, and/or politicization. These effects seem characteristic of more committed members, take some time to fully develop, and vary in importance across self-help organizations. Unlike improvements in physical health, none of these changes is inherently good or bad from an objective standpoint. Indeed, some may be both, for example an alcoholic individual may highly enjoy thinking of himself as a committed AA member and attending many AA social events with new AA friends, whereas his neglected spouse might resent these same changes. Future evaluation research should be aware that different observers will value each outcome differently.

Finally, the most reliably demonstrated effect of self-help group participation is its power to sharply reduce addiction-related healthcare costs. This outcome attracted little attention 25 years ago, but given the current international climate of cost-constraint within social policy circles, it should generate tremendous interest in the coming years. The value of voluntary associations, and civil society more generally, can never and should never be reduced to money, but within this reality policy makers should consider whether the healthcare savings produced by mutual-help organizations warrant investments in supportive infrastructure (e.g., self-help clearinghouses, self-help-related training programs for professionals).

How might professionals interact with self-help organizations?

Collaboration between external entities and self-help organizations poses some risks on both sides, as explained in Chapter 5. However, the experience of several societies shows that such risks can largely be managed through informed policy making in which both self-help group members and outside experts participate. When governments and healthcare organizations make efforts to create a positive climate for self-help organizations, both parties can better pursue their shared goal of producing positive impacts on public health.

Individual healthcare professionals have made great contributions to self-help organizations. Yet other professionals remain skeptical and competitive, and do not appreciate the vital distinction between being helpful to self-help groups and being in control of them. Professional training programs can help to correct problems that stem from lack of information, but at a broader level, full collaboration with self-help groups awaits major changes in professionals' culture. Mutual-help organizations, along with the multinational health consumerism movement, are dynamic forces within modern public health, and among their other effects may help (force?) health professionals to reconstruct their role, self-image, and socialization habits in keeping with the changing needs of developed societies.

Toward a better tomorrow

Death and suffering due to substance abuse will always be with us, but that should never discourage us from improving efforts to aid those whose lives are being destroyed by alcohol, tobacco, and illicit drugs. Given that addiction-focused healthcare systems, government agencies, and self-help organizations frequently neither understand nor cooperate with each other, the number of lives each has saved is indeed remarkable. One wonders how much more good each could do if they learned about each other's traditions, effects, shortcomings, and strengths, and found ways where concerted efforts could magnify their benefits.

Self-help organizations can help government agencies to keep in touch with grassroots' concerns about addiction; governments, in turn, can invest in infrastructure that supports self-help organizations. Treatment professionals can provide referrals and health information to self-help groups; groups, in return, can support the long-term recovery of professionals' substance-dependent patients. Healthcare systems can educate their staffs about self-help organizations; self-help organizations can reduce the fiscal and human demand on healthcare systems. Researchers can evaluate the impact of all these arrangements, and gain from each party a different, valuable perspective on how to appraise the results. In these and countless other ways, those individuals and entities that share a commitment to reducing substance and related problems can augment their collective impact. True cooperation will serve this purpose better than integration or co-optation. Governments, professionals, and self-help organizations should maintain control over their own spheres while also making collaborative efforts to combat the most serious public health problem facing the developed world.

References

Aaltonen, I. & Mäkelä, K. (1994). Female and male life stories published in the Finnish Alcoholics Anonymous Journal. *International Journal of the Addictions*, **29**, 485–495.

Ablon, J. (1974). Al-Anon family groups: impetus for learning and change through the presentation of alternatives. *American Journal of Psychotherapy*, **28**, 30–45.

(1982). Perspectives on Al-Anon family groups. In *Alcoholism: Development, Consequences and Interventions*, ed. N. J. Estes & M. E. Heinemann, pp. 319–328. St. Louis: C. V. Mosby.

Adult Children of Alcoholics World Service Organization (1997). An interview about the early history of ACA. Torrance, California: ACA World Service Organization.

Al-Anon/Alateen World Service Organization (2000). 1999 survey in the US and Canada. New York: ACA World Service Organization.

Alcoholics Anonymous (1939). *The Story of How Many Thousands of Men and Women have Recovered from Alcoholism*, 1st edn. New York: AA World Services.

(1952/1953). *Twelve Steps and Twelve traditions*. New York: AA World Services.

(1957). *Alcoholics Anonymous Comes of Age*. New York: AA World Services.

(1976). *Alcoholics Anonymous: The Story of How Many Thousands of Men and Women have Recovered from Alcoholism*, 3rd edn. New York: AA World Services.

(1984). *The AA Member – Medications and Other Drugs*. New York: AA World Services.

(1999). *Alcoholics Anonymous 1998 Membership Survey*. New York: AA World Services.

(2002). *Alcoholics Anonymous 2001 Membership Survey*. New York: AA World Services.

Alexander, F. & Rollins, M. (1984). Alcoholics Anonymous: The Unseen Cult. *California Sociologist*, **17**, 33–48.

Alford, G. S. (1980). Alcoholics Anonymous: an empirical outcome study. *Addictive Behaviors*, **5**, 359–370.

Allamani, A., Barbera, G., Calviani, L., & Tanini, S. (1994). The treatment system for alcohol-related problems in Italy. *Alcologia*, **6**(3), 247–252.

Allamani, A. & Petrikin, C. (1996). Alcoholics Anonymous and the alcohol treatment system in Italy. *Contemporary Drug Problems*, **23**, 29–42.

Allen, J. P. (2000). Measuring treatment process variables in Alcoholics Anonymous. *Journal of Substance Abuse Treatment*, **18**, 227–230.

American Psychiatric Association (1987). *DSM-III-R: Diagnostic and Statistical Manual of Mental Disorders*. Washington, DC: American Psychiatric Association.

Antonovsky, A. (1984). The sense of coherence as a determinant of health. *Advances*, **1**(3), 37–50.

Antze, P. (1979). Role of ideologies in peer psychotherapy groups. In *Self-Help Groups for Coping with Crisis*, ed. M. A. Lieberman & L. D. Borman, pp. 272–304. San Francisco: Jossey-Bass.

 (1987). Symbolic action in Alcoholics Anonymous. In *Constructive Drinking*, ed. M. Douglas, pp. 149–181. New York: Cambridge University Press.

Appel, C. (1996). Different stories: self-help groups for alcoholics and illicit drug users in Germany. *Contemporary Drug Problems*, **23**, 57–75.

Argeriou, M. & Manohar, V. (1978). Relative effectiveness of nonalcoholics and recovered alcoholics as counselors. *Journal of Studies on Alcohol*, **39**(5), 793–799.

Arnett, J. J. (2000). Emerging adulthood: a theory of development from the late teens through the twenties. *American Psychologist*, **55**, 469–480.

Asher, R. M. (1992). *Women with Alcoholic Husbands: Ambivalence and the Trap of Codependency*. Chapel Hill, NC: University of North Carolina Press.

Bailey, M. (1965). Al-Anon family groups as an aid to wives of alcoholics. *Social Work*, **10**, 68–74.

Bakker, B. & Karel, M. (1983). Support for self-help. In *Self-Help and Health in Europe: New Approaches in Health Care*, ed. S. Hatch & I. Kickbush, pp. 178–185. Copenhagen: WHO Regional Office for Europe.

Baldwin, S. & McMillan, J. (1993). Down to zero: feasibility study of court-based brief interventions with drinking offenders in England and Wales. *Addiction Research*, **1**, 157–168.

Bales, R. F. (1944). The therapeutic role of Alcoholics Anonymous as seen by a sociologist. *Quarterly Journal of Studies on Alcohol*, **5**, 267–278.

Balgopal, P., Ephross, P., & Vassil, T. (1986). Self-help groups and professional helpers. *Small Group Behavior*, **17**(2), 123–137.

Bao, Y., Sauerland, D., & Sturm, R. (2001). Changes in alcohol-related inpatient care – an international trend comparison. *Journal of Addictive Diseases*, **20**, 97–104.

Barath, A. (1991). Self-help in Europe 1979–1989, a critical review. *Health Promotion International*, **6**, 73–80.

Barber, J. G. & Gilbertson, R. (1996). An experimental study of brief unilateral intervention for the partners of heavy drinkers. *Research on Social Work Practice*, **6**, 325–336.

Barker, R. G. (1964). *Ecological Psychology: Concepts and Methods for Studying the Environment of Human Behavior*. Stanford, CA: Stanford University Press.

Barrison, I. G., Ruzek, J., & Murray-Lyon, I. M. (1987). Drinkwatchers – Description of subjects and evaluation of laboratory markers of heavy drinking. *Alcohol and Alcoholism*, **22**, 147–154.

Barrucand, D. (1984). Les mouvements d'anciens buveurs. *Alcoologie*, **35**, 237–242.

Bateson, G. (1971). The cybernetics of self: a theory of alcoholism. *Psychiatry*, **34**, 1–18.

Bayer, E. R. & Levy, S. J. (1980). Notes on the first retreat for Jewish Alcoholics. In *Alcoholism and the Jewish community*, ed. A. Blaine, pp. 333–345. New York: Federation of Jewish Philanthropies of New York.

Bean, M. (1975a). A critique of AA. *Psychiatric Annals*, **5**, 7–19.

(1975b). AA and religion. *Psychiatric Annals*, **5**, 36–42.

Beattie, M. (1987). *Codependent No More: How to Stop Controlling Others and Start Caring for Yourself*. San Francisco, CA: Harper Collins.

Beattie, M. C. & Longabaugh, R. (1997). Interpersonal factors and post-treatment drinking and subjective well-being. *Addiction*, **92**, 1507–1521.

Beckman, L. (1980). An attributional analysis of Alcoholics Anonymous. *Journal of Studies on Alcohol*, **41**(7), 714–726.

Bellah, R. N., Madsen, R., Sullivan, W. M., Swidler, A., & Tipton, S. M. (1985). *Habits of the Heart: Individualism and Commitment in American Life*. New York: Harper & Row.

Bender, E. I. (1986). The self-help movement seen in the context of social development. *Journal of Voluntary Action Research*, **5**, 77–84.

Bender, E. I., Bargal, D., & Gidron, B. (1986). Epilogue. *Journal of Voluntary Action Research*, **5**, 85–90.

Bénichou, L. (1980). Quatre questions à propos des mouvements d'anciens buveurs. *Soins*, **25**, 61–65.

Bennett, J. B. & Scholler-Jaquish, A. (1995). The Winner's Group: a self-help group for homeless chemically dependent persons. *Journal of Psychosocial Nursing*, **33**(4), 14–19.

Bennett, L. A. (1985). Treating alcoholism in a Yugoslav fashion. *East European Quarterly*, **18**(4), 495–519.

Benson, K. & Hartz, A. J. (2000). A comparison of observational studies and randomized, controlled trials. *New England Journal of Medicine*, **342**, 1878–1886.

Berger, P. L. & Luckmann, T. (1967). *The Social Construction of Reality: A Treatise in the Sociology of Knowledge*. Garden City, NJ: Doubleday.

Biegel, D. E. & Yamatani, H. (1987). Help-giving in self-help groups. *Hospital and Community Psychiatry*, **38**(11), 1195–1197.

Bishop, P. D., Jason, L. A., Ferrari, J. R., & Huang, C. F. (1998). A survival analysis of communal-living self-help, addiction recovery participants. *American Journal of Community Psychology*, **26**(6), 803–821.

B. L. (1978). Congrès national de la croix bleue. *Alcool ou Santé*, **146**(3), 25–26.

Black, C. (1981). *It will Never Happen to Me!* Denver, Co: M. A. C. Publications.

Blasi, A. (1985). Conversion. In *A Phenomenological Transformation of the Social Scientific Study of Religion*, ed. A. Blasi, pp. 91–111. New York: Peter Lang.

Blomqvist, J. (1998). The "Swedish model" of dealing with alcohol problems: historical trends and future challenges. *Contemporary Drug Problems*, **25**, 253–320.

Blondell, R. D., Looney, S. W., Northington, A. P., Lasch, M. E., Rhodes, S. B., & McDaniels, R. L. (2001). Using recovering alcoholics to help hospitalized patients with alcohol problems. *Journal of Family Practice*, **50**, 447–448.

Bloomfield, K. (1990). *Community in Recovery: A Study of Social Support, Spirituality, and Voluntarism among Gay and Lesbian Members of Alcoholics Anonymous.* Doctoral Dissertation, University of California at Berkeley School of Public Health.

(1991). *An International Comparison of Spirituality among Members of Alcoholics Anonymous in Four Countries.* Paper presented at the 17th Annual Alcohol Epidemiology Symposium, Kettill Bruun Society, Stockholm, Sweden.

(1994). Beyond sobriety: the cultural significance of Alcoholics Anonymous as a social movement. *Nonprofit and Voluntary Sector Quarterly, 23*, 21–40.

Borkman, T. J. (1976). Experiential knowledge: a new concept for the analysis of self-help groups. *Social Service Review, 50*, 445–456.

(1990). Experimental, professional and lay frames of reference. In *Working with Self-Help*, ed. T. J. Powell, pp. 3–30. Silver Springs, MD: NASW Press.

(1997). A selective look at self-help groups in the United States. *Health and Social Care in the Community, 5*, 357–364.

(1999). *Understanding Self-Help/Mutual Aid: Experiential Learning in the Commons.* New Brunswick, NJ: Rutgers University Press.

(2001). *Can Governments Assist Self-Help/Mutual Aid?* Paper presented at conference of the Association for Research on Non-Profit Organizations and Voluntary Action, Miami.

Borkman, T. J., Kaskutas, L. A., & Barrows, D. C. (1996). *The Social Model Program: A Literature Review and History.* Rockville, MD: Center for Substance Abuse Treatment.

Borman, L. D., ed. (1979). *Self-Help Groups for Coping with Crisis.* San Francisco: Jossey-Bass.

Bradshaw, J. (1988). *Healing the Shame that Binds You.* Deerfield Beach, FL: Health Communications.

Branckaerts, J. (1983). Birth of a movement: early milestones. In *Rediscovering Self-Help: Its Role in Social Care*, ed. P. P. C. Froland & D. L. Pancoast, vol. 6, pp. 203–221. Beverly Hills: Sage.

Branckaerts, J. & Deneke, C. (1983). Mutual aid: from research to supportive policy – report from a World Health Organization workshop. In *Self-Help and Health in Europe: New Approaches in Health Care*, ed. S. Hatch & I. Kickbush, pp. 186–191. Copenhagen: WHO Regional Office for Europe.

Branckaerts, J. & Richardson, A. (1989). Politics and policies on self-help: notes on the international scene. In *Self-Help in Health and Social Welfare: England and West Germany*, ed. S. Humble & J. Unell, pp. 29–46. London: Routledge.

Brandes, S. (2002). *Staying Sober in Mexico City.* Austin, TX: University of Texas Press.

Brandsma, J. M., Maultby, M. C., & Welsh, R. J. (1980). *Outpatient Treatment of Alcoholism: A Review and Comparative Study.* Baltimore, MD: University Park Press.

Breslow, L. (1990). A health promotion primer for the 1990's. *Health Affairs, 9*(Summer), 6–21.

Bridgman, L. P. & McQueen, W. M., Jr. (1987). The success of Alcoholics Anonymous: locus of control and God's general revelation. *Journal of Psychology and Theology, 15*(2), 124–131.

Brown, R. (1997). *An Introduction to the New Testament*. New York: Doubleday.

Brown, S. (1991). Adult Children of Alcoholics: the history of a social movement and its impact on clinical theory and practice. In *Recent Developments in Alcoholism*, ed. M. Galanter, vol. 9, pp. 267–285. New York: Plenum.

Brown, S. A., Mott, M. A., & Myers, M. G. (1990). Adolescent alcohol and drug treatment outcome. In *Drug and alcohol abuse prevention: Drug and alcohol abuse reviews*, ed. E. R. R. Watson, pp. 373–403. Clifton, NJ: Humana.

Browne, B. R. (1991). The selective adaptation of the Alcoholics Anonymous program by Gamblers Anonymous. *Journal of Gambling Studies*, **7**, 187–206.

Brundage, V. (1985). Gregory Bateson, Alcoholics Anonymous, and stoicism. *Psychiatry*, **48**, 40–51.

Bruun, K., Edwards, G., Lumio, M., *et al.* (1975). *Alcohol Control Policies in Public Health Perspective*. Helsinki: Finnish Foundation for Alcohol Studies.

Bryk, A. S., ed. (1983). *Stakeholder-Based Evaluation*. San Francisco: Jossey-Bass.

Bufe, C. (1991). *Alcoholics Anonymous: Cult or Cure?* San Francisco: Sharp Press.

Buxton, M. E., Smith, D. E., & Seymour, R. B. (1987). Spirituality and other points of resistance to the 12-step recovery process. *Journal of Psychoactive Drugs*, **19**, 275–286.

Cain, A. H. (1967). Alcoholics Anonymous: cult or cure? In *Human Behavior and Social Process*, ed. A. M. Rose, pp. 46–54. Boston: Houghton Mifflin.

Cain, C. (1991). Personal stories: identity acquisition and self-understanding in Alcoholics Anonymous. *Ethos*, **19**(2), 210–253.

Caison, W. (1997). *Alcohol and Drug Treatment Telephone Follow-up using Twelve Step Group Member Volunteers: Effects on A. A. and N. A. Affiliation Self-Efficacy and Behaviors among Callers and Call Recipients*. Unpublished doctoral dissertation, North Carolina State University.

Caldwell, F. J. (1983). Alcoholics Anonymous as a viable treatment resource for black alcoholics. In *Black Alcoholism: Toward a Comprehensive Understanding*, ed. T. D. Watts & R. Wright, pp. 85–99. Springfield, IL: Charles C. Thomas.

Caldwell, P. E. & Cutter, H. S. G. (1998). Alcoholics Anonymous affiliation during early recovery. *Journal of Substance Abuse Treatment*, **15**(3), 221–228.

Caldwell, S. & White, K. K. (1991). Co-creating a self-help recovery movement. *Psychosocial Rehabilitation Journal*, **15**, 91–95.

Carroll, S. (1993). Spirituality and purpose in life in alcoholism recovery. *Journal of Studies on Alcohol*, **54**, 297–301.

Cerclé, A. (1984). *L'identité de L'ancien malade alcoolique membre actif d'une association d'entraide: abstinence militante et restructuration identitaire*. Thesis submitted for a doctorate in psychology, University of Rennes, France.

Chamberlin, J. (1978). *On our Own: Patient Controlled Alternatives to the Mental Health System*. New York: McGraw-Hill.

Chang, G., Astrachan, B. M., & Bryant, K. J. (1994). Emergency physicians' ratings of alcoholism treaters. *Journal of Substance Abuse Treatment*, **11**, 131–135.

Chesler, M. A. & Chesney, B. K. (1988). Self-help groups: empowerment attitudes and behaviors of disabled or chronically ill persons. In *Attitudes Toward Persons with Disabilities*, ed. H. E. Yucker, pp. 230–245. New York: Springer.

(1995). *Cancer and Self-Help: Bridging the Troubled Waters of Childhood Illness.* Madison, WI: University of Wisconsin Press.

Cheung, Y. W. & Ch'ien, J. M. N. (1997). *Drug Policy and Harm Reduction in Hong Kong: A Socio-Historical Examination.* Paper presented at the International Conference on the Reduction of Drug-Related Harm, Hobart, Australia.

Ch'ien, J. M. N. (1980). Hong Kong: a community-based voluntary program. In *Drug Problems in the Sociocultural Context: A Basis for Policies and Programme Planning,* ed. G. Edwards & A. Arif, pp. 114–120. Geneva: WHO.

Chow, O. W. E. (1997). Empowering Chinese stroke victims through self-help/mutual aid. *Asia Pacific Journal of Social Work,* **7**, 63–76.

Christensen, A. & Jacobson, N. S. (1994). Who (or what) can do psychotherapy: the status and challenge of nonprofessional therapies. *Psychological Science,* **5**(1), 8–14.

Christo, G. & Franey, C. (1995). Drug users' spiritual beliefs, locus of control and the disease concept in relation to Narcotics Anonymous attendance and six-month outcomes. *Drug and Alcohol Dependence,* **38**, 51–56.

Christo, G. & Sutton, S. (1994). Anxiety and self-esteem as a function of abstinence time among recovering addicts attending Narcotics Anonymous. *British Journal of Clinical Psychology,* **33**, 198–200.

Christopher, J. R. (1992). *SOS Sobriety: The Proven Alternative to 12-Step Programs.* Buffalo, NY: Prometheus Books.

(1997). Secular organization for sobriety. In *Substance Abuse: A Comprehensive Textbook,* ed. J. H. Lowinson, P. Ruiz, R. B. Millman, & J. G. Langrod, pp. 397–402. Baltimore, MD: Williams & Wilkins.

Clark, H. W. (1987). On professional therapists and Alcoholics Anonymous. *Journal of Psychoactive Drugs,* **19**(3), 233–242.

Cohen, J. (1992). A power primer. *Psychological Bulletin,* **112**(1), 155–159.

Collins, S., Ottley, G., & Wilson, M. (1990). Historical perspectives and the development of community services. In *Alcohol, Social Work and Helping,* ed. S. Collins, pp. 9–42. London: Routledge.

Concato, J., Shah, N., & Horwitz, R. I. (2000). Randomized, controlled trials, observational studies, and the hierarchy of research designs. *New England Journal of Medicine,* **342**, 1887–1892.

Conlon, L. S. (1997). *Griffin v. Coughlin:* mandated AA meetings and the establishment clause. *Journal of Church and State,* **39**, 427–454.

Connors, G. J. & Dermen, K. H. (1996). Characteristics of participants in Secular Organization for Sobriety (SOS). *American Journal of Drug and Alcohol Abuse,* **22**, 281–295.

Corenblum, B. & Fischer, D. G. (1975). Some correlates of Al-Anon group membership. *Journal of Studies on Alcohol,* **36**, 675–677.

Cronbach, L. J. (1982). *Designing Evaluations of Educational and Social Programs.* San Francisco: Jossey-Bass.

Cross, G. M., Morgan, C. W., Mooney, A. J., Martin, C. A., & Rafter, J. A. (1990). Alcoholism treatment: a ten-year follow-up study. *Alcoholism: Clinical and Experimental Research,* **14**(2), 169–173.

Cutter, C. G. & Cutter, H. S. (1987). Experience and change in Al-Anon family groups: adult children of alcoholics. *Journal of Studies on Alcohol*, **48**(1), 29–32.

Davidson, L., Stayner, D. A., Lambert, S., Smith, P., & Sledge, W. H. (1997). Phenomenological and participatory research on schizophrenia: recovering the person in theory and practice. *Journal of Social Issues*, **53**, 767–784.

Davis, K. G. (1994). *Primero Dios: Alcoholics Anonymous and the Hispanic Community.* London: Associated University Presses.

Dawson, D. A. (1996). Correlates of past-year status among treated and untreated persons with former alcohol dependence: United States, 1992. *Alcoholism, Clinical and Experimental Research*, **20**, 771–779.

de Cocq, G. (1976). European and North American self-help movements: some contrasts. In *The Strength in Us: Self-Help in the Modern World*, ed. A. H. Katz & E. Bender, pp. 202–208. New York: New Viewpoints.

del Carmen Mariño, M., Medina-Mora, M. E., Velázquez, J. E., & de la Fuente, J. R. (1997). Utilización de servicios en una muestra de alcohólicos mexicanos. *Salud Mental*, **20**, 24–31.

De Leon, G. (1999). Therapeutic communities. In *Textbook of Substance Abuse Treatment*, ed. M. Galanter & H. D. Kleber, 2nd edn, pp. 447–464. Washington, DC: American Psychiatric Press.

Deneke, C. (1983). How professionals view self-help. In *Rediscovering Self-Help: Its Role in Social Care*, ed. D. L. Pancoast, P. Parker, & C. Froland, pp. 125–141. Beverly Hills, CA: Sage.

Dennis, M. L., Perl, H. I., Huebner, R. B., & McLellan, A. T. (2000). Twenty-five strategies for improving the design, implementation and analysis of health services research related to alcohol and other drug abuse treatment. *Addiction*, **95**(suppl. 3), S281–S308.

Denzin, N. K. (1987). *The Recovering Alcoholic*. Newbury Park, CA: Sage.

(1990). *The Sociological Imagination* revisited. *The Sociological Quarterly*, **31**(1), 1–22.

Devine, J. A., Brody, C. J., & Wright, J. D. (1997). Evaluating an alcohol and drug treatment program for the homeless: an econometric approach. *Evaluation and Program Planning*, **20**, 205–215.

Ditman, K. S. & Crawford, G. G. (1966). The use of court probation in the management of the alcohol addict. *American Journal of Psychiatry*, **122**, 757–762.

Ditman, K. S., Crawford, G. G., Forgy, E. W., Moskowitz, H., & Macandrew, C. (1967). A controlled experiment on the use of court probation for drunk arrests. *American Journal of Psychiatry*, **124**, 64–67.

Donovan, M. E. (1984). A sociological analysis of commitment generation in Alcoholics Anonymous. *British Journal of Addiction*, **79**, 411–418.

Dumont, M. P. (1974). Self-help treatment programs. *American Journal of Psychiatry*, **131**, 631–635.

Duncan, T. (1965). *Understanding and Helping the Narcotic Addict*. Philadelphia: Fortress Press.

Du Pont, R. L. (1999). Biology and the environment: rethinking demand reduction. *Journal of Addictive Diseases*, **18**, 121–138.

Duran, B. M. (1994). *Preliminary Findings of an Investigation into the Nature and Content of American Indian Alcoholics Anonymous.* Paper presented at the International Conference on Addiction and Mutual Help Movements in a Comparative Perspective, Toronto, Canada.

Eagly, A. H., Makhijani, M. G., & Klonsky, B. G. (1992). Gender and the evaluation of leaders: a meta-analysis. *Psychological Bulletin,* **111**, 3–22.

Edwards, B. & Foley, M. W., eds (1997). Special issue on social capital, civil society and contemporary democracy. *American Behavioral Scientist,* **40**(5), 547–678.

(1998). Special issue on beyond Tocqueville: civil society and social capital in contemporary perspective. *American Behavioral Scientist,* **42**(1), 1–139.

Edwards, G., Hensman, C., Hawker, A., & Williamson, V. (1966). Who goes to Alcoholics Anonymous? *Lancet,* **11**, 382–384.

Eisenbach-Stangl, I. (1996). Belief in medicine and belief in God: self-help of alcoholics and AA in Austria. *Contemporary Drug Problems,* **23**, 11–28.

(1997). Professional treatment and mutual aid: different offers for female alcoholics or offers for women with different alcohol-related problems? *European Addiction Research,* **3**, 22–29.

(1998). How to live a sober life in a wet society: Alcoholics Anonymous in Austria. In *Diversity in Unity: Studies of Alcoholics Anonymous in Eight Societies,* ed. I. Eisenbach-Stangl & P. Rosenqvist, pp. 131–147. NAD Publication #33. Helsinki: Nordic Council for Alcohol and Drug Research.

Eisenbach-Stangl, I. & Rosenqvist, P., eds (1998). *Diversity in Unity: Studies of Alcoholics Anonymous in Eight Societies.* NAD Publication #33. Helsinki: Nordic Council for Alcohol and Drug Research.

Ellis, A. & Schoenfeld, E. (1990). Divine intervention and the treatment of chemical dependency. *Journal of Substance Abuse,* **2**, 459–468.

Ellison, J. (1954). These drug addicts cure one another. *Saturday Evening Post,* **227**, 22–23 & 48–52.

Emrick, C. D., Tonigan, J. S., Montgomery, H., & Little, L. (1993). Alcoholics anonymous: what is currently known? In *Research on Alcoholics Anonymous: Opportunities and Alternatives,* ed. B. S. McCrady & W. R. Miller, pp. 41–77. New Brunswick, NJ: Rutgers Center for Alcohol Studies.

Etheridge, R. E., Craddock, S. G., Hubbard, R. L., & Rounds-Bryant, J. L. (1999). The relationship of counseling and self-help participation to patient outcomes in DATOS. *Drug and Alcohol Dependence,* **57**, 99–112.

Fainzang, S. (1994). When alcoholics are not anonymous. *Medical Anthropology Quarterly,* **8**(3), 336–345.

Fairweather, G. W. & Fergus, E. O. (1993). *Empowering the Mentally Ill.* Austin, TX: Fairweather Publishing.

Fédération Internationale de la Croix Bleue (2002). La Fédération Internationale. Available at www.eurocare.org/bluecross.

Finney, J. W. (1995). Enhancing substance abuse treatment evaluations: examining mediators and moderators of treatment effects. *Journal of Substance Abuse,* **7**(1), 135–150.

Finney, J. W. & Monahan, S. (1996). The cost-effectiveness of treatment for alcoholism: a second approximation. *Journal of Studies on Alcohol*, **57**, 229–243.

Finney, J. W., Noyes, C. A., Coutts, A. I., & Moos, R. H. (1998). Evaluating substance abuse treatment process models: I. Changes on proximal outcome variables during 12-step and cognitive–behavioral treatment. *Journal of Studies on Alcohol*, **59**, 371–380.

Fiorentine, R. (1999). After drug treatment: are 12-step programs effective in maintaining abstinence? *American Journal of Drug and Alcohol Abuse*, **25**, 93–116.

Fiorentine, R. & Hillhouse, M. P. (2000). Drug treatment and twelve-step program participation: the additive effects of integrated recovery activities. *Journal of Substance Abuse Treatment*, **18**, 65–74.

(in press – a). When low self-efficacy is efficacious: evidence for the addicted-self model of cessation of alcohol and drug dependent behavior. *American Journal on Addictions*.

(in press – b). Why intensive participation in treatment and twelve-step programs is associated with the cessation of addictive behaviors: an application of the addicted-self model of recovery. *Journal of Addictive Diseases*.

Fletcher, A. M. (2001). *Sober for Good: New Solutions for Drinking Problems – Advice from Those who have Succeeded*. Boston: Houghton Mifflin.

Fortney, J., Booth, B., Zhang, M., Humphrey, J., & Wiseman, E. (1998). Controlling for selection bias in the evaluation of Alcoholics Anonymous as aftercare treatment. *Journal of Studies on Alcohol*, **59**, 690–697.

Fowler, J. W. (1993). Alcoholics Anonymous and faith development. In *Research on Alcoholics Anonymous: Opportunities and Alternatives*, ed. B. S. McCrady & W. R. Miller, pp. 41–77. New Brunswick, NJ: Rutgers Center for Alcohol Studies.

Frank, J. D. (1973). *Persuasion and Healing: A Comparative Study of Psychotherapy*. Baltimore, MD: Johns Hopkins University Press.

Fredersdorf, F. (2000). Synanon in Germany: an example of a residential self-help organization for drug dependent individuals. *International Journal of Self-Help and Self-Care*, **1**, 131–144.

Fung, W. & Chien, W. (2002). The effectiveness of a mutual support group for family caregivers of relatives with dementia. *Archives of Psychiatric Nursing*, **16**, 134–144.

Galanter, M. (1984). Self-help large group therapy for alcoholism: a controlled study. *Alcoholism: Clinical and Experimental Research*, **8**(1), 16–23.

(1990). Cults and zealous self-help movements: a psychiatric perspective. *American Journal of Psychiatry*, **147**, 543–551.

(1997). Spiritual recovery movements and contemporary medical care. *Psychiatry*, **60**, 211–223.

(1999). Research on spirituality and Alcoholics Anonymous. *Alcoholism: Clinical and Experimental Research*, **23**, 716–719.

Galanter, M., Castaneda, R., & Salamon, I. (1987). Institutional self-help therapy for alcoholism: clinical outcome. *Alcoholism: Clinical and Experimental Research*, **11**, 424–429.

Galanter, M., Egelko, S., & Edwards, H. (1993). Rational Recovery: alternative to AA for addiction? *American Journal of Drug and Alcohol Abuse*, **19**(4), 499–510.

Galanter, M., Gleaton, T., Marcus, C. E., & McMillen, J. (1984). Self-help groups for parents of young drug and alcohol abusers. *American Journal of Psychiatry*, **141**, 889–891.

Gartner, A. & Riessman, F. (1976). Self-help models and consumer intensive health practice. *American Journal of Public Health*, **66**(8), 783–786.

(1977). *Self-Help in the Human Services*. San Francisco: Jossey-Bass.

Gaston, C. D. & Meissen, G. (2000). Assessing the needs of a statewide self-help organization. *International Journal of Self-Help and Self-Care*, **1**, 75–90.

George, A. A. & Tucker, J. A. (1996). Help-seeking for alcohol-related problems: social contexts surrounding entry into alcoholism treatment or Alcoholics Anonymous. *Journal of Studies on Alcohol*, **57**, 449–457.

Gidron, B. & Bargal, D. (1986). Self-help awareness in Israel: an expression of structural changes and expanding citizen participation. *Journal of Voluntary Action Research*, **5**, 47–56.

Gidron, B. & Chesler, M. (1994). Universal and particular attributes of self-help: a framework for international and intranational analysis. *Prevention in Human Services*, **11**, 1–44.

Gifford, P. D. (1991). A. A. and N. A. for adolescents. *Journal of Adolescent Chemical Dependency*, **1**, 101–120.

Gilman, S. M., Galanter, M., & Dermatis, H. (2001). Methadone Anonymous: a 12-step program for methadone maintained heroin addicts. *Substance Abuse*, **22**, 247–257.

Glaser, F. B. (1993). Matchless? Alcoholics Anonymous and the matching hypothesis. In *Research on Alcoholics Anonymous: Opportunities and Alternatives*, ed. B. S. McCrady & W. R. Miller, pp. 379–396. New Brunswick, NJ: Rutgers Center of Alcohol Studies.

Glaser, F. B. & Ogborne, A. C. (1982). Does A. A. really work? *British Journal of Addiction*, **77**, 123–129.

Godlawski, T. M., Leukefeld, C., & Cloud, R. (1997). Recovery: with and without self-help. *Substance Use and Misuse*, **32**, 621–627.

Gordon, R. E., Edmunson, E., Bedell, J. R., & Goldstein, N. (1979). Reducing rehospitalization of state mental patients. *Journal of the Florida Medical Association*, **66**, 927–933.

Gorman, J. M. & Rooney, J. F. (1979). The influence of Al-Anon on the coping behavior of wives of alcoholics. *Journal of Studies on Alcohol*, **40**(11), 1030–1038.

Gorsuch, R. (1993). Assessing spiritual variables in Alcoholics Anonymous research. In *Research on Alcoholics Anonymous: Opportunities and Alternatives*, ed. B. S. McCrady & W. R. Miller, pp. 301–318. New Brunswick, NJ: Rutgers Center for Alcohol Studies.

Gottlieb, B. H. & Peters, L. (1991). A national demographic portrait of mutual aid group participants in Canada. *American Journal of Community Psychology*, **19**, 651–666.

Grant, G. & Wenger, C. (1983). Patterns of partnership: three models of care for the elderly. In *Rediscovering Self-Help: Its Role in Social Care*, ed. D. L. Pancoast, P. Parker, & C. Froland, pp. 27–52. Beverly Hills, CA: Sage.

Greenfield, T. K., Stoneking, B. C., & Sundby, E. (1996). Two community support program research demonstrations in Sacramento: experiences of consumer staff as service providers. *Community Psychologist*, **29**, 17–21.

Greil, A. L. & Rudy, D. R. (1983). Conversion to the world view of Alcoholics Anonymous: a refinement of conversion theory. *Qualitative Sociology*, **6**(1), 5–28.

Grimsmo, A., Helgesen, G., & Borchgrevink, C. (1981). Short-term and long-term effects of lay groups on weight reduction. *British Medical Journal*, **283**, 1093–1095.

Haaken, J. (1993). From Al-Anon to ACOA: codependence and the Reconstruction of Caregiving. *Signs*, **18**(21), 321–345.

Hall, J. M. (1996). Lesbians' participation in Alcoholics Anonymous: experiences of social, personal, and political tensions. *Contemporary Drug Problems*, **23**, 113–138.

Harberden, P. V. & Raymakers, T. (1986). Self-help groups and governmental policy in the Netherlands. *Journal of Voluntary Action Research*, **5**, 24–32.

Harper, F. D. (1976). Summary, issues and recommendations. In *Alcohol Abuse and Black America*, ed. F. D. Harper, pp. 187–200. Alexandria, VA: Douglass Publishers.

Hart, K. E. (1999). A spiritual interpretation of the 12 steps of Alcoholics Anonymous: from resentment to forgiveness to love. *Journal of Ministry in Addiction and Recovery*, **6**, 25–39.

Hasin, D. & Grant, B. (1995). AA and other help seeking for alcohol problems: former drinkers in the U.S. general population. *Journal of Substance Abuse*, **7**, 281–292.

Hastie, N. (2000). Origins and activities of a self-help support center in Nottingham, United Kingdom. *International Journal of Self-Help and Self-Care*, **1**, 123–128.

Hatch, S. & Kickbush, I., eds (1983). *Self-Help and Health in Europe: New Approaches in Health Care*. Copenhagen: WHO Regional Office for Europe.

Hayes, T. A. (2002). Potential obstacles to worldview transformation: findings from Debtors Anonymous. *International Journal of Self-Help and Self-Care*, **1**, 353–368.

Helmersson Bergmark, K. (1998). The Links and Alcoholics Anonymous: two "AA movements" in Sweden. In *Diversity in Unity: Studies of Alcoholics Anonymous in Eight Societies*, ed. I. Eisenbach-Stangl & P. Rosenqvist, pp. 75–90. NAD Publication #33. Helsinki: Nordic Council for Alcohol and Drug Research.

Hermalin, J. A. (1986). Self-help clearinghouses: promoting collaboration between professionals and volunteers. *Journal of Voluntary Action Research*, **5**, 64–76.

Hermalin, J. A., Melendez, L., Kamarck, T., Klevans, F., Ballen, E., & Gordon, M. (1979). Enhancing primary prevention: the marriage of self-help groups and formal health care delivery systems. *Journal of Clinical Child Psychology*, **8** (Summer), 125–129.

Hillhouse, M. & Fiorentine, R. (2001). 12-step program participation and effectiveness: do gender and ethnic differences exist? *Journal of Drug Issues*, **31**(3), 767–780.

Hoffman, F. (1994). Cultural adaptations of Alcoholics Anonymous to serve Hispanic populations. *International Journal of Addictions*, **29**(4), 445–460.

Holden, C. (1989). Soviets seek U.S. help in combating alcoholism, *Science*, **246**, 878–879.

Holder, H. (1997). Can individually directed interventions reduce population-level alcohol-involved problems? *Addiction*, **92**, 5–7.

Horgan, C., Skwara, K. C., & Strickler, G. (2001). *Substance Abuse: the nation's Number One Health Problem*. Princeton, NJ: The Robert Wood Johnson Foundation.

Horstmann, M. J. & Tonigan, J. S. (2000). Faith development in Alcoholics Anonymous (AA): a study of two AA groups. *Alcoholism Treatment Quarterly*, **18**, 75–84.

Horvath, A. T. (1997). Alternative support groups. In *Substance Abuse: A Comprehensive Textbook*, ed. J. H. Lowinson, P. Ruiz, R. B. Millman, & J. G. Langrod, pp. 390–396. Baltimore, MD: Williams & Wilkins.

(2000). SMART Recovery. *International Journal of Self-Help and Self-Care*, **1**, 163–169.

Huber, E. (1983). Health enters green pastures: the health movement in the federal republic. In *Self-Help and Health in Europe: New Approaches in Health Care*, ed. S. Hatch & I. Kickbush, pp. 163–167. Copenhagen: WHO Regional Office for Europe.

Hudolin, V. (1984). The alcoholism programme at the University Department of Neurology, Psychiatry, Alcohology, and Other Dependencies, 'Dr. M. Stojanovic' University Hospital, Zagreb. *Alcoholism (Zagreb)*, **20**, 3–51.

Hudson, H. L. (1985). How and why Alcoholics Anonymous works for Blacks. *Alcoholism Treatment Quarterly*, **2**, 11–30.

Hughes, J. M. (1977). Adolescent children of alcoholic parents and the relationship of Alateen to these children. *Journal of Consulting and Clinical Psychology*, **45**, 946–947.

Humble, S. & Unell, J., eds (1989). *Self-Help in Health and Social Welfare: England and West Germany*. London: Routledge.

Humphreys, K. (1993a). Psychotherapy and the twelve step approach for substance abusers: the limits of integration. *Psychotherapy*, **30**, 207–213.

(1993b). *World View Transformations in Adult Children of Alcoholics Mutual Help Groups*. Unpublished doctoral dissertation, University of Illinois at Urbana-Champaign.

(1997a). Self-help/mutual aid organizations: the view from Mars. *Substance Use and Misuse*, **32**, 2105–2109.

(1997b). Clinicians' referral and matching of substance abuse patients to self-help groups after treatment. *Psychiatric Services*, **48**, 1445–1449.

(1997c). Individual and social benefits of mutual aid/self-help groups. *Social Policy*, **27**, 12–19.

(1998). Can addiction-related self-help/mutual aid groups lower demand for professional substance abuse treatment? *Social Policy*, **29**, 13–17.

(1999). Professional interventions that facilitate 12-step self-help group involvement. *Alcohol Health and Research World*, **23**, 93–98.

(2000a). Community narratives and personal stories in Alcoholics Anonymous. *Journal of Community Psychology*, **28**, 495–506.

(2000b, October). *Many Journeys, One Road: Concepts of Recovery across Different Self-Help Organizations*. Presentation to Roundtable on Models and Measurement of the Recovery Process, The Butler Research Center at Hazelden, Center City, MN.

(2002). Alcoholics Anonymous and 12-step alcoholism treatment programs. In *Recent Developments in Alcoholism (vol. XVI): Research on Alcoholism Treatment*, ed. M. Galanter., pp. 149–164. New York: Kluwer Academic.

Humphreys, K., Dearmin Huebsch, P., Moos, R. H., & Finney, J. W. (1999a). A comparative evaluation of substance abuse treatment: V. Treatment can enhance the effectiveness of self-help groups. *Alcoholism: Clinical and Experimental Research*, **23**, 558–563.

Humphreys, K., Finney, J. W., & Moos, R. H. (1994). Applying a stress and coping framework to research on mutual help organizations. *Journal of Community Psychology*, **22**, 312–327.

Humphreys, K., Greenbaum, M. A., Noke, J. M., & Finney, J. W. (1996). Reliability, validity, and normative data for a short version of the Understanding of Alcoholism scale. *Psychology of Addictive Behaviors*, **10**, 38–44.

Humphreys, K. & Hamilton, E. G. (1995). Advocacy and self-reliance: the resurgence of mutual help organizations in African American communities. *Social Policy*, **25**, 24–32.

Humphreys, K. & Kaskutas, L. A. (1995). World views of Alcoholics Anonymous, Women for Sobriety, and Adult Children of Alcoholics/Al-Anon Mutual Help Groups. *Addiction Research*, **3**, 231–243.

Humphreys, K., Kaskutas, L. A., & Weisner, C. (1998a). The relationship of pre-treatment Alcoholics Anonymous affiliation with problem severity, social resources, and treatment history. *Drug and Alcohol Dependence*, **49**, 123–131.

(1998b). The Alcoholics Anonymous Affiliation Scale: development, reliability and norms for diverse treated and untreated populations. *Alcoholism: Clinical and Experimental Research*, **22**, 974–978.

Humphreys, K. & Klaw, E. (2001). Can targeting non-dependent problem drinkers and providing internet-based services expand access to assistance for alcohol problems? A study of the Moderation Management self-help/mutual aid organization. *Journal of Studies on Alcohol*, **62**, 528–532.

Humphreys, K., Loomis, C., & Joshi, A. (2002). *Unrepresentativeness of Enrolled Participants in Clinical Trials: An Enduring Challenge for Medical Research*. Palo Alto, CA: Center for Health Care Evaluation.

Humphreys, K., Macus, S., Stewart, E., & Oliva, E. (2002). *Using Media and Education to Support Self-Help Groups: Project MESH Process and Outcomes*. Palo Alto, CA: Center for Health Care Evaluation.

Humphreys, K., Mankowski, E., Moos, R. H., & Finney, J. W. (1999b). Do enhanced friendship networks and active coping mediate the effect of self-help groups on substance use? *Annals of Behavioral Medicine*, **21**, 54–60.

Humphreys, K., Mavis, B. E., & Stöffelmayr, B. E. (1991, July). *Substance Abuse Treatment Agencies and Self-Help Groups: collaborators or Competitors? (Resources in Education)*. ERIC Document #341 927: University of Michigan, Ann Arbor.

(1994). Are twelve step programs appropriate for disenfranchised groups? Evidence from a study of posttreatment mutual help involvement. *Prevention in Human Services*, **11**, 165–179.

Humphreys, K. & Moos, R. H. (1996). Reduced substance abuse-related health care costs among voluntary participants in Alcoholics Anonymous. *Psychiatric Services*, **47**, 709–713.

(2001). Can encouraging substance abuse inpatients to participate in self-help groups reduce demand for health care? A quasi-experimental study. *Alcoholism: Clinical and Experimental Research*, **25**, 711–716.

Humphreys, K., Moos, R. H., & Cohen, C. (1997). Social and community resources and long-term recovery from treated and untreated alcoholism. *Journal of Studies on Alcohol*, **58**, 231–238.

Humphreys, K. & Noke, J. M. (1997). The influence of posttreatment mutual help group participation on the friendship networks of substance abuse patients. *American Journal of Community Psychology*, **25**, 1–17.

Humphreys, K., Noke, J. M., & Moos, R. H. (1996). Recovering substance abuse staff members' professional roles and beliefs about addiction. *Journal of Substance Abuse Treatment*, **13**, 75–78.

Humphreys, K., Phibbs, C. S., & Moos, R. H. (1996). Addressing self-selection effects in evaluations of mutual help groups and professional mental health services: an introduction to two-stage sample selection models. *Evaluation and Program Planning*, **19**, 301–308.

Humphreys, K. & Rappaport, J. (1993). From community mental health to the war on drugs: a study in the definition of social problems. *American Psychologist*, **48**, 892–901. Available in German as (1994): Von der bewegung für gemeindenaha psychsoziale versorgung zum krieg den drogen: eins studie über die definition sozialer probleme. *Psychologie und Gesellschafts Kritik*, **17**, 79–106.

(1994). Researching self-help/mutual aid groups and organizations: many roads, one journey. *Applied and Preventive Psychology*, **3**, 217–231.

Humphreys, K. & Ribisl, K. (1999). The case for a partnership with self-help groups. *Public Health Reports*, **114**, 322–327.

Humphreys, K. & Tucker, J. (2002). Towards more responsive and effective intervention systems for alcohol-related problems. *Addiction*, **97**, 126–132.

Humphreys, K. & Weingardt, K. R. (2000). Assessing readmission to substance abuse treatment as an indicator of outcome and program performance. *Psychiatric Services*, **51**, 1568–1569.

Humphreys, K. & Weisner, C. (2000). Use of exclusion criteria in selecting research subjects and its effect on the generalizability of alcohol treatment outcome studies. *American Journal of Psychiatry*, **157**, 588–594.

Humphreys, K. & Woods, M. (1993). Researching mutual help group affiliation in a segregated society. *Journal of Applied Behavioral Science*, **29**, 181–201.

Ino, A. & Hayasida, M. (2000). Before-discharge intervention method in the treatment of alcohol dependence. *Alcoholism: Clinical and Experimental Research*, **24**, 373–376.

Isenhart, C. E. (1997). Pretreatment readiness for change in male alcohol dependent subjects: predictors of one-year follow-up status. *Journal of Studies on Alcohol*, **58**, 351–357.

Jaffe, J. H. (1980). Commonalities and diversity among drug-use patterns in different countries. In *Drug Problems in the Sociocultural Context: A Basis for policies and Programme Planning*, ed. G. Edwards & A. Arif, pp. 94–105. Geneva: WHO.

James, W. J. (1890/1981). *The Principles of Psychology*, 3 vols. Cambridge, MA: Harvard University Press.

(1902/1985). *The Varieties of Religious Experience*. Cambridge, MA: Harvard University Press.

Janzen, R. (2001). *The Rise and Fall of Synanon: A California Utopia.* Baltimore: Johns Hopkins University Press.

Jarrad, J. (1997). The Brazilianization of Alcoholics Anonymous. In *The Brazilian Puzzle*, ed. D. Hess & R. da Matta, pp. 209–236. New York: Columbia University Press.

Jason, L. A. (1985). Using the media to foster self-help groups. *Professional Psychology*, **16**, 455–464.

Jason, L. A., Davis, M. I., Ferrari, J. R., & Bishop, P. D. (2001). Oxford House: a review of research and implications for substance abuse recovery and community research. *Journal of Drug Education*, **31**, 1–27.

Jason, L. A., Ferrari, J. R., Dvorchak, P. A., Groessl, E. J., & Molloy, J. P. (1997a). The characteristics of alcoholics in self-help residential treatment settings: a multi-site study of Oxford House. *Alcoholism Treatment Quarterly*, **15**, 53–63.

Jason, L. A., Ferrari, J. R., Smith, B., *et al.* (1997b). An exploratory study of male recovering substance abusers living in a self-help, self-governed setting. *Journal of Mental Health Administration*, **24**, 332–339.

Jason, L., Goodman, D., Thomas, N., Iacono, G., & Tabon, D. (1988). Clergy's knowledge of self-help groups in a large metropolitan area. *Journal of Psychology and Theology*, **16**(1), 34–40.

Jason, L. A., Gruder, C. L., Martino, S., Flay, B. R., Warnecke, R., & Thomas, N. (1987). Work site group meetings and the effectiveness of a televised smoking cessation intervention. *American Journal of Community Psychology*, **15**, 57–72.

Jason, L. A., La Pointe, O., & Billingham, S. (1986). The media and self-help: a preventive community intervention. *Journal of Primary Prevention*, **6**, 156–167.

Jensen, P. S. (1983). Risk, protective factors, and supportive interventions in chronic airway obstruction. *Archives of General Psychiatry*, **40**, 70–74.

Jilek-Aall, L. (1981). Acculturation, alcoholism and Indianstyle Alcoholics Anonymous. *Journal of Studies on Alcohol*, **9**, 143–158.

Johnsen, E. & Herringer, L. G. (1993). A note on the utilization of common support activities and relapse following substance abuse treatment. *Journal of Psychology*, **127**(1), 73–78.

Jones, R. K. (1970). Sectarian characteristics of Alcoholics Anonymous. *Sociology (Oxford)*, **4**, 181–195.

Jurik, N. C. (1987). Persuasion in a self-help group. *Small Group Behavior*, **18**, 368–397.

Kahneman, D. (1965). Control of spurious association and reliability of the controlled variable. *Psychological Bulletin*, **64**, 326–329.

Kaminer, W. (1992). *I'm Dysfunctional, You're Dysfunctional: The Recovery Movement and other Self-Help Fashions.* New York: Vintage Books.

Kanfer, F. H. & Schefft, B. K. (1988). *Guiding the Process of Therapeutic Change.* Champaign, IL: Research Press.

Kaskutas, L. A. (1992a). *An Analysis of Women for Sobriety.* Doctoral dissertation available from UMI, order number 9330441.

(1992b). Beliefs on the source of sobriety: interactions of membership in Women for Sobriety and Alcoholics Anonymous. *Contemporary Drug Problems*, **19**, (Winter), 631–648.

(1994). What do women get out of self-help? Their reasons for attending Women for Sobriety and Alcoholics Anonymous. *Journal of Substance Abuse Treatment*, **11**, 185–195.

(1996a). A road less traveled: choosing the Women for Sobriety Program. *Journal of Drug Issues*, **26**, 77–94.

(1996b). Pathways to self-help among Women for Sobriety. *American Journal of Drug and Alcohol Abuse*, **22**, 259–280.

(1998). Hip and helpful: Alcoholics Anonymous in Marin County, California. In *Diversity in Unity: Studies of Alcoholics Anonymous in Eight Societies*, ed. I. Eisenbach-Stangl & P. Rosenqvist, pp. 25–54. NAD Publication #33. Helsinki: Nordic Council for Alcohol and Drug Research.

Kaskutas, L. A., Bond, J. A., & Humphreys, K. (2002). Social networks as mediators of the effect of Alcoholics Anonymous. *Addiction*, **97**, 891–900.

Kaskutas, L. A., Weisner, C., Lee, M., & Humphreys, K. (1999). Alcoholics Anonymous affiliation at treatment intake among Whites and African Americans. *Journal of Studies on Alcohol*, **60**, 810–816.

Kassel, J. D. & Wagner, E. F. (1993). Processes of change in Alcoholics Anonymous: a review of possible mechanisms. *Psychotherapy*, **30**, 222–234.

Katz, A. H. (1981). Self-help and mutual aid: an emerging social movement? *Annual Review of Sociology*, **7**, 129–155.

(1986). Fellowship, helping and healing: the re-emergence of self-help groups. *Journal of Voluntary Action Research*, **5**, 4–13.

Katz, A. H. & Bender, E. (1976). *The Strength in Us: Self-Help in the Modern World.* New York: New Viewpoints.

Kaufmann, C. (1994). Roles for mental health consumers in self-help group research. In *Understanding the Self-Help Organization: Frameworks and Findings*, ed. T. J. Powell, pp. 154–171. Thousand Oaks, CA: Sage.

Keller, M. (1990). But "divine interventions" intervene. *Journal of Substance Abuse*, **2**, 473–475.

Kelly, J. F., Myers, M. G., & Brown, S. A. (2000). A multivariate process model of adolescent 12-step attendance and substance use outcome following inpatient treatment. *Psychology of Addictive Behaviors*, **14**, 376–389.

(2002). Do adolescents affiliate with 12-step groups: a multivariate process model of effects. *Journal of Studies on Alcohol*, **63**, 293–304.

Kennedy, M. (1995). *Ideology and Transformation in Committed Members of a Mental health Mutual Help group.* Doctoral dissertation, School of Education, University of Illinois at Urbana-Champaign.

Kennedy, M. & Humphreys, K. (1994). Understanding world view transformation in mutual help groups. *Prevention in Human Services*, **11**, 181–198.

Kessler, R. C., Mickelson, K. D., & Zhao, S. (1997). Patterns and correlates of self-help group membership in the United States. *Social Policy*, **27**, 27–46.

Kessler, R. C., Zhao, S., Katz, S. J., *et al.* (1999). Past-year use of outpatient services for psychiatric problems in the National Comorbidity Survey. *American Journal of Psychiatry*, **156**, 115–123.

Kickbush, I. & Hatch, S. (1983). A re-orientation of health care? In *Self-Help and Health in Europe: New Approaches in Health Care*, ed. S. Hatch & I. Kickbush, pp. 1–9. Copenhagen: WHO Regional Office for Europe.

Kingree, J. & Ruback, R. B. (1994). Understanding self-help groups. In *Understanding the Self-Help Organization: Frameworks and Findings*, ed. T. J. Powell, pp. 272–292. Thousand Oaks, CA: Sage.

Kingree, J. & Thompson, M. (2000). Mutual help groups, perceived status benefits, and well-being: a test with adult children of alcoholics with personal substance abuse problems. *American Journal of Community Psychology*, **28**, 325–342.

Kirkpatrick, J. (1977). *Turnabout: New Help for the Alcoholic Woman*. New York: Bantam.

(1981). *A Fresh Start*. Dubuque, IA: Kendall/Hunt Publishing.

(2000). A "new life" program: Women for Sobriety. *International Journal of Self-Help and Self-Care*, **1**, 159–162.

Kishline, A. (1994). *Moderate Drinking: The Moderation Management Guide for People who Want to Reduce their Drinking*. New York: Crown.

Klaw, E., Huebsch, P. D., & Humphreys, K. (2000). Communication patterns in an on-line mutual help group for problem drinkers. *Journal of Community Psychology*, **28**, 535–546.

Klaw, E. & Humphreys, K. (2000). Life stories of Moderation Management mutual help group members. *Contemporary Drug Problems*, **27**, 779–803.

Kleist, J. (1990). *Network Resource Utilization Patterns of Members of Alcoholics Anonymous*. Unpublished doctoral dissertation, University of Akron, Akron, Ohio.

Kloos, B. (1999). *Cultivating Identity: Meaning-Making in the Context of Residential Treatment Settings for Persons with Histories of Psychological Disorders*. Doctoral dissertation, Department of Psychology, University of Illinois at Urbana-Champaign.

Knight, B., Wollert, R. W., Levy, L. H., Frame, C. L., & Padgett, V. P. (1980). Self-help groups: the members perspectives. *American Journal of Community Psychology*, **8**(1), 53–65.

Kozlowski, L. T., Jelinek, L. C., & Pope, M. A. (1986). Cigarette smoking among alcohol abuses: a continuing and neglected problem. *Canadian Journal of Public Health*, **77**, 205–207.

Kropotkin, P. (1955). *Mutual Aid: A Factor in Evolution*. Boston: Extending Horizons Books.

Kurtz, E. (1979/1991). *Not-God: A History of Alcoholics Anonymous*. Center City, MN: Hazelden.

(1982). Why A. A. works: the intellectual significance of Alcoholics Anonymous. *Journal of Studies on Alcohol*, **43**(1), 38–80.

(1992). Commentary. In *Annual Review of Addictions Research and Treatment*, ed. J. W. Lagenbucher, B. S. McCrady, W. Frankenstein, & P. E. Nathan, vol. 2, pp. 397–400. New York: Pergamon Press.

(1993). Research on Alcoholics Anonymous: the historical context. In *Research on Alcoholics Anoymous: Opportunities and Alternatives*, ed. B. S. McCrady & W. R. Miller, pp. 13–26. New Brunswick, NJ: Rutgers Center of Alcohol Studies.

(1999a). The spirituality of William James: a lesson from Alcoholics Anonymous. In *The Collected Ernie Kurtz*, pp. 63–76. Wheeling, WV: The Bishop of Books.

(1999b). Alcoholics Anonymous: A phenomenon in American religious history. In *The Collected Ernie Kurtz*, pp. 23–38. Wheeling, WV: The Bishop of Books.

Kurtz, E. & Ketcham, K. (1992). *The Spirituality of Imperfection: Modern Wisdom from Classic Stories*. New York: Bantam.

Kurtz, L. F. (1984). Ideological differences between professionals and A. A. members. *Alcoholism Treatment Quarterly*, 1(2), 73–85.

(1985). Cooperation and rivalry between helping professionals and members of AA. *Health and Social Work*, **10**, 104–112.

(1988). Mutual aid for affective disorders: the manic depressive and depressive association. *American Journal of Orthopsychiatry*, **58**, 152–155.

(1990). Twelve-step Programs. In *Working with Self-Help*, ed. T. J. Powell, pp. 93–119. Silver Spring, MD: NASW Press.

(1994). Self-help groups for families with mental illness or alcoholism. In *Understanding the Self-Help Organization: Frameworks and Findings*, ed. T. J. Powell, pp. 293–313. Thousand Oaks, CA: Sage.

(1997a). *Self-Help and Support Groups: A Handbook for Practitioners*. Thousand Oaks, CA: Sage.

(1997b). Recovery, the 12-step movement, and politics. *Social Work*, **42**, 403–405.

Kurtz, L. F. & Chambon, A. (1987). Comparison of self-help groups for mental health. *Health and Social Work*, **12**, 275–283.

Kurtz, L. F., Garvin, C. D., Hill, E. M., Pollio, D., McPherson, S., & Powell, T. J. (1995). Involvement in Alcoholics Anonymous by persons with dual disorders. *Alcoholism Treatment Quarterly*, **12**, 1–18.

Kurube, N. (1992a). The ideological and organizational development of the Swedish Links movement. *Contemporary Drug Problems*, **19**, 649–676.

(1992b). National models: self-help groups for alcohol problems not applying the Twelve Steps program. *Contemporary Drug Problems*, **19**(4), 689–715.

Kus, R. (1991). Sobriety, friends, and gay men. *Archives of Psychiatric Nursing*, **5**, 171–177.

Kyrouz, E. M. & Humphreys, K. (1996). Do psychiatrically disabled people benefit from participation in self-help/mutual aid organizations? A research review. *Community Psychologist*, **29**, 21–25.

Lang, B. & Srdar, L. (1992). Therapeutic communities and aftercare clubs in Yugoslavia. In *Cure, Care or Control: Alcoholism Treatment in Sixteen Countries*, ed. H. Klingemann, J. P. Takala, & G. Hunt, pp. 53–63. Albany, NY: State University of New York Press.

Laudet, A. (2000). Substance abuse treatment providers' referral to self-help: review and future empirical directions. *International Journal of Self-Help and Self-Care*, **1**, 213–226.

Laudet, A., Magura, S., Vogel, H. S., & Knight, E. (2000a). Recovery challenges among dual-diagnosed individuals. *Journal of Substance Abuse Treatment*, **18**, 321–329.

(2000b, November). *Twelve Month Follow-Up on Members of a Dual Recovery Self-Help Program.* Paper presented at the American Public Health Association, Boston, Massachusetts.

Lavoie, F. (1983). Citizen participation in health care. In *Rediscovering Self-Help: Its Role in Social Care*, ed. D. L. Pancoast, P. Parker, & C. Froland, pp. 225–238. Beverly Hills, CA: Sage.

Lavoie, F., Borkman, T., & Gidron, B. (1994). Conclusion. In *Self-Help and Mutual Aid Groups: International and Multicultural Perspectives*, ed. F. Lavoie, T. Borkman, & B. Gidron, pp. 333–340. New York: Haworth.

Lavoie, F., Farquharson, A., & Kennedy, M. (1994). Workshop on "good practice" in the collaboration between professionals and mutual aid groups. *Prevention in Human Services*, **11**, 303–313.

Lazarou, J., Pomeranz, B. H., & Corey, P. (1998). Incidence of adverse drug reactions in hospitalized patients: a meta-analysis of prospective studies. *Journal of the American Medical Association*, **279**, 1200–1205.

Leach, B. (1973). Does Alcoholics Anonymous really work? In *Alcoholism: Progress in Research and Treatment*, ed. P. G. Bourne & R. Fox, pp. 245–284. New York: Academic Press.

Levy, L. H. (1984). Issues in research and evaluation. In *The Self-Help Revolution*, ed. A. Garner & F. Riessman, pp. 155–172. New York: Human Sciences Press.

Lhermitte, F. (1975). L'Alcoolique en probation l'appui des 'buveurs guéris'. *Revue de l'alcoolisme*, **12**, 65–72.

Li, E., Strohm, M., & Feifer, C. (1998). A cross-sectional comparison of locus of control in Alcoholics Anonymous and SMART Recovery treatment groups. *Journal of Addictive Disease*, **17**, 153.

Lichtenstein, E. (1999). Nicotine Anonymous: community resource and research implications. *Psychology of Addictive Behaviors*, **13**, 60–68.

Lieberman, M. (1986). Self-help groups and psychiatry. *Annual Review of Psychiatry*, **5**, 744–760.

Lieberman, M. A. & Bond, G. R. (1979). Problems in studying outcomes. In *Self-Help Groups for Coping with Crisis*, ed. L. D. Borman, pp. 323–340. San Francisco: Jossey-Bass.

Lieberman, M. A. & Videka-Sherman, L. (1986). The impact of self-help groups on the mental health of widows and widowers. *American Journal of Orthopsychiatry*, **56**(3), 435–449.

Long, P. (1985). The ebb and flow of treatment emphasis. In *Proceedings of the 31st International Institute on the Prevention and Treatment of Alcoholism*, ed. A. Tongue & E. Tongue, vol. II, pp. 69–77. Rome: Vigna.

Longabaugh, R., Wirtz, P. W., Zweben, A., & Stout, R. L. (1998). Network support for drinking, Alcoholics Anonymous and long-term matching effects. *Addiction*, **93**, 1313–1333.

López, J. A. E. (1988). Panorama actual de tratamiento y la rehabilitación de los alcohólicos en México. In *Alcohol Consumption among Mexicans and*

Mexican-Americans: A Binational Perspective, ed. M. J. Gilbert, pp. 175–197. Los Angeles: University of California.

Lorig K., Ritter, P. L., Stewart, A. L., *et al.* (2001). Chronic disease self-management program: 2-year health status and health care utilization outcomes. *Medical Care*, **39**, 1217–1223.

Lyons, J. S., O'Mahoney, M. T., Miller, S. I., Neme, J., Kabat, J., & Miller, F. (1997). Predicting readmission to the psychiatric hospital in a managed care environment: implications for quality indicators. *American Journal of Psychiatry*, **154**(3), 337–340.

Madara, E. J. (1986). A comprehensive systems approach to promoting mutual aid self-help groups: the New Jersey self-help clearinghouse model. *Journal of Voluntary Action Research*, **57**, 57–63.

(in press). Ways to increase the development, awareness, and use of self-help groups. *American Journal of Community Psychology*.

Madsen, W. (1974). Alcoholics Anonymous as a crisis cult. *Alcohol Health and Research World*, Spring, 27–30.

Mäkelä, K. (1991). Social and cultural preconditions of Alcoholics Anonymous (AA) and factors associated with the strength of AA. *British Journal of Addiction*, **86**, 1405–1413.

(1993). Implications for research of the cultural variability of Alcoholics Anonymous. In *Research on Alcoholics Anonymous: Opportunities and Alternatives*, ed. B. S. McCrady & W. R. Miller, pp. 189–208. New Brunswick, NJ: Rutgers Center of Alcohol Studies.

Mäkelä, K., Arminen, I., Bloomfield, K., *et al.* (1996). *Alcoholics Anonymous as a Mutual Help Movement: A Study in Eight Societies*. Madison, WI: University of Wisconsin Press.

Malenbaum, R., Herzog, D., Eisenthal, S., & Wyshak, G. (1988). Overeaters Anonymous: impact on bulimia. *International Journal of Eating Disorders*, **7**, 139–143.

Mann, R. E., Smart, R. G., Anglin, L., & Adlaf, E. M. (1991). Reductions in cirrhosis deaths in the United States: associations with per capita consumption and AA membership. *Journal of Studies on Alcohol*, **52**, 361–365.

Marlatt, G. A. (1978). Craving for alcohol, loss of control, and relapse: a cognitive–behavioral analysis. In *Alcoholism: New Directions in Behavioral Research and Treatment*, ed. P. E. Nathan, G. A. Marlatt, & T. Loberk. New York: Plenum Press.

Marmar, C. R., Horowitz, M. J., Weiss, D. S., Wilner, N. R., & Kaltreider, N. B. (1988). A controlled trial of brief psychotherapy and mutual-help group treatment of conjugal bereavement. *American Journal of Psychiatry*, **145**, 203–209.

Marrs, R. W. (1995). A meta-analysis of bibliotherapy studies. *American Journal of Community Psychology*, **23**, 843–870.

Martin, J. E. (1992). The evolution of Al-Anon: a content analysis of stories in two editions of its "Big Book." *Contemporary Drug Problems*, **19** (Winter), 563–585.

Martin, J. E., Calfas, K. J., Patten, C. A., *et al.* (1997). Prospective evaluation of three smoking interventions in 205 recovering alcoholics: one-year results of Project SCRAP-Tobacco. *Journal of Consulting and Clinical Psychology*, **65**, 190–194.

Maruyama, M., Higuchi, S., & Hayashida, M. (1994). A study of preventive measures for redrinking in alcoholics. *Japanese Journal of Drug and Alcohol Dependence,* **29**, 139–146.

Maslow, A. H. (1964). *Religion, Values, and Peak-Experiences.* Colombus, OH: Ohio State University.

Master, L. (1989). Jewish experiences of Alcoholics Anonymous. *Smith College Studies in Social Work,* **59**(2), 183–199.

Matijevic, I. & Paunovic, N. (1973). Rehabilitation of alcoholics in a club of treated alcoholics. *Alcoholism (Zagreb),* **9**, 50–54.

Maton, K. I. (1988). Social support, organizational characteristics, psychological well-being, and group appraisal in three self-help group populations. *American Journal of Community Psychology,* **16**(1), 53–77.

(1989). Towards an ecological understanding of mutual-help groups: the social ecology of "fit." *American Journal of Community Psychology,* **17**(6), 729–753.

Matzat, J. (1989). Some remarks on West Germany's health and welfare system and the position of self-help. In *Self-Help in Health and Social Welfare: England and West Germany,* ed. S. Humble & J. Unell, pp. 3–13. London: Routledge.

(2002). The development of self-help groups and support for them in Germany. *International Journal of Self-Help and Self-Care,* **1**, 307–322.

Maxwell, M. A. (1984). *The A. A. Experience: A Close-Up View for Professionals.* New York: McGraw-Hill.

McAuliffe, W. E. (1990). A randomized clinical trial of recovery training and self-help for opioid addicts in New England and Hong Kong. *Journal of Psychoactive Drugs,* **22**, 197–209.

McCrady, B. S., Epstein, E. E., & Hirsch, L. S. (1996). Issues in the implementation of a randomized clinical trial that includes Alcoholics Anonymous: studying AA-related behaviors during treatment. *Journal of Studies on Alcohol,* **57**, 604–612.

(1999). Maintaining change after conjoint behavioral alcohol treatment for men: outcomes at six months. *Addiction,* **94**, 1381–1396.

McCrady, B. S. & Irvine, S. (1989). Self-help groups. In *Handbook of Alcoholism Treatment Approaches: Effective Alternatives,* ed. R. K. Hester & W. R. Miller, pp. 153–169. New York: Pergamon Press.

McCrady, B. S. & Miller, W. R., eds (1993). *Research on Alcoholics Anonymous: Opportunities and Alternatives.* New Brunswick, NJ: Rutgers Center of Alcohol Studies.

McFadden, L., Seidman, E., & Rappaport, J. (1992). A comparison of espoused theories of self- and mutual-help: implications for mental health professionals. *Professional Psychology: Research and Practice,* **23**(6), 515–520.

McIntire, D. (2000). How well does AA work? An analysis of published AA surveys (1968–1996) and related analyses/comments. *Alcoholism Treatment Quarterly,* **18**, 1–18.

McKay, J. R., Alterman, A. I., McLellan, A. T., & Snider, E. C. (1994). Treatment goals, continuity of care, and outcome in a day hospital substance abuse rehabilitation program. *American Journal of Psychiatry,* **151**(2), 254–259.

McKellar, J. D., Stewart, E., & Humphreys, K. (2003). AA involvement and positive alcohol-related outcomes: cause, consequence, or just a correlate? A prospective

2-year study of 2319 alcohol dependent males. *Journal of Consulting and Clinical Psychology*, **21**, 302–308.

McKnight, J. (1995). *The Careless Society: Community and its Counterfeits*. New York: Basic Books.

McLatchie, B. H. & Lomp, K. G. (1988). Alcoholics Anonymous affiliation and treatment outcome among a clinical sample of problem drinkers. *American Journal of Drug and Alcohol Abuse*, **14**(3), 309–324.

Medvene, L. J., Wituk, S., & Luke, D. A. (1999). Characteristics of self-help group leaders: the significance of professional and founder statuses. *International Journal of Self-Help and Self-Care*, **1**, 91–105.

Meehl, P. E. (1970). Nuisance variables and the ex post facto design. In *Minnestor Studies in the Philosophy of Science*, ed. M. Radner & S. Vinokur, pp. 372–402. Minneapolis: University of Minnesota Press.

Meissen, G. J., Gleason, D. F., & Embree, M. G. (1991). An assessment of the needs of mutual-help groups. *American Journal of Community Psychology*, **19**(3), 427–442.

Meissen, G. J., Mason, W. C., & Gleason, D. F. (1991). Understanding the attitudes and intentions of future professionals toward self-help. *American Journal of Community Psychology*, **19**(5), 699–714.

Meissen, G., Powell, T. J., Wituk, S. A., Girrens, K., & Arteaga, S. (1999). Attitudes of AA contact persons toward group participation by persons with mental illness. *Psychiatric Services*, **50**, 1079–1081.

Meissen, G., Wituk, S., Warren, M. L., & Shepherd, M. D. (2000). Self-help groups and managed care: obstacles and opportunities. *International Journal of Self-Help and Self-Care*, **1**, 201–210.

Miller, G. A. & Chapman, J. P. (2001). Misunderstanding analysis of covariance. *Journal of Abnormal Psychology*, **110**, 40–48.

Miller, W. R. (1990). Spirituality: the silent dimension in addiction research. The 1990 Leonard Ball oration. *Drug and Alcohol Review*, **9**, 259–266.

   (1998). Researching the spiritual dimensions of alcohol and other drug problems. *Addiction*, **93**, 979–990.

Miller, W. R. & Kurtz, E. (1994). Models of alcoholism used in treatment: contrasting AA and other perspectives with which it is often confused. *Journal of Studies on Alcohol*, **55**(2), 159–166.

Miller, W. R. & McCrady, B. S. (1993). The importance of research on Alcoholics Anonymous. *Research on Alcoholics Anonymous: Opportunities and Alternatives*, ed. B. S. McCrady & W. R. Miller, pp. 3–12. New Brunswick, NJ: Rutgers Center of Alcohol Studies.

Miller, W. R., Meyers, R. J., & Tonigan, J. S. (1999). Engaging the unmotivated in treatment for alcohol problems: a comparison of three strategies for intervention through family members. *Journal of Consulting and Clinical Psychology*, **67**, 688–697.

Montaño Fraire, R. (2000). Entornos grupales autogestivos para la ayuda mutua: reseña de investigación. *Psicología Iberoamericana*, **8**, 3–4.

Montgomery, H., Miller, W. R., & Tonigan, J. S. (1995). Does Alcoholics Anonymous involvement predict treatment outcome? *Journal of Substance Abuse Treatment*, **12**, 241–246.

Moos, R. H. (1997a). How to become a true scientist: a guide to minimizing pesky treatment effects. *Addiction*, **92**, 481–482.

(1997b). *Evaluating Treatment Environments: The Quality of Psychiatric and Substance Abuse Programs*, 2nd edn. New Brunswick, NJ: Transaction Publishing.

Moos, R. H., Finney, J. W., & Cronkite, R. C. (1990). *Alcoholism Treatment: Context, Process, and Outcome*. New York: Oxford University Press.

Moos, R. H., Finney, J. W., Ouimette, P. C., & Suchinsky, R. T. (1999). A comparative evaluation of substance abuse treatment: treatment orientation, amount of care, and 1-year outcomes. *Alcoholism: Clinical and Experimental Research*, **23**, 529–536.

Moos, R., Schaefer, J., Andrassy, J., & Moos, B. (2001). Outpatient mental healthcare, self-help groups, and patients' one-year treatment outcomes. *Journal of Clinical Psychology*, **57**(3), 273–287.

Morawski, J. (1992). The odyssey of the Polish alcohol treatment system. In *Cure, Care or Control: Alcoholism Treatment in Sixteen Countries*, ed. H. Klingemann, J. P. Takala, & G. Hunt, pp. 39–52. Albany, NY: State University of New York Press.

Morgan, O. J. (1995). Recovery-sensitive counseling in the treatment of alcoholism. *Alcoholism Treatment Quarterly*, **13**, 63–73.

(1999). "Chemical comforting" and the theology of John C. Ford Sr.: classic answers to a contemporary problem. *Journal of Ministry in Addiction and Recovery*, **6**, 29–66.

Morgenstern, J., Labouvie, E., McCrady, B. S., Kahler, C. W., & Frey, R. M. (1997). Affiliation with Alcoholics Anonymous following treatment: a study of its therapeutic effects and mechanisms of action. *Journal of Consulting and Clinical Psychology*, **65**, 768–777.

Morgenstern, J. & McCrady, B. S. (1993). Cognitive processes and change in disease-model treatment. In *Research on Alcoholics Anonymous: Opportunities and Alternatives*, ed. B. S. McCrady & W. R. Miller, pp. 153–166. New Brunswick, NJ: Rutgers Center of Alcohol Studies.

Morrell, C. (1996). Radicalizing recovery: addiction, spirituality and politics. *Social Work*, **41**, 306–312.

Mowrer, O. H., Vattano, A., Baxley, G. B., & Mowrer, M. C. (1975). *Integrity Groups – The Loss and Recovery of Community*. Urbana, IL: Integrity Groups.

Narcotics Anonymous (1992). *An Introductory Guide to Narcotics Anonymous (revised)*. Van Nuys, CA: NA World Service Office.

(1995a). *Narcotics Anonymous: A Commitment to Community Partnerships*. Paper presented at the 37th International Congress on Alcohol and Drug Dependence, San Diego, California.

(1995b). *Facts about Narcotics Anonymous*. Van Nuys, CA: NA World Service Office.

(1996). Weekly NA meetings worldwide. *NA Update*, September, p. 1.

(2000). *Annual Report*. Van Nuys, CA: NA World Service Office.

Nash, K. & Kramer, K. D. (1993). Self-help for sickle cell disease in African-American communities. *Journal of Applied Behavioral Science*, **29**, 202–215.

Nealon-Woods, M. A., Ferrari, J. R., & Jason, L. A. (1995). Twelve-step program use among Oxford House residents: spirituality or support in sobriety? *Journal of Substance Abuse*, **7**, 311–318.

Neighbors, H. W., Elliott, K. A., & Gant, L. M. (1990). Self-help and Black Americans: a strategy for empowerment. In *Working with Self-Help*, ed. T. J. Powell, pp. 189–217. Silver Springs: NASW Press.

Nelson, G. (1994). The development of a mental health coalition: a case study. *American Journal of Community Psychology*, **22**, 229–255.

Nicholaichuk, T. P. & Wollert, R. (1989). The effects of self-help on health status and health-services utilization. *Canadian Journal of Community Mental Health*, **8**(1), 17–29.

Noda, T., Kawata, A., Ando, T., *et al.* (1988). Survey on the actual condition of alcoholics in a satellite city – Takatsui City – and a follow-up study in relation to a community support system. *Japanese Journal of Alcohol Studies and Drug Dependence*, **23**(1), 26–52.

Noordsy, D. L., Schwab, B., Fox, L., & Drake, R. E. (1994). In *Understanding the Self-Help Organization: Frameworks and Findings*, ed. T. J. Powell, pp. 314–330. Thousand Oaks, CA: Sage.

Nowinski, J., Baker, S., & Carroll, K. (1995). *Twelve-Step Facilitation Therapy Manual: A Clinical Research Guide for Therapists Treating Individuals with Alcohol Abuse and Dependence*. NIAAA (NIH Publication #94-3722). Rockville, MD: NIAAA.

O'Brien, M. (1996). *The Meaning of Recovery: An Ethnographic Study of NA in Melbourne*. Paper presented at the International Congress on Alcohol and Drug Dependence, San Diego, California.

O'Connell, T. (1989). Jewish alcoholics face unique problems. *US Journal of Drug and Alcohol Dependence*, **13**(4), 8.

Ogborne, A. C. (1996). Professional opinions and practices concerning Alcoholics Anonymous: a review of the literature and research agenda. *Contemporary Drug Problems*, **23**(Spring), 93–111.

Ogborne, A. C. & Bornet, A. (1982). Abstinence and abusive drinking among affiliates of Alcoholics Anonymous: are these the only alternatives? *Addictive Behaviors*, **7**, 199–202.

Oka, T. (1994a). Self-help groups in Japan. *Prevention in Human Services*, **11**, 69–95.

(1994b). *Self-Help Groups of Japanese Alcoholics: Their Movements and Cultural Influences*. Paper presented at the conference on addiction and mutual help in comparative perspective, Toronto, Canada.

Ólafsdóttir, H. (1986). *The growth of self-help in the response to alcohol problems in Iceland*. In *Proceedings of the 31st International Institute on the Prevention and Treatment of Alcoholism*, ed. A. Tongue & E. Tongue, pp. 99–107. Rome: Vigna.

(2000). *Alcoholics Anonymous in Iceland: From Marginality to Mainstream Culture*. University of Iceland Press.

O'Leary, M. R., Calsyn, D. A., Haddock, D. L., & Freeman, C. W. (1980). Differential alcohol use patterns and personality traits among three Alcoholics Anonymous attendance level groups: further considerations of the affiliation profile. *Drug and Alcohol Dependence*, **5**, 135–144.

Orr, A. D. (1996). SMART Recovery: a new approach to self-help. *Epikrisis*, August, p. 3.

Oxford House (2001). *History and accomplishments.* Available online at www.oxfordhouse.org.

Pancoast, D. L., Parker, P., & Froland, C., eds (1983). *Rediscovering Self-Help: Its Role in Social Care.* Beverly Hills, CA: Sage.

Patussi, V., Tumino, E., & Poldrugo, F. (1996). The development of the alcoholic treatment club system in Italy: fifteen years of experience. *Contemporary Drug Problems,* **23**, 29–42.

Payte, J. T. (1997). Methadone maintenance treatment: the first thirty years. *Journal of Psychoactive Drugs,* **29**, 149–153.

Pérez-López, C. G., González, L. U., Rosovsky, H., & Casanova, L. R. (1992). La mujer en los grupos de Alcohólicos Anónimos. *Anales del Instituto Mexicano de Psychiatria,* 125–129.

Peterson, G., Abrams, D. B., Elder, J. P., & Beaudin, P. A. (1985). Professional versus self-help weight loss at the worksite: the challenge of making a public health impact. *Behavior Therapy,* **16**, 213–222.

Petrunik, M. G. (1973). Seeing the light: a study of conversion to Alcoholics Anonymous. *Journal of Voluntary Action Research,* **1**, 30–38.

Petry, N. M. & Armentano, C. (1999). Prevalence, assessment, and treatment of pathological gambling: a review. *Psychiatric Services,* **50**, 1021–1027.

Petty, R. E. & Cacioppo, J. T. (1981). *Attitudes and Persuasion: Classic and Contemporary Approaches.* Dubuque, IO: William C. Brown Publishers.

Peyrot, M. (1985). Narcotics Anonymous: its history, structure, and approach. *International Journal of the Addictions,* **20**(10), 1509–1522.

Pini, P., Allamani, A., Basetti-Sani, I., *et al.* (1996). *The Interaction between an 'Alcohol Centre' and some Non-Governmental Organisations in Florence during 1985–93: An Overview.* Paper presented at the Kettil Bruun Society 22nd Annual Alcohol Epidemiology Symposium.

Pisani, V. D., Fawcett, J., Clark, D. C., & McGuire, M. (1993). The relative contributions of medication adherence and AA meeting attendance to abstinent outcome for chronic alcoholics. *Journal of Studies on Alcohol,* **54**, 115–119.

Porter, L., Argandoña, M., & Curran, W. J. (1999). *Drug and Alcohol Dependence Policies, Legislation and Programmes for Treatment and Rehabilitation.* Geneva, WHO.

Poshyachinda, V., Ch'ien, J. M. N., Suwaki, H., Robinson, D., & Willie, R. (1982). Treatment is a cultural process and social act. *Unesco Courier,* **35**(1), 20–24.

Powell, T. J. (1987). *Self-Help Organizations and Professional Practice.* Silver Spring, MD: NASW Press.

Powell, T. J., ed. (1990). *Working with Self-Help.* Silver Spring, MD: NASW Press.

Powell, T. J. (1994). Self-help research and policy issues. In *Understanding the Self-Help Organization: Frameworks and Findings,* ed. T. J. Powell, pp. 1–9. Thousand Oaks, CA: Sage.

Powell, T. J., Kurtz, L. F., Garvin, C. D., & Hill, E. M. (1996). A model of AA utilization by persons with a dual diagnosis (the co-occurrence of alcoholism and severe mental illness). *Contemporary Drug Problems,* **23**(Spring), 139–157.

Powell, T. J., Hill, E. M., Warner, L., Yeaton, W., & Silk, K. R. (2000). Encouraging people with mood disorders to attend a self-help group. *Journal of Applied Social Psychology*, **30**, 2270–2288.

Pristach, C. A. & Smith, C. M. (1999). Attitudes towards Alcoholics Anonymous by dually diagnosed psychiatric inpatients. *Journal of Addictive Diseases*, **18**, 69–76.

Project MATCH Research Group (1997). Matching alcoholism treatments to client heterogeneity: Project MATCH posttreatment drinking outcomes. *Journal of Studies on Alcohol*, **58**, 7–29.

——— (1998). Matching alcoholism treatments to client heterogeneity: Project MATCH three-year drinking outcomes. *Alcoholism: Clinical and Experimental Research*, **22**, 1300–1311.

Putnam, R. D. (1993). *Making Democracy Work: Civic Traditions in Modern Italy*. Princeton, NJ: Princeton University Press.

Rabinowitz, R. (1986). Alcoholism and chemical dependency in the Jewish community: Sh...Sh...Sh. In *Addictions in the Jewish Community*, ed. S. J. Levy & S. B. Blume, pp. 135–141. New York: Federation of Jewish Philanthropies of New York.

Rappaport, J. (1993). Narrative studies, personal stories, and identity transformation in the mutual help context. *Journal of Applied Behavioral Science*, **29**, 239–256.

Rappaport, J., Seidman, E., Toro, P. A., *et al.* (1985). Collaborative research with a mutual help organization. *Social Policy*, **15**, 12–24.

Rapping, E. (1997). There's self-help, and then there's self-help: women in the recovery movement. *Social Policy*, **27**, 56–61.

Rasmussen, K. & Capaldi, C. (1990). The narratives of Alcoholics Anonymous: dialectical "good reasons." In *Perspectives on Argumentation: Essays in Honor of Wayne Brockriede*, ed. R. Trapp & J. Scuetz, pp. 243–338. Prospect Heights, IL: Waveland Press.

Rehm, J. (1996). The development of AA in a country with an existing out-patient layperson help system: the case of German-speaking Switzerland. *Contemporary Drug Problems*, **23**, 77–91.

Rehm, J. & Mariolini, N. (1998). Alcoholics Anonymous in Switzerland – different organizations for different cultural traditions? In *Diversity in Unity: Studies of Alcoholics Anonymous in Eight Societies*, ed. I. Eisenbach-Stangl & P. Rosenqvist, pp. 113–129. NAD Publication #33. Helsinki: Nordic Council for Alcohol and Drug Research.

Rehm, J. & Room, R. (1992). Mutual help for alcohol-related problems: studies on Al-Anon and of alternatives to Alcoholics Anonymous. *Contemporary Drug Problems*, **19**, 555–562.

Reinert, D. F., Estadt, B. K., Fenzel, L. M., Allen, J. P., & Gilroy, F. D. (1995). Relationship of surrender and narcissism to involvement in alcohol recovery. *Alcoholism Treatment Quarterly*, **12**(1), 49–58.

Ribisl, K. (1997). *The Role of Social Networks in Predicting Substance Abuse Treatment Outcome in a Dual Diagnosis Sample*. Paper presented at the annual meeting of The Society of Behavioral Medicine, San Francisco.

Rice, J. S. (1992). Discursive formation, life stories, and the emergence of co-dependency: "power/knowledge" and the search for identity. *Sociological Quarterly*, **33**(3), 337–364.

Richardson, A. (1983a). The diversity of self-help groups. In *Self-Help and Health in Europe: New Approaches in Health Care*, ed. S. Hatch & I. Kickbush, pp. 32–42. Copenhagen: WHO Regional Office for Europe.

(1983b). English self-help: varied patterns and practices. In *Rediscovering Self-Help: Its Role in Social Care*, ed. D. L. Pancoast, P. Parker, & C. Froland, pp. 203–221. Beverly Hills, CA: Sage.

Rieff, D. (1991). Victims all? Recovery, co-dependency, and the art of blaming somebody else. *Harpers*, October, 49–56.

Rienhoff, O. (1979). Die Zusammensetzung der Anonymen Alkoholiker in der Bundesrepublik Deutschland. *Deutsche Medizinische Wochenshrift*, **104**, 81–84.

Riessman, F. (1965). The "helper-therapy" principle. *Social Work*, **10**, 27–32.

(1987). Foreword. In *Self-Help Organizations and Professional Practice*, ed. T. J. Powell. Silver Spring, MD: NASW Press.

(1990). Restructuring help: a human services paradigm for the 1990s. *American Journal of Community Psychology*, **18**, 221–230.

Riessman, F. & Carroll, D. (1995). *Redefining Self-Help: Policy and Practice*. San Francisco: Jossey-Bass.

Riordan, R. J. & Beggs, M. S. (1988). Some critical differences between self-help and therapy groups. *Journal for Specialists in Group Work*, **13**, 24–29.

Ripley, H. S. & Jackson, J. K. (1959). Therapeutic factors in Alcoholics Anonymous. *American Journal of Psychiatry*, **116**, 44–50.

Ritsher, J. B., Moos, R. H., & Finney, J. W. (2002). Relationship of treatment orientation and continuing care to remission among substance abuse patients. *Psychiatric Services*, **53**, 595–601.

Robertson, N. (1988). *Getting Better: Inside Alcoholics Anonymous*. New York: William Morrow.

Robinson, D. R. (1979). *Talking out of Alcoholism: The Self-Help Process of Alcoholics Anonymous*. London: Croom Helm.

(1980). Alcoholics Anonymous: origins and the international diffusion of a self-help group. In *Drug Problems in the Sociocultural Context: A Basis for Policies and Programme Planning*, ed. G. Edwards & A. Arif, pp. 161–167. Geneva: WHO.

Robinson, D. R. & Henry, S. (1977). *Self-Help and Health: Mutual Aid for Modern Problems*. London: Martin Robertson.

Roche, A., Parle, M. D., Stubbs, J. M., Hall, W., & Saunders, J. B. (1995). Management and treatment efficacy of drug and alcohol problems: what do doctors believe? *Addiction*, **90**, 1357–1366.

Ronel, N. (1993). *Narcotics Anonymous in Israel: Self-help Processes and Religious Faith among Drug Addicts*. Doctoral dissertation, Hebrew University, Jerusalem.

(1998). Narcotics Anonymous: understanding the "bridge to recovery." *Journal of Offender Rehabilitation*, **27**, 179–197.

(1997). The universality of a self-help program of American origin: Narcotics Anonymous in Israel. *Social Work in Health Care*, **25**, 87–101.

Ronel, N. & Humphreys, K. (1999). World view transformations of Narcotics Anonymous members in Israel. *International Journal of Self-Help and Self-Care*, 1, 107–121.

Room, R. (1993). Alcoholics Anonymous as a social movement. In *Research on Alcoholics Anonymous: Opportunities and Alternatives*, ed. B. S. McCrady & W. R. Miller, pp. 167–187. New Brunswick, NJ: Rutgers Center of Alcohol Studies.

(1997). Voluntary organizations and the state in the prevention of alcohol problems. *Drugs and Society*, 11, 11–23.

(1998). Mutual help movements for alcohol problems in an international perspective. *Addiction Research*, 6(2), 131–145.

Room, R. & Greenfield, T. (1993). Alcoholics anonymous, other 12-step movements and psychotherapy in the US population, 1990. *Addiction*, 88, 555–562.

Rootes, L. E. & Aanes, D. L. (1992). A conceptual framework for understanding self-help groups. *Hospital and Community Psychiatry*, 43(4), 379–381.

Rosenqvist, P. (1992). From the rib of AA: Al-Anon in Finland. *Contemporary Drug Problems*, 19(4), 605–629.

Rosovsky, H. (1998). Alcoholics Anonymous in Mexico: a strong but fragmented movement. In *Diversity in Unity: Studies of Alcoholics Anonymous in Eight Societies*, ed. I. Eisenbach-Stangl & P. Rosenqvist, pp. 165–194. NAD Publication #33. Helsinki: Nordic Council for Alcohol and Drug Research.

Rosovsky, H., Casanova, L., & Pérez, C. (1991). Las características de los grupos y de los miembros de Alcohólicos Anónimos. *Anales del Instituto Mexicano de Psiquitría*, 138–142.

Rosovsky, H., Garcia, G., Gutierrez, R., & Casanova, L. (1992). Al-Anon groups in Mexico. *Contemporary Drug Problems*, 19, 587–603.

Ross, M. (1989). Relation of implicit theories to the construction of personal histories. *Psychological Review*, 96, 341–357.

Rotgers, F. & Kishline, A. (2000). Moderation management: a support group for persons who want to reduce their drinking, but not necessarily abstain. *International Journal of Self-Help and Self-Care*, 1, 145–158.

Rudy, D. R. (1986). *Becoming Alcoholic: Alcoholics Anonymous and the Reality of Alcoholism*. Carbondale: Southern Illinois University Press.

Rudy, D. R. & Greil, A. L. (1988). Is Alcoholics Anonymous a religious organization? Meditations on marginality. *Sociological Analysis*, 50, 41–51.

Ruzek, J. (1987). The drinkwatchers experience: a description and progress report on services for controlled drinkers. In *Helping the Problem Drinker: New Initiatives in Community Care*, ed. T. Stockwell & S. Clement, pp. 35–60. London: Croom Helm.

Ruzek, J. & Vetter, C. (1983). *Drinkwatchers Handbook: A Guide to Healthy Enjoyment of Alcohol and How to Achieve Sensible Drinking Skills*. London: Accept Publications.

Rychtarik, R. G., Connors, G. J., Dermen, K. H., & Stasiewicz, P. R. (2000). Alcoholics Anonymous and the use of medications to prevent relapse: an anonymous survey of member attitudes. *Journal on Studies on Alcohol*, 61, 134–138.

Sadler, P. O. (1977). The 'Crisis Cult' as a voluntary association: an interactional approach to Alcoholics Anonymous. *Human Organization*, 36, 207–210.

Salem, D. A., Bogat, G. A., & Reid, C. (1997). Mutual help goes on-line. *Journal of Community Psychology*, **25**, 189–207.

Salem, D. A., Reischl, T. M., Gallacher, F. & Randall, K. W. (2000). The role of referent and expert power in mutual help. *American Journal of Community Psychology*, **28**, 303–324.

Salzer, M. S., Rappaport, J., & Segre, L. (1999). Professional appraisal of professionally led and self-help groups. *American Journal of Orthopsychiatry*, **69**, 536–540.

Sanchez-Craig, M., Wilkinson, D. A., & Davila, R. (1995). Empirically based guidelines for moderate drinking: 1-year results from three studies with problem drinkers. *American Journal of Public Health*, **85**, 823–828.

Sarason, S. B. (1972). *The Creation of Settings and the Future Societies*. San Francisco: Jossey-Bass.

(1981). An asocial psychology and a misdirected clinical psychology. *American Psychologist*, **36**(8), 827–836.

Saulnier, C. F. (1994). Twelve steps for everyone? Lesbians in Al-Anon. In *Understanding the Self-Help Organization: Frameworks and Findings*, ed. T. J. Powell, pp. 247–271. Thousand Oaks, CA: Sage.

Schaef, A. W. (1986). *Codependence: Mistreated, Misunderstood*. Minneapolis, MN: Winston Press.

Schank, R. C. (1990). *Tell Me a Story: A New Look at Real and Artificial Memory*. New York: Scribner.

Schmidt, E. (1996). Rational Recovery: finding an alternative for addiction treatment. *Alcoholism Treatment Quarterly*, **14**, 47–57.

Schmidt, L. A. & Weisner, C. M. (1999). Public health perspectives on access and need for substance abuse treatment. In *Changing Addictive Behavior: Bridging Clinical and Public Health Strategies*, ed. J. A. Tucker, D. M. Donovan, & G. A. Marlatt, pp. 67–96. New York: Guilford.

Schubert, M. A. & Borkman, T. J. (1991). An organizational typology for self-help groups. *American Journal of Community Psychology*, **19**, 769–787.

Schwartz, C. E. & Sendor, R. M. (1999). Helping others helps oneself: response shift effects in peer support. *Social Science and Medicine*, **48**, 1563–1575.

Seixas, F. A., Washburn, S., & Eisen, S. V. (1988). Alcoholism, Alcoholics Anonymous attendance, and outcome in a prison system. *American Journal of Drug and Alcohol Abuse*, **14**, 515–524.

Sewell, V. H. (1998). *Narcotics Anonymous Way of Life*. Marietta, GA: N. A. Foundation Group. Available online at www.nawol.org/.

Sharma, H. K. & Mohan, D. (1994). *The Philosophy and Practice of Self-Help among Traditional and Non-Traditional Drug Users in India*. Paper presented at the International Conference on Addiction and Mutual Help Movements in a Comparative Perspective, Toronto, Canada.

Shaw, S. (1982). What is problem drinking? In *Drinking and Problem Drinking*, ed. M. A. Plant, pp. 1–22. London: Junction Books.

Sheeren, M. (1987). The relationship between relapse and involvement in Alcoholics Anonymous. *Journal of Studies on Alcohol*, **49**, 104–106.

Shido, M., Yamada, K., Muraoka, H., *et al.* (1986). A survey on the members of volunteer groups in the metropolitan area. *Japanese Journal of Alcohol Studies and Drug Dependence*, **21**(1), 49–63.

Sibthorpe, B., Fleming, D., & Gould, J. (1994). Self-help groups: a key to HIV risk reduction for high-risk injection drug users? *Journal of Acquired Immune Deficiency Syndromes*, **7**, 592–598.

Sikic, B. I., Walker, R. D., & Peterson, D. R. (1973). An evaluation of a program for the treatment of alcoholism in Croatia. *International Journal of Social Psychiatry*, **18**, 171–182.

Silverman, P. R. (1970). The widow as a caregiver in a program of preventive intervention with other widows. *Mental Hygiene*, **54**, 540–547.

Simmons, D. (1992). Diabetes self help facilitated by local diabetes research: the Coventry Asian diabetes support group. *Diabetes Medicine*, **9**(9), 866–869.

Simoni, J. M. & Perez, L. (1995). Latinos and mutual support groups: a case for considering culture. *American Journal of Orthopsychiatry*, **65**(3), 440–445.

Sisson, R. W. & Mallams, J. H. (1981). The use of systematic encouragement and community access procedures to increase attendance at Alcoholics Anonymous and Al-Anon meetings. *American Journal of Drug and Alcohol Abuse*, **8**, 371–376.

Smart, R. G. & Mann, R. E. (1993). Recent liver cirrhosis declines: estimates of the impact of alcohol abuse treatment and Alcoholics Anonymous. *Addiction*, **88**, 193–198.

(1998). Treatment, Alcoholics Anonymous and alcohol controls during the decrease in alcohol problems in Alberta: 1975–1993. *Alcohol and Alcoholism*, **33**, 265–272.

Smart, R. G., Mann, R. E., & Anglin, L. (1989). Decreases in alcohol problems and increased Alcoholics Anonymous membership. *Addiction*, **84**, 507–513.

Smith, D. I. (1986). Evaluation of a residential AA program. *International Journal of the Addictions*, **21**, 33–49.

Smith, S. R. (1997). Alcohol in Japanese society. *Social History of Alcohol Review*, **34/35**, 37–43.

(1998). Good old boy into alcoholic: Danshukai and learning a new drinking role in Japan. In *Learning in Likely Places: Varieties of Apprenticeship in Japan*, ed. J. Singleton, pp. 286–303. Cambridge: Cambridge University Press.

Smith, W. C. (1963). *The Meaning and End of Religion: A New Approach to the Religious Traditions of Mankind*. New York: MacMillan.

Sobell, M. B. & Sobell, L. B. (1999). Stepped care for alcohol problems: an efficient method for planning and delivering clinical services. In *Changing Addictive Behavior: Bridging Clinical and Public Health Strategies*, ed. J. A. Tucker, D. M. Donovan, & G. A. Marlatt, pp. 331–343. New York: Guilford.

Speiglman, R. (1994). Mandated AA attendance for recidivist drinking drivers: ideology, organization, and California criminal justice practices. *Addiction*, **89**, 859–868.

Spitz, H. I. (1987). Cocaine abuse: therapeutic group approaches. In *Cocaine Abuse: New Directions in Treatment and Research*, ed. H. I. Spitz & J. S. Rosecan, pp. 156–200. New York: Brunner/Mazel.

Sproule, J., O'Halloran, K., & Borkman, T. (2000). Initiating a quasi-self-help group in North Ireland: a case study of new groups for tranquilizer addicts. *International Journal of Self-Help and Self-Care*, 1, 267–280.

Steffen, V. (1994). Individualism and welfare – Alcoholics Anonymous and the Minnesota model in Denmark. *Nordisk Alkoholtidskrift* (English suppl.), 11, 13–20.

Stewart, E., Klaw, E., Horst, D., & Humphreys, K. (2002). Expectations and experience in Moderation Management: Established and potential members' perceptions of an alternative self-help setting for problem drinkers. Manuscript submitted for publication.

Stewart, M. (1990). Professional interface with mutual-aid self-help groups: a review. *Social Science and Medicine*, 31(10), 1143–1158.

Stewart, M., Banks, S., Crossman, D., & Poel, D. (1994). Partnerships between health professionals and self-help groups: meanings and mechanisms. *Prevention in Human Services*, 11, 199–240.

Stone, R. (1997). *My Years with Narcotics Anonymous*. Joplin, Missouri: Hulon Pendleton.

Stroul, B. A. (1987). *Crisis Residential Services in a Community Support System*. Rockville, MD: National Institute of Mental Health, Community Support Program.

Stunkard, A., Levine, H., & Fox, S. (1970). The management of obesity: patient self-help and medical treatment. *Archives of Internal Medicine*, 125, 1067–1072.

Sugita, T., Suzuki, Y., Suzuki, S., *et al.* (1985). Survey on the actual condition of ex-alcoholics – by using the questionnaire to the members of "Danshukai" in Shizuoka prefecture. *Japanese Journal of Alcohol Studies and Drug Dependence*, 20(3), 250–262.

Suler, J. (1984). The role of ideology in self-help groups. *Social Policy*, 14(3), 29–36.

Suler, J. & Barthelomew, E. (1986). The ideology of Overeaters Anonymous. *Social Policy*, 16, 48–53.

Surgeon General Koop's Workshop on Self-Help and Public Health (1990). *Conference Report*. US Department of Health and Human Services, Washington, DC: US Government Printing Office.

Sutro, L. D. (1989). Alcoholics Anonymous in a Mexican peasant–Indian village. *Human Organization*, 48(2), 180–186.

Suwaki, H. (1979). *Naikan* and *Danshukai* for the treatment of Japanese alcoholic patients. *British Journal of Addiction*, 74, 15–19.

  (1980). Japan: culturally based treatment of alcoholism. In *Drug Problems in the Sociocultural Context: A Basis for Policies and Programme Planning*, ed. G. Edwards & A. Arif, pp. 139–143. Geneva: WHO.

  (1988). Trends and issues in alcoholism treatment in Japan. In *Biomedical and Social Aspects of Alcohol and Alcoholism*, ed. K. Kuriyama, A. Takada, & H. Ishii, pp. 597–600. Amsterdam: Elsevier.

Świątkiewicz, G. (1992). Self-help abstainer clubs in Poland. *Contemporary Drug Problems*, 19(4), 677–687.

Świątkiewicz, G. & Zieliński, A. (1998). Alcoholics Anonymous in Poland. In *Diversity in Unity: Studies of Alcoholics Anonymous in Eight Societies*, ed.

I. Eisenbach-Stangl & P. Rosenqvist, pp. 149–164. NAD Publication #33. Helsinki: Nordic Council for Alcohol and Drug Research.

Tattersall, M. L. & Hallstrom, C. (1992). Self-help and benzodiazepine withdrawal. *Journal of Affective Disorders*, **24**, 193–198.

Taylor, M. C. (1979). *Alcoholics Anonymous: How it Works Recovery Processes in a Self-Help Group*. Unpublished doctoral dissertation, University of California, San Francisco.

Thaller, V., Breitenfeld, D., Pintaric, S., *et al.* (1996). Self-help groups of alcoholics and war in Croatia. *Alcoholism (Zagreb)*, **32**(1), 29–33.

Thurstin, A. H., Alfano, A. M., & Nerviano, V. J. (1987). The efficacy of AA attendence for aftercare of inpatient alcoholics: some follow-up data. *International Journal of the Addictions*, **22**(11), 1083–1090.

Tiebout, H. M. (1954). The ego factors in surrender in alcoholism. *Quarterly Journal of Studies on Alcohol*, **15**, 610–621.

Timko, C., Finney, J. W., Moos, R. H., Moos, B. S., & Steinbaum, D. P. (1993). The process of treatment selection among previously untreated help-seeking problem drinkers. *Journal of Substance Abuse*, **5**, 203–220.

Timko, C., Moos, R., Finney, J. W., & Moos, B. S. (1994). Outcome of treatment for alcohol abuse and involvement in AA among previously untreated problem drinkers. *Journal of Mental Health Administration*, **21**, 145–160.

Toch, H. (1965). *The Social Psychology of Social Movements*. Indianapolis, IN: Bobbs-Merrill.

Tonigan, J. S. (2001). Benefits of Alcoholics Anonymous attendance: replication of findings between clinical research sites in Project MATCH. *Alcoholism Treatment Quarterly*, **19**, 67–78.

Tonigan, J. S., Connors, G. J., & Miller, W. R. (1998). Special populations in Alcoholics Anonymous. *Alcohol Health and Research World*, **22**(4), 281–285.

(2002). Participation and involvement in Alcoholics Anonymous. In *Treatment Matching in Alcoholism*, ed. T. Babor & Del Boca, F. Cambridge: Cambridge University Press.

Tonigan, J. S., Miller, W. R., & Schermer, C. (in press). Atheists, agnostics and Alcoholics Anonymous. *Journal of Studies on Alcohol*.

Tonigan, J. S., Toscova, R., & Miller, W. R. (1996). Meta-analysis of the literature on Alcoholics Anonymous: sample and study characteristics moderate findings. *Journal of Studies on Alcohol*, **57**, 65–72.

Toro, P. A., Reischl, T. M., Zimmerman, M. A., *et al.* (1988). Professionals in mutual help groups: impact on social climate and members' behavior. *Journal of Consulting and Clinical Psychology*, **56**(4), 631–632.

Toseland, R. W., Rossiter, C. M., & Labrecque, M. S. (1989). The effectiveness of two kinds of support groups for caregivers. *Social Service Review*, **34** (September), 415–432.

Toumbourou, J. W., Hamilton, M., & Smith, R. (1994). Surveying the drug service users' perspective through self-help groups. *Journal of Community and Applied Social Psychology*, **4**, 131–140.

Toumbourou, J. W., Hamilton, M., U'Ren, A., Stevens-Jones, P., & Storey, G. (2002). Narcotics Anonymous participation and changes in substance use and social support. *Journal of Substance Abuse Treatment*, **23**, 61–66.

Tournier, R. E. (1979). Alcoholics Anonymous as treatment and as ideology. *Journal of Studies on Alcohol*, **40**, 230–239.

Trainin, I. N. (1986). Alcoholism in the Jewish community. In *Addictions in the Jewish Community*, ed. S. J. Levy & S. B. Blume, pp. 15–27. New York: Federation of Jewish Philanthropies of New York.

Trainor, J., Shepherd, M., Boydell, K. M., Leff, A., & Crawford, E. (1997). Beyond the service paradigm: the impact and implications of consumer/survivor initiatives. *Psychiatric Rehabilitation Journal*, **21**(1), 132–140.

Trevino, A. J. (1992). Alcoholics Anonymous as a Durkheimian religion. *Research in the Social Scientific Study of Religion*, **4**, 183–208.

Trice, H. M. (1955). *A Study of the Process of Affiliation with Alcoholics Anonymous*. Doctoral dissertation, University of Wisconsin. Available from University Microfilms, High Wycombe, England (no ID number).

Trice, H. M. & Roman, P. M. (1970). Sociopsychological predictors of affiliation with Alcoholics Anonymous: a longitudinal study of "treatment success." *Social Psychiatry*, **5**, 51–59.

Trimpey, J. (1988). *Rational Recovery from Alcoholism: The Small Book*. Lotus, CA: Lotus Press.

Trojan, A. (1989). Benefits of self-help groups: a survey of 232 members from 65 disease-related groups. *Social Science and Medicine*, **29**(2), 225–232.

Trojan, A., Halves, E., & Wetendorf, H. W. (1986). Self-help groups and consumer participation: a look at the German health care self-help movement. *Journal of Voluntary Action Research*, **5**, 14–23.

Tucker, J. A. (1999). Changing addictive behavior: historical and contemporary perspectives. In *Changing Addictive Behavior: Bridging Clinical and Public Health Strategies*, ed. J. A. Tucker, D. M. Donovan, & G. A. Marlatt, pp. 3–66. New York: Guilford.

Tudiver, F., Hilditch, J., Permaul, J., & McKendree, D. (1992). Does mutual help facilitate newly bereaved widowers? Report of a randomized controlled trial. *Evaluation and the Health Professions*, **15**(2), 147–162.

Unell, J. (1989). Introduction. In *Self-Help in Health and Social Welfare: England and West Germany*, ed. S. Humble & J. Unell, pp. ix–xii. London: Routledge.

Unhooked online newsletter (1999). *Press release May 23, 1999: largest chapter of SOS changes name to LifeRing Secular Recovery*. Available online at www.unhooked.com.

US Department of Health and Human Services (1990). *Healthy People 2000: National Health Promotion and Disease Prevention Objectives*. DHHS Publication #91-50212. Washington: US Government Printing Office.

Vachon, M. L. S., Lyall, W. A. L., Rogers, J., Freedman-Letofsky, K., & Freeman, S. J. J. (1980). A controlled study of self-help intervention for widows. *American Journal of Psychiatry*, **137**(11), 1380–1384.

Vaillant, G. E. (1995). *The Natural History of Alcoholism Revisited*. Cambridge, MA: Harvard University Press.

Vaillant, G. E. & Milofsky, E. S. (1982). Natural history of male alcoholism: IV. Paths to recovery. *Archives of General Psychiatry*, **39**, 127–133.

Van der Avort, A. & Van Harberden, P. (1983). On identification resonance. In *Self-Help and Health in Europe: New Approaches in Health Care*, ed. S. Hatch & I. Kickbush, pp. 148–152. Copenhagen: WHO Regional Office for Europe.

Van de Velde, J. G., Schaap, G. E., & Land, H. (1998). Follow-up at a Dutch addiction hospital and effectiveness of therapeutic community treatment. *Substance Abuse and Misuse*, **33**(8), 1611–1627.

(1985). Helping self-help groups: a developing theory. *Psychotherapy*, **22**, 269–272.

Vex, S. L. & Blume, S. B. (2001). The JACS Study I: characteristics of a population of chemically dependent Jewish men and women. *Journal of Addictive Diseases*, **20**, 71–89.

Vogel, H. S., Knight, E., Laudet, A., & Magura, S. (1998). Double Trouble in Recovery: self-help for the dually diagnosed. *Psychiatric Rehabilitation Journal*, **21**, 356–364.

Voipio, M. (1987). The development of voluntary care of alcoholics in Finland. *Globe*, **1**, 19–21. Hamburg: International Organization of Good Templars.

Von Appen, U. (1994). The development of self-help in German's new provinces (former East Germany): the case of Schwerin. *Prevention in Human Services*, **11**, 97–116.

Walsh, D., Hingson, R., Merrigan, D., *et al.* (1991). A randomized trial of treatment options for alcohol-abusing workers. *New England Journal of Medicine*, **325**, 775–782.

Wegscheider-Cruse, S. (1985). *Choicemaking: For Co-Dependents, Adult Children and Spirituality Seekers*. Pompano Beach, FL: Health Communications.

Weick, K. E. (1976). Educational organizations as loosely coupled systems. *Administrative Science Quarterly*, **21**, 1–19.

(1984). Small wins: redefining the scale of social issues. *American Psychologist*, **39**, 40–49.

Weiss, R. D., Griffin, M. L., Gallop, R., *et al.* (2000). Self-help group attendance and participation among cocaine dependent patients. *Drug and Alcohol Dependence*, **60**, 169–177.

Weiss, R. D., Griffin, M. L., Najavits, N. M., *et al.* (1996). Self-help activities in cocaine dependent patients entering treatment: results from the NIDA collaborative cocaine treatment study. *Drug and Alcohol Dependence*, **43**, 79–86.

Weiss, S. (1990). Characteristics of the Alcoholics Anonymous Movement in Israel. *British Journal of Addiction*, **85**, 1351–1354.

(1995). From a medical, psychiatric, individual problem to a public health–social problem: the development over time of the Israeli governmental alcohol treatment system. *Addiction Research*, **3**(1), 49–56.

Wells, B. (1994). Narcotics Anonymous in Britain. In *Heroin Addiction and Drug Policy: The British System*, ed. J. Strang & M. Gossop, pp. 240–247. New York: Oxford University Press.

Wells, K. B. (1999). Treatment research at the crossroads: the scientific interface of clinical trials and effectiveness research. *American Journal of Psychiatry*, **156**, 5–10.

White, B. & Madara, E. (1998). *The Self-Help Sourcebook: Your Guide to Community and Online Support Groups*, 6th edn. Denville, NJ: American Self-Help Clearinghouse.

White, W. L. (1998). *Slaying the Dragon: The History of Addiction Treatment and Recovery in America*. Bloomington, IL: Chesnut Health Systems.

Whitfield, C. (1985). *Alcoholism, Attachments & Spirituality: A Transpersonal Approach*. East Rutherford, NJ: Thomas W. Perrin.

Wilson, A. N. (1999). *God's Funeral: The Decline of Faith in Western Civilization*. New York: Norton.

Wilson, E. O. (1988). *On Human Nature*. Cambridge, MA: Harvard University Press.

Wilson, L. (1979). *Lois Remembers: Memoirs of the Co-Founder of Al-Anon and Wife of the Co-Founder of Alcoholics Anonymous*. New York: Al-Anon Family Group Headquarters.

Winters, A. (1978). Review and rationale of the Drinkwatchers International Program. *American Journal of Drug and Alcohol Abuse*, **5**, 321–326.

Winzelberg, A. (1997). The analysis of an electronic support group for individuals with eating disorders. *Computers in Human Behavior*, **13**, 393–407.

Winzelberg, A. & Humphreys, K. (1999). Should patients' religious beliefs and practices influence clinicians' referral to 12-step self-help groups? Evidence from a study of 3,018 male substance abuse patients. *Journal of Consulting and Clinical Psychology*, **67**, 790–794.

Wituk, S. A., Shepherd, M. D., Warren, M., & Meissen, G. (2002). Factors contributing to the survival of self-help groups. *American Journal of Community Psychology*, **30**, 349–366.

Woff, I., Tombourou, J., Herlihy, E., Hamilton, M., & Wales, S. (1996). Service providers' perceptions of substance use self-help groups. *Substance Use and Misuse*, **31**, 1241–1258.

Woititz, J. G. (1983). *Adult Children of Alcoholics*. Pompano Beach, FL: Health Communications.

Wolf/Altschul/Callahan Inc. (1990). *Analysis of 1990 Al-Anon/Alateen Membership Survey*. New York: Wolf/Altschul/Callahan Inc.

Wong, D. & Chan, C. (1994). Advocacy on self-help for patients with chronic illness: the Hong Kong experience. *Prevention in Human Services*, **11**, 117–139.

Wordes, M., Freitag, R., Poe-Yamagata, E., & Wolf, A. (2002). *Parents Anonymous Process Evaluation Report*. Oakland, CA: National Council on Crime and Delinquency.

World Health Organization (1995). *WHO European Charter on Alcohol*. Available online at www.eurocare.org/charter.htm.

(1999). *Global Status Report on Alcohol*. Geneva: WHO.

Woronowicz, B. T. (1992, October). *Abstainer Clubs in Poland and their Working Relationship to the Alcoholics Anonymous Community*. Paper presented at the 4th Working Meeting of the International Collaborative Study of Alcoholics Anonymous, Mexico City, Mexico, 1992.

Wright, J. D. & Devine, J. A. (1995). Factors that interact with treatment to predict outcomes in substance abuse programs for the homeless. *Journal of Addictive Diseases*, **14**(4), 169–181.

Wright, K. B. (1997). Shared ideology in Alcoholics Anonymous: a grounded theory approach. *Journal of Health Communication*, **2**, 83–99.

Wright, K. D. & Scott, T. B. (1978). The relationship of wives' treatment to the drinking status of alcoholics. *Journal of Studies on Alcohol*, **39**, 1577–1581.

Wulff, D. M. (1991). *Psychology of Religion: Classic and Contemporary Views*. New York: John Wiley.

Yalom, I. D. (1975). *The Theory and Practice of Group Psychotherapy*. New York: Basic Books.

Zaslav, P. (1993). The role of self-help groups in the treatment of the dual diagnosis patient. In *Dual Diagnosis*, ed. J. Solomon, S. Zimberg, & E. Sholler, pp. 105–127. New York: Plenum.

Zinman, S. (1987). Issues of power. In *Reaching Across: Mental Health Clients Helping Each Other*, ed. S. Zinman, H. T. Harp, & S. Budd, pp. 182–187. Sacramento, CA: California Network of Mental Health Clients.

Zinman, S., Harp, H. T., & Budd, S. (1987). *Reaching Across: Mental Health Clients Helping Each Other*. Sacramento, CA: California Network of Mental Health Clients.

Zweben, J. E. (1986). Recovery oriented psychotherapy. *Journal of Substance Abuse Treatment*, **3**, 255–262.

Zywiak, W. H., Hoffman, N. G., & Floyd, A. S. (1999). Enhancing alcohol treatment outcomes through aftercare and self-help groups. *Medicine and Health / Rhode Island*, **82**(3), 87–90.

Index

Abstainers Clubs 43–6
  approach 44–5
  funding 156
  government support 45, 91
  history 43–4
  media campaign 159
  membership 45–6
  optimism 131
  origins 43–4
  philosophy 44–5
  professional support 43–4, 45, 58, 59
  Sobriety International membership 68
  "Way of Sobriety" 44
abstinence 38, 45
  Blue Cross 56
  Clubs of Treated Alcoholics 59–60
  commitment augmenting with AA 119,
    120, 123
  Danshukai 53
  Double Trouble in Recovery 103
  Free Life 65
  Kishline's views 71
  Narcotics Anonymous 75
  opiates 106
  Oxford House organization 107
  Project MATCH 117
  Rational Recovery 83
  SMART Recovery 85
  SOS 87
abstinence violation effect (AVE) hypothesis
  125
addicted-self model of recovery 120
addiction
  health care 19
  multi-modal interventions 122
  stepped care concept 167

stigmatization 142
addiction-related groups 33–5
  membership numbers 35
  see also named groups
addictive behavior
  cross-cultural diversity 9
  modification 85
adolescents 46, 50, 101, 173–4
adult-children movement 47–8
Adult Children of Alcoholics (ACA) 48
  evaluation 101
  friendship networks 145–6
  identity 141–2
  spiritual alienation 136
  spiritual change 135–6, 137–8
advocacy 91, 92
  loss of potential 153
  political 19, 162
African–American mutual-aid organizations
  27
Al-Anon Family Groups 46–50
  approach 48–50
  history 46–8
  lifetime involvement 142
  membership 47, 50
  origins 46–8
  outcome studies 100–1
  philosophy 48–50
  rituals 50
  spiritual change 135–6, 137–8
  spiritual principle 49
  12 steps 48–9
  see also Adult Children of Alcoholics
    (ACA)
Alateen 46, 50
  evaluation 101

alcohol, problem drinkers 70–3
  adverse consequence reduction 104
  healthcare costs 150–1
alcohol consumption, declining 124
Alcoholics Anonymous (AA) 6–7, 9, 35–43
  24-Hour-a-Day Movement (Mexican) 21
  approach 38–41
  attitudes of professionals 165–6
  "conversion" experience 133
  couples therapy 118
  disapproval of government funding 156
  dropouts 125–6
  dual-diagnosis patients 170
  effectiveness in combination with treatment
    115–19
  exit strategy 142
  experimental studies 111–15
  growth 41, 42
  harm potential 125–6
  Higher Power 39, 40, 140
  history 35–8
  Hong Kong 80
  influence on other organizations 92–3
  interpersonal mediators 120
  Italy 58
  Japan 53, 54
  Kishline's attendance 71
  lifetime attendance 125–6, 142
  longitudinal studies 115–19
  mediator effectiveness specificity 122–3
  mediators of influence on drinking
    outcomes 119–23
  medical treatment support 171–2
  meetings 36, 40
  membership 35, 41–3, 144
  meta-analysis 110–11
  motivation to change 118
  Native Americans 173
  origins 35–8
  outcome studies 109–19
  philosophy 38–41, 120
  Poland 44
  population-level benefits 123–5
  professional visitors 176
  Project MATCH 116–17
  psychopathology 118
  quasi-experimental studies 114–15
  recovery process 133, 144
  relationships with The Links 68
  ritual 40
  Scandinavia 68
  self-efficacy 122
  selfish trait minimizing 134
  severely troubled individuals 115–16
  shared community narrative 143
  social environment 120–1

  spiritual aspects as barrier to attendance
    135, 172–3
  spiritual change 36, 133–5, 137–8
  spiritual emphasis 18, 36, 39
  spiritual surrender measure 133
  12 steps 18, 22, 38, 39–40, 115–16
    Al-Anon use 48–9
    counseling 120
    evaluation 116–17, 118–19
    friendships 145–6
    patients on medication 171–2
    political activity 146–8
    proximal changes 122
    spiritual change 133, 134
  story-telling 40–1
  Switzerland 55, 57
  weaknesses 125–6
  Women for Sobriety members' spirituality
    136–7
  women members 42
  "work the program" concept 126
  world view 143
  Yugoslavia 58
alcoholism
  AA 35–43
    philosophy 38–41, 120
  Abstainers Clubs 43–6
  abstinence 38
  Al-Anon Family Groups 46–50, 100–1
  Blue Cross 54–7
  Clubs of Treated Alcoholics 57–60, 103
  Danshukai 51–4, 102–3
  Double Trouble in Recovery 63
  families 46–50
  Free Life 63–5
  inpatient treatment 43
  JACS 65–7
  Moderation Management 70–3, 104
  nicotine dependence 78
  Oxford House organization 78–80, 107–8
  physical dependence 43
  problems with other drugs 93
  Rational Recovery 82–4, 108
  recovery process 133, 144
  SOS 86–8, 109
  Women for Sobriety 88–90, 109
All Nippon Sobriety Association
  approach 52–3
  evaluation 102–3
  funding 156
  history 51–2
  membership 53–4
  origins 51–2
  philosophy 52–3
  Sobriety International membership 68
altruism 120, 122

amphetamine abuse 88
anonymity tradition 91
anti-heavy-drinking Zeitgeist 125
antisocial behavior of Oxford House residents
    80, 108
anxiety
    control 18
    reduction with Narcotics Anonymous
        attendance 105
atheism 172–3
Australia, attitudes of professionals 165–6
Austria, Blue Cross 57

"The Beast" 83
behavioral norms in self-help groups 129
behaviors
    addictive 9, 85
    enabling 49
    see also criminal behavior
Belgium, media campaign 159
The Big Book (AA) 37, 140
Bill W. *see* Wilson, William Griffith
bipolar disorder 63
Blue Cross 54–7, 92
    approach 55–6
    history 54–5
    membership 57
    origins 54–5
    philosophy 55–6
books, self-help 21–2
Buchman, Frank 35

Canada
    consumer-operated organizations 156
    professionals' phased withdrawal 174
    self-help group attitudes toward
        professionals 166
    widows' mutual-help group 164
change
    motivation 118
    perspectives 128–48
    program of 17–18
children of alcoholics 47–8
    identity 141–2
    see also Adult Children of Alcoholics
        (ACA)
Christianity 172–3
Christopher, James 86
church groups 144
civil sector *see* voluntary sector
clearinghouses *see* self-help clearinghouses
clinical trials, randomized 95–9
    self-help group evaluation 97–8
clinicians
    strategies for 163–6
    see also professionals

Clubs of Treated Alcoholics 57–60, 91
    approach 58–60
    evaluation 103
    history 57–8
    membership 60
    origins 57–8
    philosophy 58–60
co-dependent relationships 47
cocaine abuse
    Double Trouble in Recovery 63
    Rational Recovery 84
Cocaine Anonymous (CA) 104
cognitive antidote 120
cognitive–behavioral methods 117
    Moderation Management 70, 72
    Project MATCH 116
    SMART Recovery 84
community narrative, shared 143
Compassionate Friends 14
confidentiality 175–6
conscience, collective 140
consumer-operated organizations 156
consumer participation in health care 153–4
consumerism 30–1
coping strategies 10
correctional facilities 157
counseling, recovery sensitive 149
counselors, recovering/non-recovering 175–6
couples therapy 118
covariance adjustments 98–9
crack abuse 63
criminal behavior
    alcohol-related 124
    Oxford House residents 80, 108
Croix Bleue *see* Blue Cross
cross-cultural diversity 9
cults 138–9
cultural forces 178

Danshukai 51–4
    alcoholism treatment unit relationships 157
    approach 52–3
    evaluation 102–3
    history 51–2
    membership 53–4
    origins 51–2
    philosophy 52–3
    professional visitors 176
    referral strategies 167
democratic society 153, 154
Denmark, The Links 68, 69, 70
depression
    control 18
    identity change 141
    online groups 73
    unipolar major 63

detoxification services 80
disease models 22
Double Trouble in Recovery 60–3, 93
  approach 62
  evaluation 103–4
  history 60–2
  membership 62–3
  origins 60–2
  philosophy 62
Dr. Bob *see* Smith, Dr. Robert Holbrook
drinking, problem *see* alcohol, problem
  drinkers
Drinkwatchers 71
drug abuse
  infectious disease risk 106
  post-treatment 12-step self-help group
    attendance 105–6
  SOS members 88
dysfunctional families 47

Ellis, Albert 82
Emotions Anonymous 37
empowerment, political 129, 146–8, 179
enabling behaviors 49
entry to groups, barriers 16, 135, 172–3

facilitator role of professionals 23, 174
families
  dysfunctional 47
  support 92
    Blue Cross 56
  tie weakening 27–8
family groups
  Al-Anon Family Groups 46–50
  Clubs of Treated Alcoholics 59
  Danshukai 52–3, 54, 102–3
  JACS 67
  The Links 70
fees, lack of 16
feminist movement 47
  Women for Sobriety 88
foundations, private funding 156, 160
France
  Blue Cross 57
  Free Life 19, 34, 63–5
Free Life (Vie Libre) 19, 34, 63–5
  approach 64–5
  history 63–4
  membership 65
  origins 63–4
  philosophy 64–5
friendship-network composition 144–6, 179
friendships in self-help groups 130, 131, 144–6
  potentially adverse effects 146
funding
  acceptance of external 21

consistency need 158–9
  external 91, 92
  media campaigns 160
  private 156, 160
  psychiatric self-help organizations 156
  substance abuse organizations 156

Gamblers Anonymous 37
gender relations 47
Germany
  attitudes of professionals 165
  consumer participation 153
  healthcare system 30–1
  self-help clearinghouses 158
  support commitment 159
  Synanon communities 21, 139
Gold Cross 55, 63
government advisory/policy boards 163
government agencies 149
  collaboration 152–4
  rhetoric 155
government policy 155
governmental support, strategies for 154–63
  financial 156
  funding consistency 158–9
groups, barriers to entry 16, 135, 172–3
GROW 23–4

halfway houses 78–80, 80–1
hashish abuse 84, 88
Hazard, Rowland 36
healing, concept of 120
health benefits of self-help group membership
  149–50
health care
  addiction-related 19
  consumerism 30–1
  cost offsets 151–2
  cost reductions 150–2, 179–80
  utilization reduction 150–1
healthcare practitioners
  guidelines 4–5
  interactions with self-help organizations
    149
  see also professionals
healthcare systems
  consumer participation 153–4
  fiscal strain 150
helper-therapy principle 120
helping, reciprocal 15–16
heroin abuse 63
Higher Power 39, 40
  see also spiritual change; spiritual
    principles; spirituality
HIV-positive individuals, mutual support 18
Hong Kong

AA 80
Pui Hong Self-Help Association 80–2
hope instillation 122
hospitals 157
human values 129
humanism, secular 86

identity transformation 129, 130, 141–3, 179
addiction incorporation 142
information campaigns 159–60
information dissemination 160–1
inpatient facilities 80
inpatient treatment, compulsory 112–13
insight therapy 112
institutions, opening to self-help groups 157
Internet 19, 35, 90–1
Moderation Management communication 71, 73
investments 157–9
Islamic societies
AA 42
12-step groups 173
Israel
JACS 66
spiritual change 134
12-step groups 173
Italy
AA 58
Clubs of Treated Alcoholics 58, 60, 103

Japan
AA 53, 54
funding 156
space-sharing 157
see also Danshukai
Jewish Alcoholics, Chemically Dependent
Persons, and Significant Others (JACS)
65–7, 93
12-step recovery 66
approach 66–7
history 65–6
membership 67
origins 65–6
philosophy 66–7
Judaism 65–7, 173
Jung, Carl 36

Kinnon, Jimmy 74–5
Kirkpatrick, Jean 88–90
Kishline, Audrey 70–3
knowledge 15

leadership
peer 15, 20
professional–peer 20
self-directed 14–15

lectures 174
life expectancy 26
life-story transformation 143–4, 179
destruction 144
LifeRing Secular Recovery 86–8
The Links 67–70
approach 69–70
history 67–8
membership 70
origins 67–8
philosophy 69–70
Seven Points 69
literature, accessible 7
liver cirrhosis rate reduction 124
Lost Weekend (film) 37
loving detachment 49

marijuana abuse
Rational Recovery 84
SOS members 88
matching hypothesis 116
media campaigns 159–60
media referral persons 174
medications 171–2
meetings
AA 36, 40–1
mutual-support 36
online 19, 71, 73
membership of self-help groups
AA 35, 41–2, 144
Abstainers Clubs 45–6
Al-Anon Family Groups 47
Blue Cross 57
Clubs of Treated Alcoholics 60
coercion of individuals 153
Danshukai 53–4
direct health benefits 149–50
Double Trouble in Recovery 62–3
healthcare system need reduction 150–2
JACS 67
The Links 70
Moderation Management 73
Narcotics Anonymous 76–7
Nicotine Anonymous 77–8
Oxford House organization 79–80
Pui Hong Self-Help Association 81–2
Rational Recovery 83–4
by relations 19
in self-conception 142
SMART Recovery 86
SOS 87–8
Women for Sobriety 90
mental health
Adult Children of Alcoholics 101
Al-Anon Family Groups 100

mental health (*cont.*)
  Double Trouble in Recovery 61–2, 63,
    103–4
  professionals 176
mental illness *see* psychiatric disorders
Methadone Anonymous 171
mind harmony with good in life 137
Minnesota Model treatment programs 37
  Scandinavia 68
Moderation Management 70–3
  approach 72–3
  collaborative research projects 104
  evaluation 104
  history 70–2
  Internet use 19
  membership 73
  origins 70–2
  philosophy 72–3, 144
Molloy, Paul 78
motivation to change 118
motivational enhancement therapy 116
mutual-aid organizations *see* self-help
    organizations
mutual-help groups 13
  nested within larger organizational
    structures 18–19
  see also self-help organizations

Narcotics Anonymous 14, 37, 74–7, 93
  approach 75–6
  evaluation 104–6
  history 74–5
  infectious disease risk effects 106
  membership 76–7
  origins 74–5
  outcomes 105
  philosophy 75–6
  professional visitors 176
  recovery process 133
  spiritual aspects as barrier to attendance
    135, 172–3
  spiritual change 133–5, 137–8
  spiritual Higher Power 131
  sponsorship 76
  12 steps 75
National Federation of the Societies of Links
  18
Native Americans 173
needs assessments 161–2
Netherlands
  funding 156
  in-kind resources 157
  support for self-help organizations 153–4
neurofibromatosis 27
Nicotine Anonymous 77–8, 93

evaluation 106–7
Norway, The Links 68, 69, 70
Nottingham Self-Help Support Centre 158

online meetings 19
  depression self-help groups 73
  Moderation Management 71, 73
  see also Internet
opiate addiction 80, 93
  evaluation of self-help groups 106
Overeaters Anonymous 37, 159
The Oxford Group 35–7
Oxford House organization 21, 78–80, 93
  approach 79
  evaluation 107–8
  history 78
  membership 79–80
  origins 78
  philosophy 79
  spiritual change 133

participation benefits 31–2
patient-education programs 22–4
peer leadership 15, 20
personal change goals 17
Poland
  Abstainers Clubs 43–6, 58, 59
  media campaign 159
  Solidarity Period 44
policy
  government 155
  participation/planning 163
  public 155
political advocacy 19, 162
political empowerment 129, 146–8, 179
political views in self-help groups 130
population-level benefits 123–5
population size 27
power, personal 144
prisons 157
professional bias 6–7
professional treatment programs 5
professionals 22–4, 91, 92, 149
  AA relationship 109–10, 112
  Abstainers Clubs support 43–4, 45, 58, 59,
    91
  addicted 175–6
  a priori matching 168–9
  attending self-help groups 175–6
  attitudes to self-help groups 164–6
  Blue Cross relationship 56
  Clubs of Treated Alcoholics 59
    relationships 58, 91
  collaboration with self-help groups 152–4,
    164–6

avenues for 166–76
consultation 168–9
defined role 20
dissatisfaction with 28–9
Double Trouble in Recovery relationship 61
education 160–1
ethical constraints 23, 129
facilitator role 23, 174
founding of self-help groups 174
guidelines 4–5
help limitations 29–30
interactions 180
    with patients 23
    with self-help groups 149, 180
lectures 174
legal constraints 23
media referral persons 174
mental health 176
Moderation Management relationship 72
phased withdrawal plans 174
protection from/for self-help organizations 95
referrals
    adolescents 174
    concerns 169–70
    consultation 168–9
    dual-diagnosis patients 170–1
    effective 167
    empirically supported strategies 167–8
    psychiatric disorders 170–1
research support 174
role in self-help organizations 20
shortcomings 28–9
SMART Recovery relationship 85
strategies for 163–6
technical assistance 174
training 160–1
treatment interventions 149
visits of non-addicted to groups 176
waiting list patients 167
Project MATCH 98, 116–17, 120
dual-diagnosis patients 170–1
referral 168
psychiatric disorders 23–4
AA evaluation 117
cross-person similarity in life-stories 144
Double Trouble in Recovery 61, 62, 63, 103–4
group communication processes 143
identity change 142
patient referrals 170–1
psychiatric self-help organizations, funding 156
psychological problems 108

psychopathology 118
public health 26–7
public policy 155
public responsibility, denial 153
public spending, addiction-related health care 19
Pui Hong Self-Help Association 34, 80–2, 92, 93
approach 81
evaluation 108
history 80–1
membership 81–2
origins 80–1
philosophy 81

Quebec, healthcare policy 31

rational analysis 82
rational behavioral therapy 112
Rational Recovery 82–4
approach 82–3
"The Beast" 83
evaluation 108
history 82
membership 83–4
origins 82
philosophy 82–3
spiritual surrender measure 133
rational–emotive therapy 82
rationality, Moderation Management philosophy 144
reciprocal helping 15–16
recovery
counselors 175–6
process 133, 144
programs 149
Recovery Inc. 18
recovery-sensitive counseling 149
referrals
adolescents 174
concerns 169–70
consultation 168–9
dual-diagnosis patients 170–1
effective 167
empirically supported strategies 167–8
psychiatric disorders 170–1
relations
membership of groups 19
see also families
religions 139–40
see also atheism; Christianity; Judaism
religious emphasis 18
research, randomized clinical trials 95–9
research support 161–3
professionals 174

residential structure of organizations 21, 90
  Oxford House organization 78–80
resources
  in-kind 156–7
  see also funding
retinitis pigmentosa 27
rituals
  AA meetings 40
  Al-Anon Family Groups 50
role models 121, 122

Scandinavia
  AA 68
  The Links 67–70
schizophrenia 63
scientific studies 161
Secular Organization for Sobriety *see* SOS
sedative abuse 88
self-conception changes 141–4
self-control 82, 83
  Moderation Management philosophy 144
self-efficacy
  augmenting with AA 119, 123
  decreased 120
self-esteem 141
self-examination, cognitive 82
self-help books 21–2
self-help clearinghouses 158, 159, 161–2
self-help group movement 1–2
  consumerism 30–1
  family tie weakening 27–8
  generic factors 24–5
  inter-related forces fostering 26–32
  participation benefits 31–2
  professional assistance limits 28–30
  public health 26–7
  wealth growth 27
self-help organizations
  addiction-related 2–3, 11–12
  attitudes
    of professionals 164–6
    toward professionals 166
  barriers to entry 16, 135, 172–3
  clinical interactions 4–5
  coalition of leaders 160
  coercion of individuals 153
  collaboration of professionals 164–6
    avenues for 166–76
  collaboration with
    professional–governmental bodies
    152–4
  countries 8–9
  cross-cultural diversity 9
  cult distinctions 138–9
  defined role for professionals 20

differentiation from other interventions 21–4
direct health benefits 149–50
distinctions from other treatments 178
diversity 1–2
empowerment 147–8
essential characteristics 13–17
evaluation 94–5, 179–80
  analogy to healthcare interventions
  95–6
  covariance adjustments 98–9
  naturalistic 98–9
  stakeholder-based 162
experiential knowledge valuation 15
exploitation potential 152–3
external funds acceptance 21
external support 149–54
facilitation intervention 167
fees lack 16
friendship-network composition 144–6
friendships 130, 131, 144–6
funding for quasi-professionalization 152
generalization 178
governmental support strategies 154–63
groups nested within 18–19
health-related organization guidelines 4–5
healthcare
  cost reductions 150–2
  practitioner guidelines 4–5
identity transformation 143–4
individual passions 5–6
interactions of members 4
Internet presence 19
investments 157–9
involvement 3–4
life-story transformation 141–3
national data-gathering 163
needs assessments 161–2
nomenclature 12–13
non-addiction-related 11–12
optional features *14*, 17–21
outcome studies 99–119
participation outcomes 94–5, 179–80
peer-operated 20
personal change goals 17
philosophy 17–18
  changes 129, 130
policy interactions 4–5
political advocacy 19
politicization 146–8
professional bias 6–7
program of change 17–18
protection from professional guilds 95
randomized clinical trials in evaluation
  97–8
range of organizations 11–12

reciprocal helping 15–16
religion distinctions 139–40
religious emphasis 18
residential structure 21
self-directed leadership 14–15
service agency culture risks 152
shared problems/status 13–14
social network 129, 130
social responsibility for evaluation 94–5
societies examined 7–8
spiritual emphasis 18
    changes 129, 130, 179
starting 174
technical assistance from professionals 174
traditions 178
treatment-evaluation perspective 95–6
voluntary nature 16–17
see also addiction-related groups;
    membership of self-help groups;
    professionals; referrals
Self-Management and Recovery Training *see*
    SMART Recovery
shared problems/status 13–14
sickle cell anemia 27
The Small Book (Trimpey) 82
SMART Recovery 82, 84–6
    approach 84–5
    atheistic patients 172–3
    four-point program 85
    history 84
    membership 86
    origins 84
    philosophy 84–5
    spiritual surrender measure 133
Smith, Dr. Robert Holbrook 36
smoking cessation program 106–7
sobriety 38–9
Sobriety Friends Society
    approach 52–3
    evaluation 102–3
    history 51–2
    membership 53–4
    origins 51–2
    philosophy 52–3
Sobriety International 68
social model recovery programs 149
social network of self-help groups 129, 130
social support, generic 120
social trends 177–8
social welfare 30
Society for the Aid and Rehabilitation of Drug
    Addicts (SARDA) 80–1
SOS 86–8
    approach 86–7
    atheistic patients 172–3

evaluation 109
history 86
membership 87–8
origins 86
philosophy 86–7
space-sharing 157
Spain, self-help clearinghouses 159
spiritual alienation 136
spiritual change 129, 130, 131–41
    AA 133–5, 137–8
    Adult Children of Alcoholics 135–6,
        137–8
    Al-Anon Family Groups 135–6, 137–8
    definition 131
    Narcotics Anonymous 133–5, 137–8
    phenomenological 132
    recovery process 133
    study 132
    substance-abuse-related self-help
        organizations 137–41
    Women for Sobriety 136–7, 137–8
spiritual principles 18, 39, 91, 92
    Al-Anon Family Groups 49
    barrier to attendance at AA/NA 135, 172–3
    Blue Cross 55–6
    cult distinction 138–9
    JACS 66
    Narcotics Anonymous 75
    religion distinction 139–40
    SMART Recovery 84
    spiritual transformation 36, 122
spirituality 132
    changes 179
    patients averse to 172–3
sponsorship, Narcotics Anonymous 76
stakeholder-based evaluations 162
12-step programs 18, 22, 38, 39–40, 115–16
    adolescents 173–4
    Al-Anon use 48–9
    counseling 120
    evaluation 116–17, 118–19
    friendships 145–6
    JACS 66
    medical treatment support 171–2
    political activity 146–8
    proximal changes 122
    spiritual change 133, 134
    spirituality 172–3
stepped care concept 167
stigmatization of addiction 142
stimulant abuse 88
Stone, Robert 75
story-telling
    AA meetings 40–1
    Danshukai 52–3

substance abuse 33–4
  adolescents 173–4
  alcohol and other drugs 93
  appraisal as source of harm 120
  Double Trouble in Recovery 61, 62, 63, 103–4
  JACS 65–7
  reduction 179
support, external 149–54
support groups, professionally operated 22–4
supporter attendance 92
Sweden, The Links 67–70
Switzerland
  AA 55, 57
  Blue Cross 54–7
Synanon communities 21, 139

temperance movement 38
  Blue Cross 55–6
  influences 91–2
  Japan 51
  The Links 67–8
Thatcher, Edwin 36
third sector *see* voluntary sector
tobacco products 77–8, 93, 106–7
tranquilizer abuse 88
treatment
  professionally operated 22–4
  programs 157
treatment agencies, strategies for 163–6
treatment-evaluation perspective 95–6
treatment research, randomized clinical trials 95–9
treatment-evaluation perspective 129
Trimpey, Jack 82
Twelve Step Facilitation Handbook (Project MATCH) 168
Twelve Steps and Twelve Traditions (AA) 37

undermanned settings 15
United Kingdom
  Drinkwatchers 71
  self-help group support 158
  Thatcherite discrediting of public services 153
United States 91–2
  attitudes of professionals 165
  governmental support strategies 155
  healthcare companies' reduction of benefits 153
  JACS 65–7
  Jewish substance abuse 173
  media campaign 159–60

Moderation Management 70–3
Narcotics Anonymous 74–7
Nicotine Anonymous 77–8
Oxford House organization 78–80
Rational Recovery 83–4
self-help clearinghouses 29, 158, 159, 161–2
SOS 86–8
spiritual change 134
Synanon communities 139

validity
  external 98
  internal 96–7, 98
Vie Libre *see* Free Life (Vie Libre)
voluntary care 22
voluntary sector 16–17

"Way of Sobriety" 44
wealth increase 27
websites 19
widow peer-helping programs 164
"Will Training" 18
Wilson, Lois 46, 68
  shoe anecdote 49, 146
Wilson, William Griffith 36–7, 68
women
  Al-Anon Family Groups 46, 47, 50, 100
  Blue Cross membership 57
  Clubs of Treated Alcoholics 60
  Danshukai 52–3, 54
  Free Life 65
  JACS 67
  Oxford Houses 78, 80
Women for Sobriety 88–90
  approach 88–90
  evaluation 109
  history 88
  membership 90
  origins 88
  philosophy 88–90
  spiritual change 136–8
women's movement 47, 88
World Health Organization (WHO) 9, 155
World Service Board of Al-Anon Family Groups 18
world view 128
  AA 143
  transformation 131, 141, 179

Yugoslavia
  AA 58
  Clubs of Treated Alcoholics 57–60, 103